Talking Business

A Guide to the Language of Business

Linda A. Donville
B.A., M.Educ., CELTA, Centennial College

Emily R. Donville
B.A., M.A., Centennial College

PEARSON
Prentice Hall
Toronto

Library and Archives Canada Cataloguing in Publication

Donville Linda A. (Linda Ann), 1947–
Talking Business: A Guide to the Language of Business / Linda A. Donville, Emily R. Donville.

ISBN 978-0-13-205200-9

1. English language—Textbooks for foreign speakers. 2. English language—Business English—Problems, exercises, etc. 3. Business writing—Problems, exercises, etc. I. Donville, Emily R. (Emily Rose), 1974– II. Title.

PE1128.D653 2009 808'.06665 C2007-907072-8

ISBN-13: 978-0-13-205200-9
ISBN-10: 0-13-205200-8

Vice President, Editorial Director: Gary Bennett
Acquisitions Editor: Karen Elliott
Executive Marketing Manager: Cas Shields
Developmental Editor: Lisa Cicinelli/Pamela Voves
Production Editor: Cheryl Jackson
Copy Editor: Martin Tooke
Proofreader: Elspeth McFadden
Production Coordinator: Andrea Falkenberg
Permissions Researcher: Lynn McIntyre
Art Director: Julia Hall
Cover Designer: Brett Miller
Cover Image: Photodisc

For permission to reproduce copyrighted material, the publisher gratefully acknowledges the copyright holders listed throughout the sourcelines in the book, which are considered an extension of this copyright page.

1 2 3 4 5 12 11 10 09 08

Printed and bound in Canada.

PEARSON
Prentice Hall

Contents

Contents

Preface

It is evident to most of us who teach at the college and university levels that ESL students often struggle in their core courses. Because of the great mass of new language that students must acquire in order to progress, many students will simply memorize key vocabulary and will miss out on a deeper comprehension of the concepts involved. Most ESL students are willing to put in the extra work required to familiarize themselves with the materials, but instructors do not have the time to take the students through this process, particularly in classes that mix ESL students with native English speakers. This workbook was designed to aid instructors in their facilitation of introductory business concepts for ESL students.

The chapters in the workbook are organized to correspond functionally with chapters that are typically included in introductory business textbooks. Each chapter is based on a selection of key terms that are likely to be covered in most introductory business textbooks. Instructors can assign portions of the workbook to correspond to the functional areas that they cover in class. The Glossary, Audio Key Terms List, and Answer Key included in this workbook are tools that allow students to work independently on enhancing their understanding of the concepts that instructors are dealing with in class.

This workbook gives ESL students the opportunity to put in focused work that will manifestly increase their understanding of the materials involved in an introductory business course. The activities incorporate multiple language skills in order to give students a comprehensive familiarity with important business concepts. The activities are also designed to utilize varying levels of abstraction and appeal to students with different learning styles.

This companion book will support instructors in their efforts to ensure that ESL students progress with a deeper comprehension of the materials presented in their courses.

Organization

Chapters are ordered to follow the general approach of most introductory business texts. However, each chapter is designed to stand alone, so instructors have flexibility in terms of utilizing the materials to enhance the functional areas as they cover them in class.

Each chapter includes:

- key terms with an audio component for pronunciation
- exercises that reinforce students' knowledge of conceptual clusters of the key terms
- current articles from *Canadian Business* magazine, *The Globe and Mail*, and the *Toronto Star* with exercises based on these readings
- audio dialogues with exercises
- short grammar lessons that incorporate business terminology with some of the trickier elements of English grammar
- a Test Your Knowledge exercise that draws from all of the conceptual areas covered in the chapter

Features

- An audio component for the key terms in each chapter is included so that students are comfortable using each term in both their written and spoken class work.
- The glossary is arranged alphabetically so that students can access vocabulary even when a different functional area is being covered.
- Multiple language skills are utilized in the activities in every chapter, including reading, listening, pronunciation, and critical thinking.
- Various learning styles are accommodated in the activities, which take varying approaches to the vocabulary and language of business.
- Fresh and engaging articles on current issues in the business world, taken from respected sources, are included. These provide students with a context around which to learn—enhancing their knowledge of the contemporary business world, familiarizing them with specific business language, and equipping these students with the reading skills necessary to stay current in their field.
- Grammar lessons and activities reinforce some of the more challenging areas of English grammar and usage for ESL learners.
- Audio dialogues enhance students' ability to listen both for the overall picture and for specific content.
- A Test Your Knowledge activity in each chapter provides a review of chapter concepts before students move on to a new functional area.

Acknowledgments

We would like to thank Alice Stutt for being so supportive and encouraging and we'd also like to thank Kay for not eating the manuscript.

Chapter 1

Business Systems and Environments

Before You Start

Study the terms below and be sure that you understand each one. If any of the terms are unclear to you, you can find definitions in the Glossary.

Key Terms

balance of trade
business
business cycle
capital
capitalism
command economy
communism
competition
consumer price index (CPI)
deficit
deflation
demand
demand and supply schedule
depression
economics
entrepreneur
factors of production
fiscal policy
free-market economy
gross domestic product (GDP)
industrial policy
inflation
labour
law of demand
law of supply
loss
macroeconomics
market
market economy
market price
marketing boards
mass production
microeconomics
mixed economies
monetary policy
monopolistic competition
monopoly
national debt
oligopoly
perfect competition
productivity
profit
purchasing power parity
recession
revenue
risk
socialism
specialization
stability
standard of living
supply
surplus
transfer payments
unemployment

Now, listen to the chapter's Audio Key Terms List for the correct pronunciation of each term.

Exercise 1

There are four stages to the **business cycle**. Use the stages listed to label the graph below. Check the glossary if you are unclear about any of the stages.

recovery	recession (or depression)
peak	trough

Business Cycle Graph

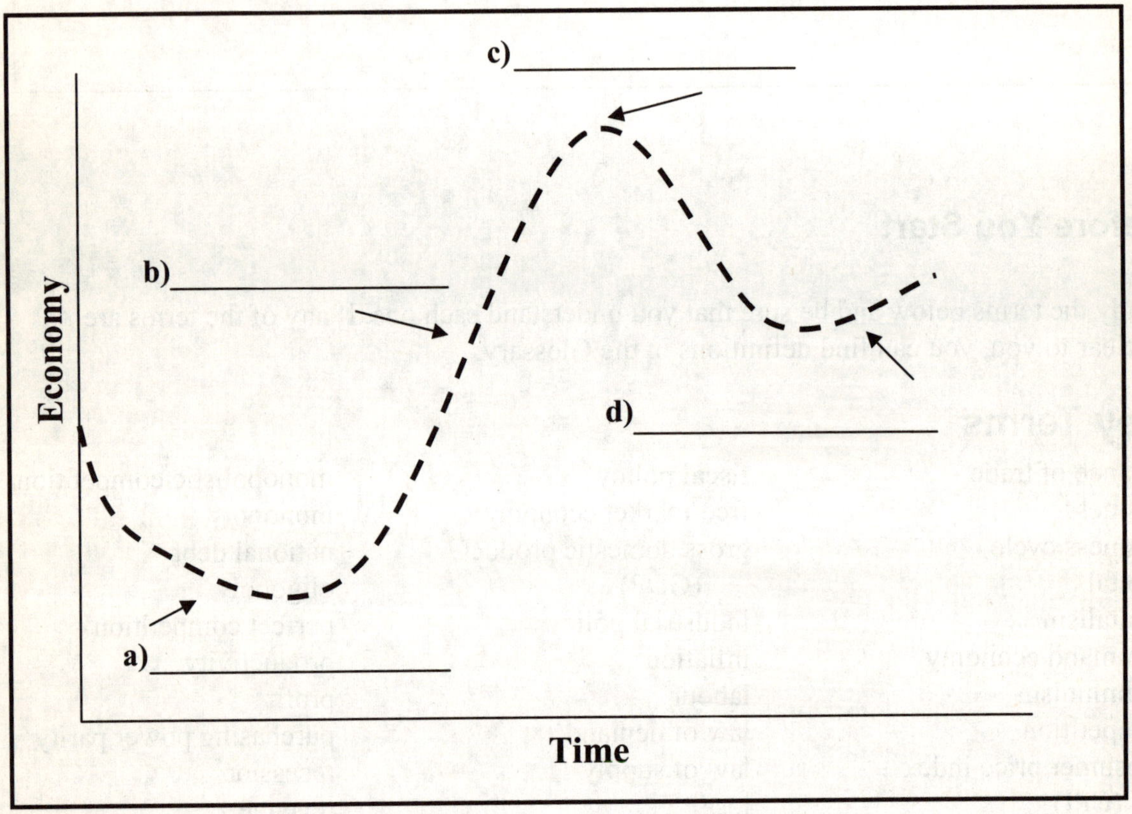

Check your answers in the Answer Key.

Exercise 2

There are many different ways to measure economic growth. Match each term below with the description of the economic factors that it measures. The first one is completed for you.

Gross Domestic Product (GDP)

Gross National Product (GNP)

General Progress Indicator (GPI)

standard of living

aggregate output

GDP per capita

real GDP

nominal GDP

a) This relatively new measurement is not yet widely utilized. It assigns negative value to economic activity that harms the environment or general social welfare.

b) This measures the value of the total production of any economic system. It can be applied to nations or, more locally, to communities or specific firms.

c) This measures the general economic power of a population; specifically, it measures the goods and services available for purchase against the purchasing power of the population in a given economy.

d) This measures the value of the total domestic production of a nation divided by its population.

e) This measurement includes the value of the total domestic production of a nation without adjustments for inflation or currency fluctuations.

f) This measures the value of the total goods and services produced domestically in a given period of time. It includes the output of any foreign companies operating domestically.

g) This measures the value of the total domestic production of a nation and adjusts for inflation and currency fluctuations.

h) This measurement includes the value of the total national production, including the output of domestic companies operating abroad.

Check your answers in the Answer Key.

Exercise 3a

Business terms often come in pairs used to describe contrasting or opposing forces or trends in economics or business operations.

Match the pairs of terms below.

a) command economy	demand
b) deficit	surplus
c) deflation	loss
d) profit	market economy
e) supply	inflation

Check your answers in the Answer Key.

Exercise 3b

Now, match the pairs of terms with the definition that best describes them.

a) These terms describe the increase or decrease in the price of a product compared to the price at a historical point in time.

b) These two terms describe different ways that countries manage business. One refers to business that is primarily controlled by government, and the other refers to business that is left to regulate itself according to the forces of supply and demand.

c) This pair of terms refers to the amount of a certain product available to be sold in a market, and the willingness of customers to buy that product in the market.

d) These terms describe situations in which businesses produce too much or too little of a product compared to the consumer demand.

e) These terms refer to the money that a firm makes from selling a product compared to the money spent in making the product.

Check your answers in the Answer Key.

Exercise 4

The paragraph below describes the experience of an individual firm. Fill the general business terms from the list below into the correct spaces in the paragraph.

capital	factors of production	profit
competition	labour	natural resources
entrepreneur	risk	information resources

George Stefopoulos decided to open a small landscaping company. George is an a) ______________________. First, George needs some b) ________________. He borrows some money from a relative to open his business. In terms of c) ______________________, George decides to use the services of a marketing firm to help him decide where to locate and how to advertise his business. The marketing firm will also identify all of the other landscaping firms in the local market; that is, George's d) ______________________. Next, George needs to acquire some e) _________________________, including some land on which to locate his business, and some plants, rock, and soil. George can't do all of the work himself, so he has to hire some f) _______________. At this point, George has considered all of the g) ___________________________ involved in his new business. George hopes that after paying for all of this, the money he is paid by his customers will exceed the money he has spent. George wants to make a h) ___________________ from his new business. As with any new business, George's landscaping business is a i)__________, but if George manages things well, he will be successful.

Check your answers in the Answer Key.

Exercise 5

Match the following terms that describe forms of competition with the correct definitions.

a) perfect competition	i) This term describes a complete lack of competition, in which all of the demand in a market is supplied by one producer.
b) monopolistic competition	ii) This term refers to a market that consists of a large number of smaller firms that work to supply the market demand.
c) oligopoly	iii) This term refers to a market that has a small number of large firms that supply the market demand.
d) monopoly	iv) This term refers to a market with many producers whose products are relatively similar. Firms work to make their product seem different from those offered by other firms.

Check your answers in the Answer Key.

In the News 1.1

Wal-Mart Rolling Out Green Label

Dana Flavelle

After years of competing mainly on price, the Canadian unit of the world's largest retailer says the environment is now part of the "value" equation for consumers.

Wal-Mart Canada will introduce its own green label today to identify products that have been certified as environmentally friendly.

The company says it will also flex its considerable muscle with suppliers, working with them to develop more products that qualify for its logo, "For the Greener Good."

"Wal-Mart is not just about cost," said Wal-Mart Canada's chief executive officer, Mario Pilozzi.

"Wal-Mart is about delivering value to our customers so they can live better lives. I don't think we want to be known only as selling for less than anyone else."

The new logo is part of a branding initiative aimed at reducing corporate waste, cutting energy use and generally becoming a better neighbour, the company said.

"I want to change how we conduct business," Pilozzi said in a telephone interview yesterday. "I want to change the mindset of the company and make us a much more responsible company. Not to say that we haven't always been responsible."

Other retailers have undertaken similar initiatives. Home Depot Canada introduced its own "Eco Options" logo nearly three years ago. Loblaws Cos. Ltd. re-launched its 20-year-old PC Green program earlier this month, adding what it calls the world's "greenest" shopping bag to the assortment.

The moves by some of the country's biggest retailers to tap into the environmental craze aren't surprising. However, it's far from clear how many of Wal-Mart's customers are ready to follow its lead.

Some U.S. reports have said Wal-Mart's mainly lower-income customers can't or won't pay the higher price of being green. Environmentally friendly products usually cost more than conventional products.

Pilozzi said he doesn't see that as an issue, and if anything Wal-Mart is helping making it easier by driving down the price of such goods, partly due to its enormous buying power and by working with suppliers to develop lower-price store brands.

Its private label compact fluorescent bulb, for example, is one of the lowest priced on the market, the retailer said.

The first products to bear Wal-Mart's new logo are the appliances rated by Energy Star, the internationally recognized symbol of energy efficiency, the company said. The next category will likely be its new line of organic cotton clothing.

The retailer says only those items certified by independent authorities will get the Wal-Mart logo, an approach other retailers have taken.

"We're looking for third parties to certify these products so we're not just slapping labels on our shelves," Pilozzi said.

This approach means only 100 items out of the 40 000 carried in a typical Wal-Mart store currently bear the Greener Good label, Pilozzi said. But thousands more likely qualify, a spokesperson said later.

The retailer said it would be using its considerable clout with suppliers to develop more.

"There are times when being the large retailer that we are comes in handy. We can leverage that sort of power with the vendor," Pilozzi said.

Source: Dana Flavelle, "Wal-Mart Rolling Out Green Label," *Toronto Star*, April 26, 2007, pp. C1, C10.

Exercise 6

Please reread the article above, "Wal-Mart Rolling Out Green Label." Match the terms below with the statements from the article that best fit the meaning of the term. You may need to refresh your mind about the definitions in each case. However, definitions can be misleading, so check your text for the broader meanings of the terms before you do the matching. The first one is done for you.

Term	**Article Statement**
demand	a) "Some U.S. reports have said Wal-Mart's mainly lower-income customers can't or won't pay the higher price of being green."
competition	b) "Wal-Mart is about delivering value to our customers...I don't think we want to be known only as selling for less than anyone else."
output market	c) "Wal-Mart is...driving down the price of such goods...due to its...buying power and by working with suppliers to develop lower-price store brands."
factors of production	d) "The moves by some of the country's biggest retailers to tap into the environmental craze aren't surprising."

Check your answers in the Answer Key.

Grammar Tip

Coordinating Conjunctions

Coordinating conjunctions are used to link two equal ideas or clauses (grammatical units containing a subject and a verb) together. They include the words *and*, *or*, *but*, *so*, *nor*, *for*, and *yet*. An easy way to remember the **coordinating conjunctions** is the acronym FANBOYS (**F**or, **A**nd, **N**or, **B**ut, **O**r, **Y**et, **S**o).

These **coordinating conjunctions** are not interchangeable; they each have a different meaning. Study each **coordinating conjunction** and its meaning in the table below.

and	links two similar ideas together
but/yet	link two contrasting ideas
or	links two alternatives; can be used with **either**
so	links cause (first idea) and effect (second idea)
nor	links two negative alternatives; must be used with **neither**
for	links effect (first idea) and cause (second idea). This is not commonly used in speech; the subordinating conjunction "because" is much more common.

Coordinating conjunctions can be used to link together two ideas within a single sentence. These ideas can be words or phrases. Study the examples below.

I like *math* **and** *science.*
They *visited* **but** *left* early.
She lives *in* **or** *around* the city centre.
He *worked all day* **but** *went to bed early.*
We want to *finish our work tonight* **or** *get up early tomorrow.*

Coordinating conjunctions can also be used to join two separate sentences or **clauses** (units containing a subject and verb) together. When **coordinating conjunctions** are used in this way, they must be preceded by a comma. Study the examples below.

They started to cook dinner, **and** *she suggested* they eat outside.
We have to finish tonight, **or** *the report will* be late.
There *is a problem* with the computer, **but** *he will fix* it quickly.

Exercise 7

Fill in the blanks in the sentences below with the correct coordinating conjunction. Use each coordinating conjunction once.

a) Jay-Hoon wanted to get a good grade, ________ he studied hard.

b) In his hometown, Sajid worked as a paperboy, _______ when he moved to the city, he got a job as a server.

c) We should fix this bicycle ________ buy a new one.

d) When she won the contest, Sonia received a plaque ________ some prize money.

e) Jose neither ate ________ slept during the six-hour flight.

f) Tim couldn't buy the stereo he wanted, _______ he didn't have any money.

g) It was sunny ________ cool on the shore of the lake.

Check your answers in the Answer Key.

Exercise 8

The sentences below relate to **In the News 1.1**, above. Reread the article. Then, choose the best coordinating conjunction for each sentence. Add commas where appropriate.

a) Wal-Mart's new green logo is about reducing corporate waste _______ cutting energy use.

b) Canada's largest stores are "going green" ________ the writer isn't sure if Wal-Mart's customers will find this idea appealing.

c) Wal-Mart is having its green products certified by independent authorities _______ its customers know that the products really are environmentally responsible.

d) Some critics believe that Wal-Mart's customers can't afford _______ won't be willing to pay for environmentally friendly products.

e) Wal-Mart expects to make environmentally friendly products cheaper ________ it is a powerful company in the international market.

f) Wal-Mart currently offers a line of energy-efficient appliances _______ hopes to offer a line of organic clothing in the near future.

g) In the past, Wal-Mart has chiefly been known as a discount chain ________ now it plans to compete in the growing market in environmentally friendly products.

Check your answers in the Answer Key.

In the News 1.2

Energy Fuels Strong Growth

Louise Egan

OTTAWA—Canada's economy grew faster than expected in February as the energy sector expanded at its fastest rate in nearly four years, increasing the chances of an eventual Bank of Canada interest rate hike.

Statistics Canada reported Monday that gross domestic product expanded 0.4 percent in February, double the average forecast of analysts in a Reuters poll and up sharply from 0.1 percent in January. The economy grew 2.1 percent in February from a year earlier.

The data sent the Canadian dollar racing up to a seven-month high against the U.S. dollar.

The upturn in growth, combined with higher-than-expected inflation, fits into the very slight tightening bias introduced by the Bank of Canada last week. Despite keeping interest rates on hold, it flagged inflation as a key risk to its outlook.

"The February GDP report is solid, yet should not really be seen as having altered the monetary landscape since Friday," said Stewart Hall, market strategist at HSBC, in a note.

The bank held its overnight lending target at 4.25 percent last Tuesday. The comparable U.S. rate is 5.25 percent.

"Canadian rates market continues to underperform the U.S. in keeping with the upside data surprises that now have come to characterize Canada," said Hall, adding there appeared to be no concerted effort to re-price rate expectations.

In its revised projections for the Canadian economy on Thursday, the bank slightly raised its GDP forecast for the first quarter of this year to 2.5 percent from 2.4 percent. It sees growth easing to 2.3 percent in the second half of the year. However, it now sees inflation staying above its target of 2 percent for longer than previously thought.

At 9:30 a.m., the Canadian dollar was at $1.1100 to the U.S. dollar, or 90.09 U.S. cents, up from $1.1160 to the U.S. dollar, or 89.61 U.S. cents, at Friday's close.

"This is just yet another sign that the Canadian economy is faring well in the face of a U.S. slowdown, and is clearly good news for the already high-flying Canadian dollar," said Doug Porter, deputy chief economist at BMO Capital Markets.

For the complete article, visit *www.thestar.com/printArticle/208819*

Exercise 9a

Read the article, "Energy Fuels Strong Growth," above. Then, use the information in the article to fill in the spaces in the sentences below.

a) Because the energy sector has expanded so quickly, Canada's ____________ has grown faster than expected.

b) The increase in Canada's ____________________ doubled the average forecasted by analysts for the month of February.

c) With _____________ and growth higher than forecasted, the Bank of Canada might be expected to show a tendency toward increasing interest rates.

d) The Bank of Canada has decided to maintain interest rates at their current level, although it intends to be cautious about the risk of ________________.

e) Although the ________________ findings for February are strong, some market strategists may feel that it's too minor an increase to change the market significantly.

f) In terms of projections for the Canadian ________________, the bank has adjusted its ________________ forecast for the first quarter of 2007.

g) The bank is also changing its projections about ____________ and is accepting that it may stay higher than the previously projected target of 2 percent.

h) This new information about Canada's ____________ indicates that the Canadian ________________ is doing very well in spite of the turndown in the U.S. ____________.

Check your answers in the Answer Key.

Exercise 9b

The questions below relate to **In the News 1.2**, above.

a) Which government body publishes regular reports on the gross domestic product?

b) When Canada's economy is expanding rapidly, what action can we expect from the Bank of Canada?

c) To which other currency does Canada usually compare its dollar?

d) How often is the gross domestic product reported? Monthly, quarterly, or yearly?

e) Since the U.S. economy has slowed down, does it necessarily follow that the Canadian economy will slow down?

Check your answers in the Answer Key.

Test Your Knowledge 1

Answer the following questions in order to fill in the puzzle below. When you have correctly filled in each of the answers, the mystery word will appear.

a) ________________________ is a measurement of the number of people without work who are actively pursuing work.

b) The measurement that compares the amount produced with the resources required to produce it is called ________________________.

c) The general economic trend of decreasing prices is called ________________________.

d) The umbrella economic policy that covers a government's monetary and fiscal policies is called the ______________________________ policy.

e) The general economic trend of increasing prices is called ______________________________.

f) The ______________________ policy deals with control over the supply of money in any given nation.

g) The state in which an economy's supply of money and availability of goods and services for sale are growing at a similar rate is called ______________________________.

h) The value of a nation's total exported goods and services minus the value of its total imported goods and services is called its ____________________________ of trade.

i) A government's ________________ policy deals with the collection and spending of government revenues.

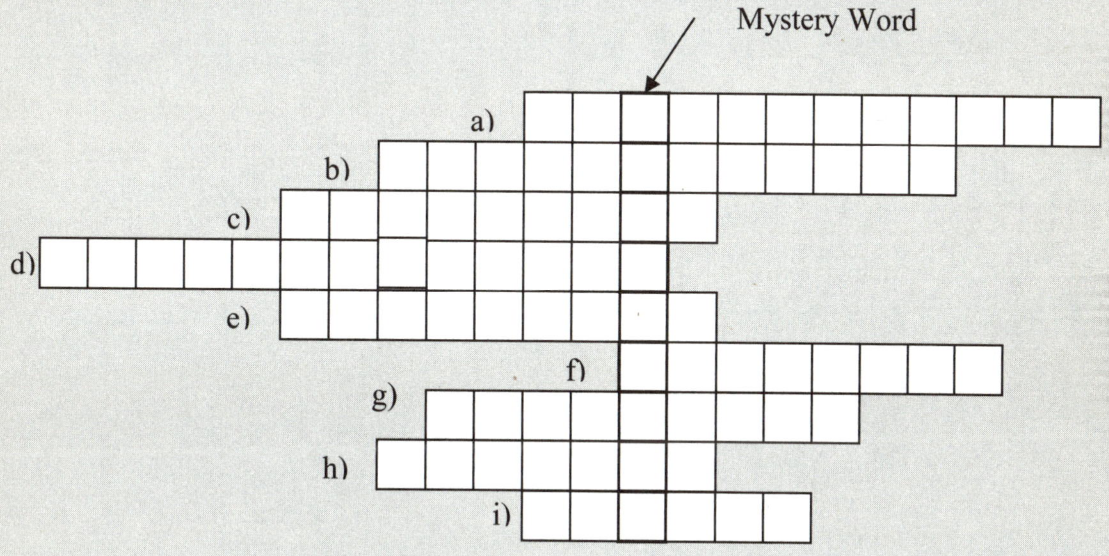

The Mystery Word is ____.

Check your answers in the Answer Key.

Chapter 2

International Business Concepts

Before You Start

Study the terms below and be sure that you understand each one. If any of the terms are unclear to you, you can find definitions in the Glossary.

Key Terms

absolute advantage
balance of payments
balance of trade
branch office
business practice law
cartel
common market
comparative advantage
contract manufacturing
countertrading
dumping
embargo
Euro
European Union (EU)
exchange rate
export
foreign direct investment
foreign subsidiary
franchising
free trade
General Agreement on Tariffs and Trade (GATT)
globalization
import
independent agent
international firm
International Monetary Fund (IMF)
joint venture
licensing
local content law
multinational firm
national competitive advantage
North American Free Trade Agreement (NAFTA)
per capita income
protectionism
quota
strategic alliance
subsidy
tariff
trade deficit
trade surplus
World Bank
World Trade Organization (WTO)

Now, listen to the chapter's Audio Key Terms List for the correct pronunciation of each term.

Exercise 1

Acronyms (words formed from the *first letters* of a title or common noun phrase) are frequently used in speaking about organizations and concepts in international business and economics.

Match the descriptions below with the correct circled acronym. Check the Glossary or the list of key terms at the beginning of this chapter if you forget any of the full titles or noun phrases. The first one is completed for you.

a) Agreement between most major European states to eliminate or standardize most of the trade barriers that affect the member states.

b) An organization that helps member nations to resolve trade disputes and negotiates new trade agreements.

c) An agreement to remove most of the tariffs and other barriers to trade between Canada, the United States, and Mexico.

d) An international trade agreement designed to make trade freer between all member states.

e) An international bank that helps countries achieve a balance of trade or a stronger economy through short- and long-term loans.

- GATT
- IMF
- NAFTA
- WTO
- EU

Check your answers in the Answer Key.

Exercise 2

The concepts of *absolute advantage*, *comparative advantage*, and *national competitive advantage* help to explain why countries import and export certain products. Read the descriptions of the three types of competitive advantage below and put the correct terms in the spaces provided.

If you need to, review the terms in the Glossary before you start.

a) When a country specializes in the efficient production of one type of product over all others, that country is said to have a(n) ____________________ advantage.

b) A country's ____________________ advantage in any given area is determined by a complex evaluation of factor conditions, demand conditions, related and supporting conditions, and strategies, structures, and rivalries.

c) When a country can cheaply and easily supply itself with all of a certain product that it needs, that country is said to have a(n) ____________________ advantage.

Check your answers in the Answer Key.

Exercise 3

Match these concepts of import/export balance with the picture that best represents them. The first one is completed for you.

balance of trade

a)

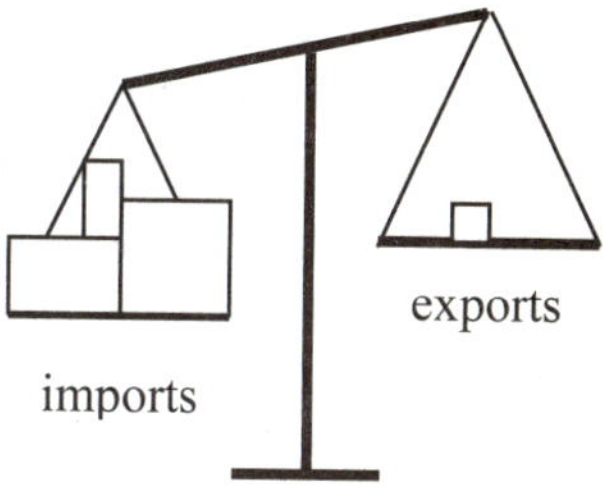

trade deficit

b)

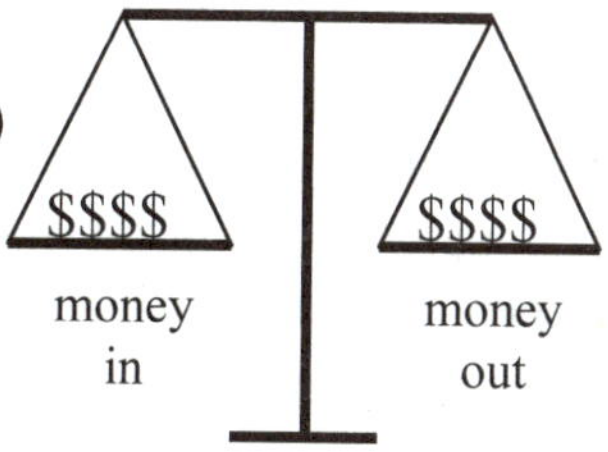

trade surplus

c)

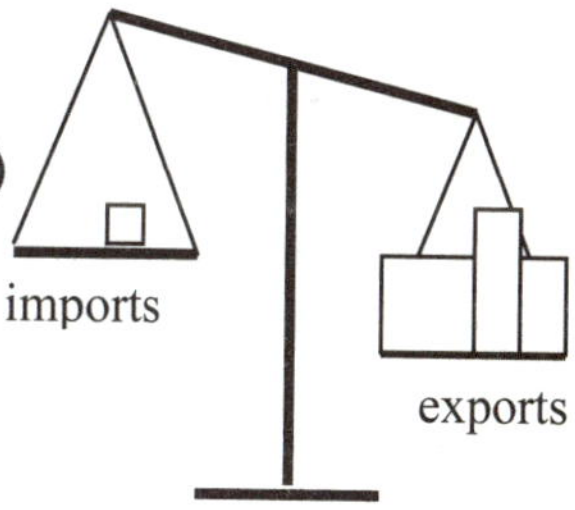

balance of payments

d)

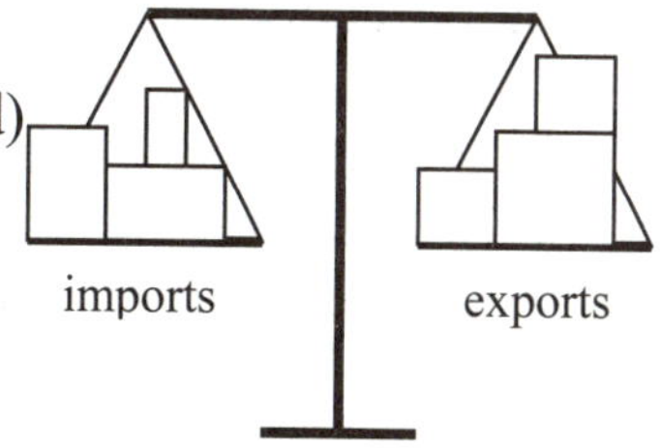

Check your answers in the Answer Key.

Grammar Tip

Relative Pronouns and Relative Clauses

Relative pronouns usually function as the subject in **relative clauses**. Words that can function as **relative pronouns** include *that, which, who, what, whom, whose, where, when,* and *why*. **Relative clauses** are sometimes called adjective clauses because they function like adjectives, modifying a noun that has already been specified in the main clause of the sentence. Look at the examples below. The **relative pronouns** are in *italics* and the nouns that the **relative clauses** modify are in **bold** type.

> She ate the **cake** *that* was sitting on the counter.
> He chose the **sweater,** *which* was on sale.
> They liked the **actor** *who* starred in their favourite movie.
> I enjoy the **times** *when* we are all together.

* Notice that *the* is used in all of these examples to introduce the noun that the relative clause modifies. The *the* often signifies that a relative clause will follow.

Defining and Non-Defining Relative Clauses

Relative clauses can be *defining* or *non-defining*. A *defining* **relative clause** gives information that is needed to identify the noun that is being modified. A *non-defining* **relative clause** gives extra information that may be interesting but is not necessary. A *non-defining* **relative clause** is separated from the main clause with a comma. *That* is commonly used to indicate a *defining* **relative clause** and *which* is used to indicate a *non-defining* **relative clause**. Look at the examples below.

> *Defining* **relative clauses**:
>
> I wanted the sweater *that* was lying on the chair.
> We spoke to the man *who* was sitting next to us.
> They moved into the house *that* they bought.
>
> *Non-defining* **relative clauses**:
>
> I wanted the red sweater, *which* was lying on the chair.
> We spoke to our friend, *who* was sitting next to us.
> They moved into their new house, *which* they bought last week.

Different **relative pronouns** have different functions. Study the chart below, then create a sentence using each **relative pronoun**.

Pronoun(s)	Function	Example
that, which	modify a thing or things, amount or superlative (that only)	
who, whom	modify a person or people	
where	modify a place	
when	modify an occasion or time	
why	modify a reason	
whose	possessive form of who; indicates ownership of something by the person it modifies	
what	means *the things that*	

Prepositions of Verbs in Relative Clauses

As you probably already know, some verbs are commonly combined with prepositions to create prepositional verbs (i.e. agree *with*, belong *to*, pay *for*). When this type of verb is used in a **relative clause**, the preposition can come at the beginning or the end of the **relative clause**.

It is considered correct in formal writing for the preposition to come at the *beginning of the* **relative clause**. However, in speaking, that often sounds artificial, and the preposition usually comes at the *end of the* **relative clause** in spoken English. Look at the examples below.

Formal and written English:

He practises the faith *in* which he *believes*. (*believe in*)
She loves the children *for* whom she must *care*. (*care for*)
They were waiting for the radio program *to* which they *listen* every Saturday night. (*listen to*)

Informal and spoken English:

He practises thc faith that he *believes in*.
She loves the children who she *cares for*.
They were waiting for the radio program which they *listen to* every Saturday night.

* Notice that *who* changes to *whom* after a preposition. Also, *that* is never used after a preposition.

Exercise 4

Put the correct relative pronoun into the following sentences. Use each of the following once in the exercise: *that*, *which*, *who*, *whom*, *what*, *whose*, *where*, *when*, and *why*.

a) We enjoyed the movie ____________ we watched on Friday night.

b) I saw the teacher ___________ class I was in last semester.

c) She wanted to know the reason ____________ he was so unhappy.

d) They remembered the time ____________ they were young and single.

e) I ran to my telephone, _____________ was on the wall in my kitchen.

f) It was her mother to _____________ she owed money.

g) He visited the house ____________ he lived as a child.

h) We showed our friends the new car ______________ we bought.

i) Tom was the friend _____________ liked hockey the best.

Check your answers in the Answer Key.

Exercise 5

Read the scenario below and fill in the appropriate relative pronouns.

It isn't difficult to understand how the terrorist attacks of September 11, 2001, on the United States, affected the lives of those a) _______ lost loved ones in that tragedy. The events of 9/11 have had a great political and social impact, b) ________ is still felt today. However, it may be less obvious just how this tragedy affected the world economy.

Globalization has turned "local" events into "global" events. Which areas of the global economy were affected by 9/11? It would be easier to ask about the areas c) _______were not affected. An immediate slowdown in global trade was a short-term result. Every company d) ________ traded internationally suddenly became vulnerable to the larger implied threat e) ________ characterized this event. Long-term effects include higher prices in many of the logistically connected services f) ________ facilitate international trade, such as the following: insurance rates (because of higher perceived risks); the necessity of ramping up security services; losses incurred because of longer border-crossing times; risks to just-in-time inventory systems and, therefore, the costs of having to retain higher inventories; tighter immigration policies g) ________ impede the ability to find skilled workers; and the list goes on.

It doesn't matter to h) ________ you speak today, everyone has had to change the way i) ___ they do business since 9/11.

Check your answers in the Answer Key.

Exercise 6

Match the definitions with these types of international business structures.

a) A branch office...	i) is a company that produces goods in one country and then transports and sells its products in other countries.
b) An exporter...	ii) is a company that buys products from other countries to sell in its domestic market.
c) Foreign direct investment...	iii) is a company that creates a partnership with a company in the foreign target market in order to produce and sell goods there.
d) A franchise...	iv) is a person or company that conducts business on behalf of an exporter in foreign markets.
e) An importer...	v) is the purchase or creation of assets in a foreign market by a person or company.
f) An independent agent...	vi) is a company involved in a kind of licensing arrangement in which the parent company maintains control over the practices of the licensed operations.
g) An international firm...	vii) is a company's granting of exclusive permission to foreign companies to produce and sell its product.
h) A joint venture/strategic alliance...	viii) is a company that conducts a large part of its business in foreign markets.
i) Licensing...	ix) is a company that structures its operations for the international market and is not firmly connected to any particular domestic market.
j) A multinational firm...	x) is part of a company that operates in foreign markets but under the same management structure as its domestic operations.

Check your answers in the Answer Key.

Exercise 7

Review the following examples of different types of international business structures. Then, listen to the scenarios on the CD accompanying this workbook and fill in the spaces below with the scenario that best represents each type of business structure. If you are having difficulty or would like to read more about any of these international business ventures, check the websites given at the end of this exercise.

These are the international business terms that you must match to the scenarios:

a) joint ventures and strategic alliances ____________________

b) exporting ____________________

c) contract manufacturing ____________________

d) foreign direct investment ____________________

e) franchising ____________________

f) licensing ____________________

Check your answers in the Answer Key.

For more information about the businesses described in the scenarios, go to the following websites:

Robeez: *www.robeez.com/en-us/about/sandra.htm*

FUN Technologies:
www.canadianbusiness.com/shared/print.jsp?content=20061121_021507_1_ccn_cn

Metal Supermarkets: *www.canadianbusiness.com/shared/print.jsp?content=49718*

Ciara Technologies: *www.ciara-tech.com/html_en/about_us.asp*

Sherritt International: *http://en.wikipedia.org/wiki/Sherritt_International*.

Salzgitter AG: *www.rbcinvest.theglobeandmail.com*

Exercise 8

The following terms describe barriers to international trade. Use those terms to complete the real-life scenarios below.

business practice law
cartel
dumping
embargo
local content law
quota
subsidy
tariff

a) During apartheid (enforced racial segregation policies) in South Africa, most western countries refused to export goods to or import goods from South Africa in protest against government practices. Those countries had an ______________________ on South African trade.

b) Embraer of Brazil and Bombardier of Canada are companies that manufacture executive jets. An ongoing battle has developed between the two companies, each complaining that the other is receiving huge amounts of financial assistance from its government, compromising free-market competition. Each believes that the other's government is giving the company a __________________.

c) In the past, there have been concerns that the member countries of OPEC (Organization of Petroleum Exporting Countries) were purposely fixing the price of oil on the international market. If this were true, OPEC would be considered an oil ___________________.

d) In South Korea, the government protects the domestic film industry by requiring cinemas in the country to play a certain percentage of South Korean films at all times. South Korea's cinemas must obey this __________________________________.

e) In order to protect its domestic market, Japan has limited imports of foreign automobiles. In other words, Japan has a _____________________ on foreign automobiles.

f) The Argentinean government imposes a high import tax on beef products in order to protect its domestic beef producers. This __________________ discourages beef producers from other countries from exporting to Argentina.

g) Oxfam, an international NGO (Non-Governmental Organization), has concerns about European practices that use export subsidies to flood the world market with sugar every year. This ___________________ closes off access to the world market for poorer countries producing sugar.

Check your answers in the Answer Key.

Exercise 9

Use the clues below to fill the names of internationally famous companies in the puzzle below. Use your knowledge and the internet to find the answers to the clues.

Clues

Across

3. This famous French producer of cosmetics and perfumes is also the parent company of L'Oreal and Biotherm brand cosmetics.
6. This Danish company produces a popular children's toy that consists of interlocking, coloured plastic bricks.
8. This German company produces comfortable shoes and sandals that are sold all over the world.
9. This Japanese electronics manufacturer is a Fortune 500 company.
10. This is a South Korean automotive manufacturer that also trades in steel and chemical products, electronic products, ocean-going vessels, and plants and machinery.

Down

1. This American discount department store chain has become a household name and now has stores in major cities throughout the world.
2. This Canadian company produces executive jets, regional aircraft, snowmobiles, and other transportation-related equipment.
4. This company produces and sells designer casual clothing and uses racial diversity in its popular magazine and billboard advertisements.
5. This Finnish manufacturer is currently the world's largest producer of mobile phones.
7. Probably the world's most famous fast-food restaurant chain, this company has recently been asked by Beijing to remove its famous golden arches in order to make the city more beautiful for the 2008 Olympics.

Check your answers in the Answer Key.

In the News 2.1

U.S. and Brazil Launch International Forum to Promote World Trade in Biofuels

Alexandra Olson

UNITED NATIONS—The world's two top ethanol producers—the U.S. and Brazil—announced the creation of an international forum to help turn biofuels into a globally traded commodity, just days before the two countries are expected to sign a separate agreement promoting the industry across the Western Hemisphere.

The International Biofuel Forum will meet regularly for a year to draft global standards for biofuel production, find ways to open markets and encourage investment in countries with the potential to develop the industry, officials said Friday. The forum also includes China, India, South Africa and the European Union Commission in an effort to involve the world's biggest potential consumers and producers.

"By working together we will be able to identify ways to help countries with agricultural potential become major energy suppliers," said Thomas A. Shannon, Assistant Secretary of State for Western Hemisphere Affairs. "We think this is a huge step forward in the development of a new international understanding of energy."

The announcement comes a week before President Bush travels to Brazil for talks in which renewable biofuels will top the agenda. Bush and Brazilian President Luiz Inacio Lula da Silva are expected to sign an agreement—separate from the international forum—to share scientific and technological research for an industry that has burgeoned in both countries.

"Biofuel cannot be promoted by just one country," Silva told journalists in Brazil on Thursday. "It is a global issue."

Brazil is the world's biggest ethanol exporter, using sugar cane to produce it. Eight out of 10 Brazilian cars run on ethanol, which emits far less greenhouse gases than fossil fuels. In the United States, where farmers use corn to make ethanol, production surpasses that in Brazil.

Brazil's method of producing ethanol is better than the American way, Silva suggested, noting that sugar cane–based ethanol is far cheaper to make than corn-based ethanol, and warm-weather climates like Brazil are the only places where sugar cane thrives.

Neither country produces enough ethanol to meet growing domestic demand. And while countries from Asia to Europe are pursuing biofuels as a way to reduce dependency on oil imports, international trade of alternative fuels is minimal.

Hoping to promote the emergence of such a market, participants in the forum created Friday will try to come up with technical quality standards for biofuels production, said Antonio Patriota, Brazil's Ambassador to the United States. Although the forum can only make recommendations for the rest of the world, Patriota said the eventual goal is to convene an international biofuel conference in Brazil next year.

Source: Alexandra Olson, "U.S. and Brazil Launch International Forum to Promote World Trade in Biofuels," Associated Press, March 3, 2007.

For the complete article online, visit
www.canadianbusiness.com/markets/market_news/article.jsp?content=D8NKI9E00

Exercise 10

Read the article, "U.S. and Brazil Launch International Forum to Promote World Trade in Biofuels," above. Then, use the information in the article to fill in the spaces in the sentences below.

a) Brazil and the U.S. are the world's top ______________ ______________.

b) In order to help turn biofuel into an internationally traded commodity, Brazil and the U.S. have announced the creation of an ______________ ______________.

c) China, India, South Africa, and the EUC have been included in the forum because they are considered the world's biggest ______________ consumers and producers.

d) Brazilian President Luis Inacio Lula de Silva claims that biofuel is a ______________ issue.

e) Brazil uses ______________ to produce ethanol.

f) The U.S. uses ______________ to produce ethanol.

g) The world's biggest ethanol exporter is ______________.

h) The U.S. ______________________ more ethanol than Brazil.

i) President Silva suggests that it is better to produce ethanol from sugar cane because it is __________________ to make than corn-based ethanol.

j) Although many countries are interested in biofuel as an alternative to oil, __________________ __________________ of biofuels is minimal.

k) Participants in the international biofuel forum will try to establish ________________ __________________ in order to promote an international alternative fuels market.

Check your answers in the Answer Key.

Test Your Knowledge 2

Try to choose the best answer for the following questions without looking back at the chapter or the Glossary. If you can't answer any of the questions, review that section and try again.

1. When a country imports more than it exports, it is said to have a _______.
   - a) trade surplus
   - b) trade deficit
   - c) absolute advantage
   - d) balance of trade

2. "Our country has a balance of trade, ________ is good for our economy."
   - a) which
   - b) whom
   - c) that
   - d) where

3. Financial support from government for domestic industry is called a ________.
   - a) tariff
   - b) subsidy
   - c) franchise
   - d) IMF

4. When a country can cheaply and easily produce all of a product that it needs, it is said to have ________.
   - a) a franchise
   - b) a comparative advantage
   - c) an absolute advantage
   - d) a business practice law

5. An acronym is a word made up of _______.
   a) a noun and a verb
   b) the first letters of a title or noun phrase
   c) an international firm
   d) the local content laws of a country

6. A foreign company in a partnership with a domestic company to do business in a country is called a _______.
   a) franchise
   b) trade surplus
   c) embargo
   d) joint venture

7. The North American Free Trade Act involves these countries:
   a) Canada, Brazil, and Argentina
   b) Canada, the United States, and England
   c) Canada, the United States, and Mexico
   d) Mexico, Brazil, and Argentina

8. The letters WTO stand for ________.
   a) Worst Tariff Organization
   b) World Trade Organization
   c) World Tariff Organization
   d) Worst Trade Organization

9. Large companies, like Coca-Cola, often sell permission to companies around the world to manufacture and sell their product. This relationship is called ________.
   a) licensing
   b) franchising
   c) subsidy
   d) globalization

10. When a company manufactures component parts for a company in another country that manufactures the complete product, the relationship between the companies is called _______.
    a) foreign direct investment
    b) contract manufacturing
    c) dumping
    d) relative clause

Check your answers in the Answer Key.

Chapter 3

Small Business, Entrepreneurship, and Business Ownership

Before You Start

Study the terms below and be sure that you understand each one. If any of the terms are unclear to you, you can find definitions in the Glossary.

Key Terms

acquisition
board of directors
business plan
chief executive officer
common stock
conglomerate merger
co-operative
corporate governance
divestiture
double taxation
employee stock ownership plan
entrepreneur
franchise
franchising agent
friendly takeover
general partner
horizontal merger
hostile takeover
initial public offering
inside directors
limited liability
limited partner
merger
microenterprise
outside directors
parent corporation
partnership
preferred stock
private corporation
public corporation
small business
sole proprietorship
spinoff
stock
stockholders (or shareholders)
strategic alliance
subsidiary corporation
tender offer
unlimited liability
vertical merger

Now, listen to the chapter's Audio Key Terms List for the correct pronunciation of each term.

Grammar Tip

A **phrase** is a group of two or more words that act like a single word. The simplest kind of phrase is called a **noun phrase**. In a **noun phrase**, two or more words act like a single noun, both in meaning and grammatical function. For example, the phrase *college professor* refers to one person and acts as a single noun in the following sentence: *The college professor opened the door.*

Many nouns are often found in the form of **noun phrases**. This is especially true in business language. The **noun phrases** in the exercise below are very common in business English.

Exercise 1a

Match up the two parts of these corporate noun phrases. The first one is completed for you.

a) double	executive officer
b) public	public offering
c) chief	liability
d) tender	corporation
e) inside	taxation
f) preferred	of directors
g) initial	offer
h) board	governance
i) corporate	directors
j) limited	stock

Check your answers in the Answer Key.

Exercise 1b

Use the phrases from the first part of the exercise to fill in the blanks in the sentences below.

a) Selling shares of stock in a company for the first time to a general investing public is called a(n) ______________________________.

b) ______________________________ are members of a corporation's board of directors who are also full-time employees of a corporation.

c) Shares whose owners have first claim on the corporation's assets and profits but who usually have no voting rights in the firm are called ______________________________.

d) A ________________________________ is a business whose stock is widely held and available for sale to the general public.

e) With __________________________, investor liability is limited to their personal investments in the corporation.

f) The relationship between shareholders, the board of directors, and other top managers in a corporation is called ________________________________.

g) The fact that a corporation must pay taxes on its profits, and shareholders must also pay taxes on the money they make from their investment, is referred to as

_______________________.

h) A ____________________________ is a group of individuals elected by a firm's shareholders and charged with overseeing, and taking legal responsibility for, the firm's decisions.

i) The person who is responsible for a firm's overall performance is called the

___________________________.

j) A ____________________________ is an offer to buy shares made by a prospective buyer directly to a corporation's shareholders.

Check your answers in the Answer Key.

Grammar Tip

A **preposition** is a word that links nouns, pronouns, and phrases to other words in a sentence. A **preposition** usually indicates the relationship in time, space, or logic of its object to the rest of the sentence. Look at the examples below.

> The newspaper is *on* the table.
> The newspaper is *about* current events.
> I read the newspaper *before* work.

Each of these sentences describes the newspaper's relationship to what comes after it in the sentence, either in time, space, or logic. Common **prepositions** include *on*, *in*, *over*, *under*, *beside*, *to*, *of*, *for*, *with*, *before*, *after*, and *about*.

Exercise 2

Choose one of the following prepositions to fill in the blanks below: *on, in, under, beside, to, of, for, with, before,* or *about.*

a) I work __________ many co-workers.

b) My computer sits __________ my desk.

c) __________ graduation, I worked at a bank.

d) We are going __________ the boardroom for a meeting.

e) The meeting is ___________ next year's budget.

f) His desk is __________ his office.

g) They all work __________ their boss.

h) She passed the report to the person __________ her.

i) The subway runs __________ the street.

j) I have had five cups __________ coffee today!

Check your answers in the Answer Key.

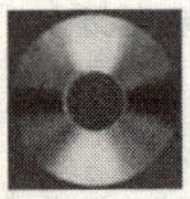

Exercise 3a

Listen to the dialogue. Number these concepts in the order that you hear them.

a) ____ franchises

b) ____ sole proprietorship

c) ____ succession planning

d) ____ entrepreneur

e) ____ partnership

Check your answers in the Answer Key.

Exercise 3b

Now, listen again and write the correct preposition in the blanks in the statements below.

a) I have been __________ business for over 30 years.

b) We operated mainly out __________ malls and food courts.

c) I am in a partnership ___________ my brother.

d) We run them all, with a manager ___________ each shop.

e) We'd like to pass the business ___________ to someone else.

Check your answers in the Answer Key.

Exercise 4

Match these concepts of business ownership with the picture that best represents them.

a) horizontal merger

b) friendly takeover

c) acquisition

d) spinoff

e) conglomerate merger

f) divestiture

g) vertical merger

h) hostile takeover

i)
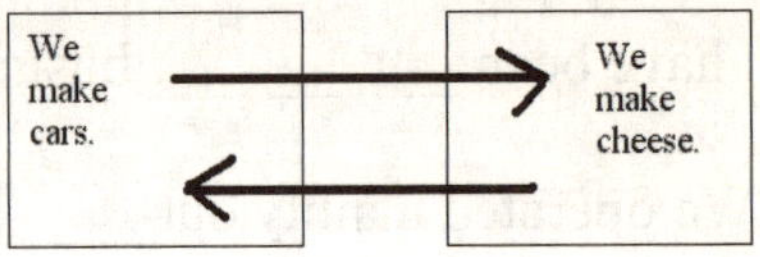

ii)
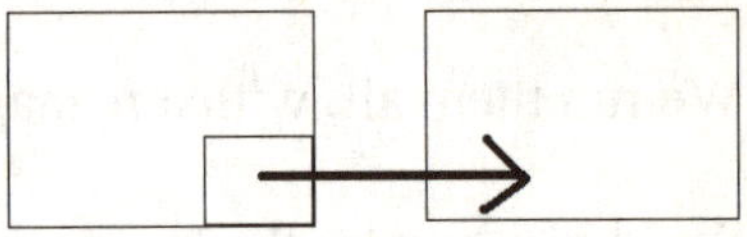

iii)
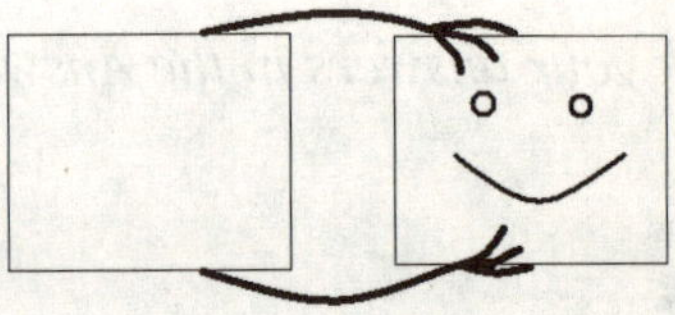

iv)
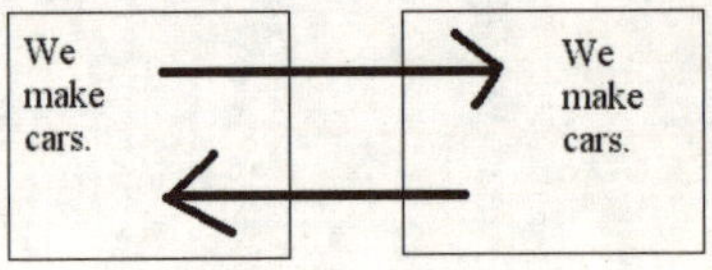

v)
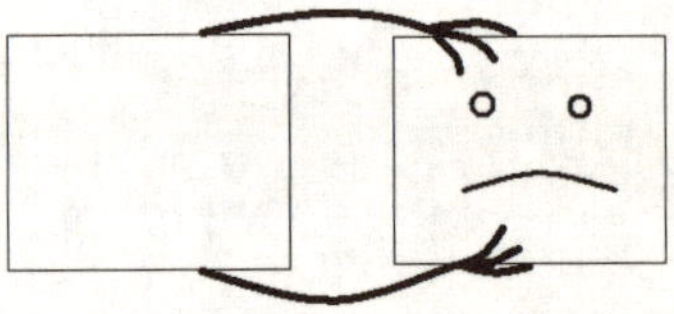

vi)
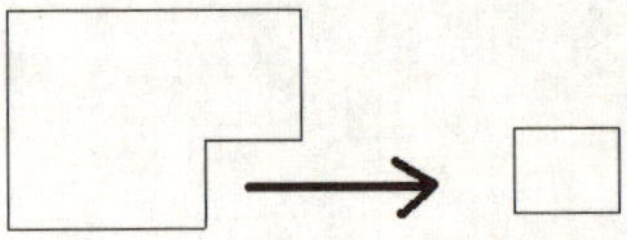

vii)
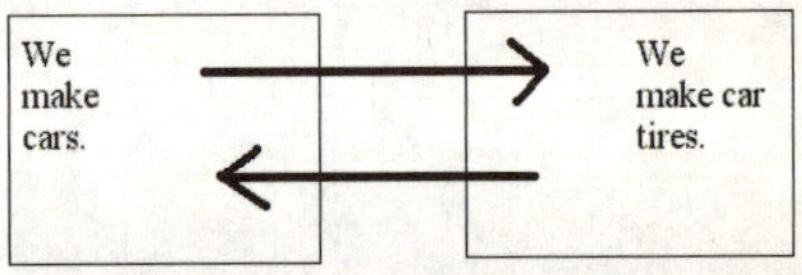

viii)
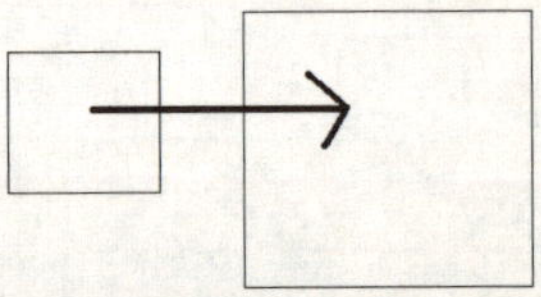

Check your answers in the Answer Key.

In the News 3.1

Clock's Ticking on Succession Planning

Sasha Nagy

The president of the Business Development Bank of Canada (BDC) has a message for small business owners who haven't made a succession plan.

The clock's ticking.

"Because of population aging, the Canadian economy will experience an unprecedented wave of business ownership transitions in the next few years," said Jean-Rene Halde, at a luncheon meeting at the Vancouver Board of Trade on Thursday. "It is estimated that trillions of dollars in assets will change hands in the next ten years. But the most disturbing aspect is that a large number of entrepreneurs do not have a succession plan in place."

Mr. Halde says some people will end up selling, willingly or unwillingly, their business without any assurance of continuity.

And if that happens, a lifetime spent building a business could be for naught.

According to a study done by the Canadian Federation of Independent Business (CFIB), 70 percent of Canadian entrepreneurs will retire in the next ten years, and nearly half of those who plan to retire in the next five years do not have a succession plan in place.

A poorly prepared or non-existent business ownership transition process can harm the Canadian economy, with a drop in productivity, job losses and an increase in the business bankruptcy rate.

"It is important for the main financial and political stakeholders to make entrepreneurs aware of the fact that they will have to hand over the reins sooner or later," Mr. Halde said.

The BDC president stressed the importance of conveying to entrepreneurs the advantages of planning the transition process, and pointing out the support role that outside consultants can play in managing the financial, tax and legal implications.

According to Mr. Halde, there is growing interest regarding business ownership transition in British Columbia, citing as one example UBC's Sauder School of Business' unique venture dedicated to helping family businesses succeed from one generation to the next called Business Families Centre.

But transition planning is an issue for non-family businesses as well.

"Business ownership transitions can be considered successful if the sellers achieve the financial security they are looking for and believe that they obtained a fair price and found the right person to take over, who will ensure the survival of the business," Mr. Halde explained. "As for the buyers, they will want to make sure that the conditions of the sale increase their chances of success."

Since financing is often the first obstacle to carrying out a business ownership transition plan, Canadian financial institutions are trying to meet this need by offering entrepreneurs financial solutions tailored to their particular situation. For example, BDC offers entrepreneurs an integrated solution that includes consulting services. It can help businesses on both sides of the equation, the primary goal being the continuity of Canadian businesses.

Source: Sasha Nagy, "Clock's Ticking on Succession Planning," *The Globe and Mail*, February 9, 2006. Reprinted with permission from *The Globe and Mail*.

For the complete article, visit
www.theglobeandmail.com/servlet/story/RTGAM.20060209.wsuccession09/BNStory/specialSmallBusiness

Exercise 5

Read the article, "Clock's Ticking on Succession Planning," above, then circle the correct preposition in the summary statements below.

a) The lack of succession planning in Canadian small businesses could be harmful **to/of** the Canadian economy.

b) Succession planning can help family businesses to succeed **for/from** one generation to the next.

c) The aging of Canada's population means that there will soon be a large number **to/of** business ownership transitions.

d) Business owners must accept that they will need to hand over control **of/from** their businesses eventually.

e) Outside consultants can help **in/with** practical issues involved in transition planning. Succession planning is an issue **of/for** both family and non-family businesses.

f) Sellers consider a transition successful if they get the financial security they are looking **for/to**, believe they got a fair price, and believe they found a buyer who will ensure the survival **for/of** the business.

g) Buyers want to know that the conditions of sale will increase their chances **to/of** success.

h) Canadian financial institutions are offering solutions, including consulting services, to help with the continuity **of/to** Canadian businesses.

Check your answers in the Answer Key.

Exercise 6

Do you have what it takes to be an entrepreneur? Rate yourself for the following statements by circling a number between 0 and 5. (A rating of 5 means that the statement is very true for you. A rating of 0 means that it is absolutely not true for you.)

a) I deal well with uncertainty and risk.

0 1 2 3 4 5

b) I would really like to be my own boss someday.

0 1 2 3 4 5

c) I am very good at developing and maintaining relationships with others.

0 1 2 3 4 5

d) I enjoy and seek out challenges.

0 1 2 3 4 5

e) I don't get discouraged by small failures. I just keep on trying.

0 1 2 3 4 5

f) People would say of me that I have a certain charisma that attracts them to me.

0 1 2 3 4 5

g) I have a high degree of creativity.

0 1 2 3 4 5

h) My improvisational skills are excellent and assist me in finding solutions to problems.

0 1 2 3 4 5

i) I have a great deal of stamina and work toward achievement through action.

0 1 2 3 4 5

j) I am open-minded and therefore am able to see opportunities as they arise.

0 1 2 3 4 5

k) I know my talents and abilities; I am self-confident.

0 1 2 3 4 5

l) I like adventure—trying new things and being responsible for favourable outcomes.

0 1 2 3 4 5

m) I am assertive.

0 1 2 3 4 5

n) I am able to make decisions.

0 1 2 3 4 5

o) I believe that having one's own business gives one more control over one's life.

0 1 2 3 4 5

Now add together your score from each question to get your final total. *Check your results in the Answer Key.*

Exercise 7

Use the terms listed below to fill in the blanks in the following paragraph.

weak control	insufficient
success	competence
managerial	failure
market demand	dedication

Four basic factors explain most small-business (a)__________________: the first is hard work, drive, and (b) ________________; the second is (c) ___________________ for the products or services being provided; the third is managerial (d) ___________________; and the fourth is luck. Four other factors contribute to small-business (e)_______________: the first is (f) ______________ incompetence or inexperience; the second is neglect; the third is (g) ______________ systems; and the fourth is (h) ___________________ capital.

Check your answers in the Answer Key.

Exercise 8

Draw lines to connect the forms of business ownership with the correct definition. The first one is completed for you.

a) partnership

b) corporation

c) sole proprietorship

d) co-operative

i) business formed to benefit its owners in the form of reduced prices and/or the distribution of surpluses at year-end

ii) business owned and usually operated by one person who is responsible for all of its debts

iii) business with two or more owners who share in the operation of the firm and in financial responsibility for the firm's debts

iv) business considered a legal entity separate from its owners and in which the liability of the owners is limited to their investment in the firm

Check your answers in the Answer Key.

In the News 3.2

Director Elections Campaign Pays Off

Janet McFarland

More than 20 major Canadian companies have pledged to introduce new voting provisions for electing directors following an aggressive behind-the-scenes lobbying campaign by the Canadian Coalition for Good Governance (CCGG).

The powerful coalition, which represents 46 institutional investors with more than $1-trillion in assets under management, has contacted the chairmen of Canada's 150 largest public companies since last fall, urging them to adopt the new voting standard.

The CCGG wants firms to implement a policy requiring directors to tender their resignations if they fail to receive majority support from shareholders in board elections.

CCGG managing director David Beatty said such a requirement gives "an outward and visible sign" to shareholders that their views on director elections do matter.

"It overcomes literally generations of meaningless voting," Mr. Beatty said in an interview.

In Canada and the United States, shareholders receive ballots allowing them to vote "for" a director or to "withhold" their votes. However, the ballots do not allow them to vote against a director, which means board members can be elected with even a single vote cast in their favour.

To address the gap, the CCGG is urging companies to require their directors to voluntarily resign if they do not get at least 50-percent support from shareholders.

Mr. Beatty said the CCGG has decided to ask companies individually to change their policies because it is easier than lobbying the federal government to change legislation governing all director elections.

"We just want the board and individual directors to be conscious that there are shareholders out there and their views do count."

All of the major banks have announced they are adopting new policies requiring directors to voluntarily resign if they fail to get the support of a majority. Manulife Financial Corp. and Sun Life Financial Inc. have also agreed to adopt similar standards.

Mr. Beatty said the CCGG has written to the chairmen of the 150 largest Canadian companies, encouraging them all to implement the same voting policy. The CCGG subsequently sent them copies of the new provisions announced by the major banks in their proxy circulars released early this year.

He said CCGG members are phoning chairmen of 50 large companies to talk to them about the policy.

Including the banks, at least 17 of Canada's top 50 companies have indicated they are adopting a new policy, and another six smaller companies have said they will introduce the rule, he said.

Among the companies implementing new majority voting policies are Canadian Pacific Railway Ltd., TSX Group inc., Goldcorp inc., Potash Corp. of Saskatchewan Inc. and TransCanada Corp.

Potash Corp. spokeswoman Betty-Ann Heggie said the board responded to the wishes of investors.

"Our board is really sensitive to what they think investors are looking for," she said. "It's a big issue on people's agendas right now."

Mr. Beatty credits Toronto securities lawyer James Baillie for leading the "breakthrough" on getting companies to adopt the policy.

Mr. Baillie, a former chairman of the Ontario Securities Commission, lobbied Canada's big banks last fall on CCGG's behalf. He also sought an advance ruling from the federal banking regulator to ensure the banks knew they had the clear authority to change their policies.

Mr. Baillie said yesterday it was an easy decision to get involved. "I thought it was a good idea, and I said: 'Sure I'll give you some help.' Somebody who can't get a majority of the votes available cast in his or her favour, I have no trouble with the proposition that that person should not become a director."

Most of the new policies require directors to tender their resignations if they fail to win majority support, but leave the board discretion to choose to reject the offer.

Mr. Beatty said the CCGG is willing to allow some discretion. For example, he said many large institutional investors have policies requiring them to vote against directors who have bad attendance records, even if they were ill and have since recovered.

Source: Janet McFarland, "Director Elections Campaign Pays Off," *The Globe and Mail*, March 9, 2006. Reprinted with permission from *The Globe and Mail*.

For the complete article, visit
www.globeandmail.com/servlet/Page/document/v5/content/subscribe?user_URL

Exercise 9

Read the article, "Director Elections Campaign Pays Off," above, and then answer the comprehension questions below. If you need to, review corporate terms in the Glossary.

a) Is the CCGG's call for changes to director elections likely focused on public or private corporations?

b) Who does the CCGG work to protect?

c) In a corporation that has not changed to the CCGG's recommended system, what can shareholders do to express their disapproval of a current director?

d) What discretionary power do boards of directors have over the new system?

e) Why is the CCGG trying to get corporations to agree to voluntarily adopt the new voting provisions for electing directors?

f) What advantage is there for companies that adopt the new system?

Check your answers in the Answer Key.

Exercise 10

Fill in the business terms that describe each of the following real-life scenarios.

a) Mary works as a law clerk. In her spare time, she shops for vintage clothes and sells them on the internet. Her internet store is very successful. Mary's internet business is called a ______________________________.

b) Charles wants to open a restaurant but he doesn't have enough capital to do it by himself. Charles is looking for investors. He has written down all of his ideas and his financial projections. He shows these documents to possible investors. These documents are Charles' ____________________________.

c) Anwar owns a car dealership. His dealership is not incorporated and it is a sole proprietorship. If Anwar's dealership has financial trouble, Anwar could lose his house and all of his other belongings. Anwar has __________________________.

d) Juicy Beverages Incorporated sells a popular line of sports beverages. Tough Guy Incorporated runs a successful chain of fitness clubs for men. These two companies have decided to work together to increase both of their profits. These two companies are in a ____________________________.

e) Last year, Juanita opened a bar. Her father-in-law invested money in the bar but he is not involved in the management of the bar. Juanita's father-in-law is a ________________________ in the bar business.

f) Juicy Beverages Incorporated makes only sports beverages. However, Juicy is owned by a larger corporation that produces standard carbonated beverages and juices. Juicy is a ______________________ of the larger corporation.

g) Anita only eats organic fruits and vegetables. Many other people in her neighbourhood share the same lifestyle. Last year, a group of people in Anita's neighbourhood got together and decided to start purchasing organic produce regularly in bulk in order to save money. Anita invested some money in the organization. Anita is part of a ________________________.

h) Sheila is on the board of directors of a large shipping company. She helps to make the business decisions that will make the company successful. However, Sheila does not work in the company's day-to-day operations. Sheila is an ______________________.

i) Sajid works for an internet provider. The company is owned by the people who work there. They each own stock in the company. Because Sajid has been there for a long time, he owns a lot of the company's stock. Sajid's company works on a ___________________________.

j) Vlad is on the board of directors of a large cheese manufacturing company. Vlad is also the company's chief accountant. Vlad is an _________________________.

Check your answers in the Answer Key.

Exercise 11

Read the following list of items and place them in the correct section of the business plan chart below.

a brief history of the company
capital sources
promotional strategy
break-even analysis
assignment of responsibilities
detailed financial statements
distribution strategy
production facilities and equipment needed
the training/skills needed
explanation of the business strategy
form of ownership
cash-flow forecast
detailed management biographies
competitive analysis
inventory requirements
all production processes
industry overview

Business Plan Section	Items
Executive Summary	
Background	
Marketing	
Production and Manufacturing	
Finance	
Human Resources	
Appendices	

Check your answers in the Answer Key.

Test Your Knowledge 3

Use your new knowledge and skills to solve the clues and complete the puzzle!

Clues

Across

6. Occurs when a company sells part of its existing business operations to another company.
11. The purchase of a company by another, larger firm, which absorbs the smaller company into its operations.
12. Shares whose owners usually have last claim on the corporation's assets but who have voting rights in the firm are owners of ___________ stock.

13. Members of a corporation's board of directors who are not also employees of the corporation on a day-to-day basis are called ____________ directors.
14. An enterprise in which two or more persons or companies temporarily join forces to undertake a particular project is called a ____________ alliance.
15. A ____________ corporation is owned by another corporation.
16. When a person buys stock in a company, they are said to ____________ in that company.
18. An arrangement that gives one business entity the right to sell the products of another.

Down

1. A person who has limited financial responsibility in a business enterprise is said to have limited ____________.
2. A ____________ takeover is an acquisition in which the management of the acquired company fights the firm's buyout by another company.
3. A ____________ corporation is a business whose stock is widely held and available for sale to the general public.
4. A ____________ merger is a merger of two firms that have previously been direct competitors in the same industry.
5. A business enterprise is also often called a business ____________.
6. In the event of failure, the bankruptcy courts may seize a corporation's assets and sell them to pay ____________.
7. A business person who accepts both the risks and the opportunities involved in creating and operating a new business.
8. An enterprise that the owner operates part-time from home while continuing regular employment elsewhere.
9. The person responsible for the firm's overall performance.
10. Shares of ownership in a corporation.
17. The strategy of setting up one or more corporate units as new, independent corporations.

Check your answers in the Answer Key.

Chapter 4

Social Responsibility, the Environment, and Ethics

Before You Start

Study the terms below and be sure that you understand each one. If any of the terms are unclear to you, you can find definitions in the Glossary.

Key Terms

accommodative stance
acid rain
business ethics
collusion
compliance-based ethics codes
consumerism
corporate philanthropy
corporate responsibility
corporate social responsibility (CSR)
defensive stance
ethical behaviour
ethics
insider trading
integrity-based ethics codes
managerial ethics
obstructionist stance
organizational stakeholders
pollution
proactive stance
recycling
social audit
special social initiatives
toxic waste
unethical behaviour
whistle blower

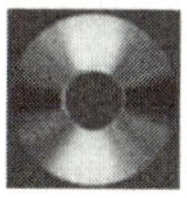

Now, listen to the chapter's Audio Key Terms List for the correct pronunciation of each term.

Exercise 1a

There is a broad spectrum of approaches that businesses can take to corporate social responsibility, ranging from socially irresponsible to very socially responsible. Although it is often difficult to put such labels on real-life businesses, there are four terms used to describe approaches to social responsibility. Place the four terms in the correct place on the spectrum of social responsibility below.

accommodative stance
defensive stance
obstructionist stance
proactive stance

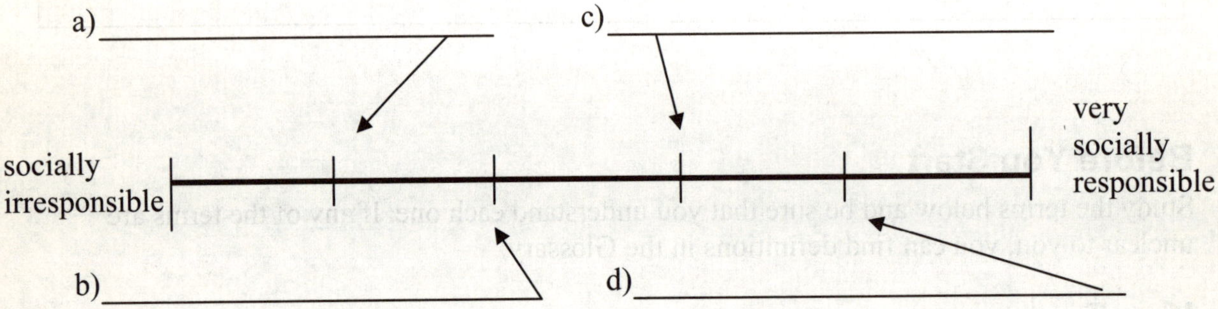

Check your answers in the Answer Key.

Exercise 1b

Now, use the four terms from the exercise above to label the examples of approaches to social responsibility below.

a) A popular chain of coffee shops switched to recycled paper cups years ago and has recently started using recycled toilet tissue in its bathrooms. The company has looked into the cost of Fair Trade coffee and is planning to switch over to Fair Trade coffees in all of its stores. For years, a portion of the company's profits has been donated to local literacy programs. This business takes a(n) ______________________ stance to social responsibility.

b) This industrial supplier of cleaning products used to dump its waste into a local water source. When legislation was passed to prohibit this dumping, the company was careful to follow the letter of the law. They know that they will eventually have to add filters to the exhaust from their plants, but they aren't going to add the filters until they have to. This company takes a(n) ______________________ stance to social responsibility.

c) This auto manufacturer is actively fighting the adoption of the Kyoto protocols in its country. Industry watchdogs have suspected for years that the accounting practices of this company are dishonest or even illegal, but the company actively denies these charges and has so far avoided an investigation. This company takes a(n) ______________________ stance to social responsibility.

d) This large electronics company adheres to all environmental regulations. Recently, employees expressed an interest in switching to recycled paper products in all offices and cafeterias. Management researched the suggestion, found it was workable, and adopted it. This company takes a(n) ____________________________ stance to social responsibility.

Check your answers in the Answer Key.

Exercise 2

In the last three decades, environmental considerations have become an important issue in business ethics. Match the following environmental terms with their definitions. The first one is completed for you.

acid rain	a)...is the contamination of the environment, including land, water, and air, by chemical or radioactive emissions.
pollution	b)...is the practice of breaking down used products, like glass bottles, newspapers, and plastic containers, and using the resulting materials to create new products.
recycling	c)...is the dangerous chemical or radioactive byproduct of industry. Special measures must be taken in the disposal of these byproducts to ensure that land, water, and air are not contaminated.
toxic waste	d)...is the result of sulfur dioxide or nitrous oxides released into the atmosphere by industry, which then falls to the earth again in the form of highly acidic precipitation.

Check your answers in the Answer Key.

In the News 4.1

Idol Puts Its Celebrity to Good Use

Vinay Menon

Television's most powerful brand will temporarily rebrand itself with a two-night extravaganza that promises to meld the show's vapid karaoke vibe with a newfound spirit of altruism.

Idol Gives Back is a "historic television event" that's part concert, part fundraiser, part new trick, part same old.

The same old: the Top 6 finalists will perform tonight. After they sing "Life Anthems," you, the viewer, will be encouraged to vote for your favourite.

The new trick: for every vote, corporate sponsors will donate an undisclosed sum to various charities that are fighting extreme poverty in Africa and America.

The fundraiser: viewers can also donate via phone, the Web and, for fusty traditionalists, the post office.

The concert: the show will broadcast live tomorrow from the Walt Disney Concert Hall in Los Angeles, where Ellen DeGeneres will emcee the proceedings.

And as confirmed yesterday, Bono—*Bono!*—will take part in Wednesday's show to discuss his charitable work in Africa. The Top 6 will also sing "American Prayer," a song co-written by the U2 front man.

Other scheduled guests (note: there could be changes) for *Idol Gives Back* include: Jack Black, Helen Mirren, Annie Lennox, Gwen Stefani, Daniel Radcliffe, Sacha Baron Cohen, Michael Bublé, Teri Hatcher, Brad Garrett, Brian McKnight, Rowan Atkinson, Helena Bonham Carter, Forest Whitaker, Keira Knightley, Hugh Grant, Céline Dion, Pink, Earth, Wind & Fire, and Il Divo.

Hmmm. Does Hatcher know that Ryan Seacrest still works for *Idol*? And isn't there some kind of international treaty that prohibits Harry Potter, Borat, and Mr. Bean from appearing on the same show?

So is *Idol Gives Back* good, bad, or somewhere in between? Maybe old age is making me mushy—or I'm too tired for sniggering cynicism—but I'm going with an unqualified "good."

Seriously.

In recent years, celebrity activism has become a sort of cultural imperative.

Stars are still rich and famous, sure, but many have added a new dimension to their public personas: conspicuous compassion.

Put it this way: when George Clooney delivers a speech on the genocide ravaging Darfur, he does so at the United Nations Security Council.

Scratch any issue—from the environment to poverty to disease to third-world debt relief—and you'll find a celebrity. Make that, many celebrities.

To an entire generation, Live Aid was a watershed, a revelation, a flashbulb memory.
As such, Live Aid is there, in spirit, for everything that has followed—from Farm Aid to the Human Rights Now! tour, the Concert for New York City to the SARS benefit concert...in Toronto.

Undoubtedly, *Idol Gives Back* will elicit some griping and sniping since there will be those who find it impossible to extract this one-off charitable act from the show's superficial DNA.

But here's the thing: *American Idol* is now itself a "celebrity." So it was only a matter of time before it would start acting like one. Meaning, it deserves praise when it uses its power for good.

Source: Vinay Menon, "Idol Puts Its Celebrity to Good Use," *Toronto Star*, April 24, 2007. Reprinted with permission – Torstar Syndication Services.

For the complete article, visit *www.thestar.com/printArticle/206387*

Exercise 3

a) What is the above article, "*Idol* Puts Its Celebrity to Good Use," really about?
- i) corporate philanthropy
- ii) celebrities getting together to support a good cause
- iii) getting viewers to donate money to help stop poverty
- iv) *American Idol* getting on the fundraiser bandwagon
- v) all of the above

b) The article calls *Idol Gives Back* a "historic television event." Name the four components that make this broadcast special, according to the author of the article.

c) *Idol Gives Back* is attempting to raise money to put a stop to poverty in which countries?

d) Re-read the article and find the expressions or words that are defined as:
- i) changing the image or qualities of the program
- ii) concern for the welfare of others; selflessness
- iii) organizations that support a particular cause
- iv) presenting as a gift to a fund or a cause; to contribute
- v) to act as master of ceremonies
- vi) to prevent; to hinder; to hold back
- vii) being scornful of the motives or actions of others; mocking
- viii) obligatory; mandatory
- ix) attracting attention with generosity; being noticed for supporting a cause
- x) the systematic, planned annihilation of a racial, political, or cultural group
- xi) grumbling; complaining

Check your answers in the Answer Key.

Grammar Tip

In **Chapter 1** you studied coordinating conjunctions, which are used to link two ideas or two clauses (grammatical units containing a subject and verb) together. **Subordinating conjunctions** are also used to link two clauses together. However, **subordinating conjunctions** work to subordinate one clause, or make one clause less important than the other. Study the sentences below.

She was late for work **because** she missed her train.
(subordinate clause)
He will look for a new job **if** his boss doesn't give him a raise.
(subordinate clause)

The word *because* makes the clause *because she missed her train* less important than the clause that comes before it, which is called the main clause. The most important information in the sentence is *she was late for work*. It is a complete thought and a complete sentence on its own. The reason why she was late is extra information and therefore subordinate to the main clause in the sentence.

The **subordinate clause** can also come before the main clause. Study the examples below.

Because she missed her train, she was late for work.
(subordinate clause)
If his boss doesn't give him a raise, he will look for a new job.
(subordinate clause)

When the **subordinate clause** comes before the main clause, it must be separated from the main clause with a comma. When the main clause comes first, no comma is necessary.

The table below lists some of the most common **subordinating conjunctions** and their functions.

function	**conjunctions**	**example**
reason or cause	**because, since**	**Because** he was good with numbers, he studied economics. She expected a bonus **since** she worked so hard on the project.
condition	**if, unless**	**If** the company makes money, the stockholders will be pleased. He has a meeting every Monday **unless** it is a holiday.
contrast	**although, while**	**Although** he was tired, he worked on the project all night. Jamil works in accounting, **while** Sam works in media relations.

time	*same time*	**when, while**	**When** Sophia arrived, Tran was in the office. Luigi worked on the computer **while** Anita completed the budget.
	earlier time	**before, until**	**Before** he got to the office, Will stopped to buy some coffee. They kept records on paper **until** the system was computerized.
	later time	**after, since**	**After** the meeting, Carlos and Robert went for lunch. The company has reduced its emissions **since** the Kyoto protocol came through.

Exercise 4

Use the subordinating conjunctions listed below to fill in the blanks in the paragraph.

after
until
while
because
if
although

Social responsibility was not a substantial factor in business practices **a)** ______________ the second half of the twentieth century. **b)** ______________ social responsibility has become a bigger issue for business in the last 30 years, all companies do not approach the issue in the same way. Some companies adopt an obstructionist or defensive stance, **c)** ______________ other, forward-thinking companies adopt an accommodative or proactive stance. Some companies do not address social responsibility **d)** ________________ they are worried that it will cut into their profits. However, **e)** ________________ the government becomes more aggressive about meeting the Kyoto protocol, companies will have little choice. Furthermore, many companies are experiencing greater profits **f)** ___________________ they have adopted a proactive stance toward social responsibility. Consumer priorities and the Kyoto protocol are making it essential that business take social responsibility seriously.

Check your answers in the Answer Key.

Exercise 5

Use subordinating conjunctions to fill in the blanks in the sentences below relating to the **In the News 4.1** article, "Idol Puts Its Celebrity to Good Use," by Vinay Menon. In some cases, more than one answer is possible.

a) Menon suggests that ____________________ *Idol Gives Back*, the TV series *American Idol* had a "vapid karaoke vibe."

b) Menon explains that some elements of the show will be something new_____________ other elements of the show will be the same old thing.

c) Corporate sponsors will donate money for each vote from viewers. Therefore, ______________ viewers want to help fight poverty, they should vote.

d) Guests will include Bono, Daniel Radcliffe, and Keira Knightley ______________ there are changes.

e) ______________ Teri Hatcher and Ryan Seacrest dated and broke up, they are both appearing on *Idol Gives Back.*

f) ______________ the Live Aid concert in 1985, which featured many famous musicians, the public has expected celebrities to be rich, famous, *and* engaged in activism.

g) Menon anticipates some "griping and sniping" from the public regarding *Idol Gives Back* ______________ *American Idol* is such a "superficial" show.

h) Menon argues that *American Idol* "deserves praise" ______________ it is "us[ing] its power for good."

Check your answers in the Answer Key.

Exercise 6

Listen to the dialogue. Number the concepts in the order that you hear them. Listen again if necessary.

a) ____ accommodative stance
b) ____ acid rain
c) ____ consumerism
d) ____ ethics
e) ____ organizational stakeholders
f) ____ pollution
g) ____ proactive stance
h) ____ recycling
i) ____ social audit
j) ____ social responsibility
k) ____ toxic waste

Check your answers in the Answer Key.

Exercise 7

Corporations and organizations can implement ethics codes in two different ways: integrity-based ethics codes and compliance-based ethics codes. Examples of business practices are listed below. Sort the list by letter (a, b, c…) into the categories provided. If you need to, review the definitions of integrity-based and compliance-based ethics codes in the Glossary.

a) All documents that originate with management use proper documentation of sources for research and studies so that no copyright laws are broken.

b) A copy of the main points of the company's code of ethics is visibly posted in all offices and work areas.

c) Employees who are caught accepting bribes are dismissed without severance pay.

d) Instructional seminars on ethical practices are conducted regularly for staff.

e) Accounts are double-checked by an independent agent.

f) Contracts with suppliers include strict quality controls and an assurance of ethical practices.

g) Employees are kept up to date on philanthropic projects and donations.

h) When they are hired, employees must sign a contract promising to adhere to the organization's ethics code.

compliance-based ethics codes	**integrity-based ethics codes**

Check your answers in the Answer Key.

Exercise 8

Use the listed terms related to business ethics to fill in the blanks in the definitions below.

collusion
consumerism
insider trading
organizational stakeholders
social audit
whistle blower

a) ________________________ are the groups that are most affected by a firm or company's practices. They include consumers, investors, employees, suppliers, and the surrounding community.

b) The social movement that advocates on behalf of purchasers is called

________________________.

c) A systematic evaluation of a company's investment in and progress toward its social goals is called a ______________________.

d) ____________________ occurs when companies work together to artificially raise prices.

e) A ____________________ is an employee who reports wrongdoing within the company or industry he or she works for.

f) When an individual uses privileged corporate information to benefit themselves, their family, or their friends, it is called ____________________.

Check your answers in the Answer Key.

Test Your Knowledge 4

Use your new knowledge and skills to solve the clues and complete the puzzle!

Clues

Across

2. The dangerous chemical or radioactive byproducts of industry are called __________ waste.
4. The result of sulfur dioxide or nitrous oxides released into the atmosphere is called __________ rain.

5. Corporate ethics codes that focus on rules and penalties are called ______________-based ethics codes.
9. A company that actively seeks out ways to improve its social responsibility takes a ______________ stance to social responsibility.
12. Employees who report wrongdoing on behalf of the company or industry they work for.
13. A subordinating conjunction that indicates reason or cause.

Down

1. The contamination of the environment, including land, water, and air, by chemical or radioactive emissions.
3. The groups that are most affected by a firm or company's practices are called ______________ stakeholders.
6. The social movement that advocates on behalf of consumers.
7. When companies work together to artificially raise prices.
8. A systematic evaluation of a company's investment in and progress toward its social goals is called a social ____________.
10. A subordinating conjunction that indicates contrast.
11. The practice of breaking down used products and using the resulting materials to create new products.

Check your answers in the Answer Key.

Chapter 5

Management: Planning, Organizing, and Controlling

Before You Start

Study the terms below and be sure that you understand each one. If any of the terms are unclear to you, you can find definitions in the Glossary.

Key Terms

accountability
authority
board of directors
brainstorming
chain of command
conceptual skills
contingency planning
controlling
crisis planning
decision making
delegation
departmentalization
goals
human relations skills
leading
management
middle management
mission statement
objectives
operational planning
organizational structure
organizing
planning
PMI (Pluses, Minuses, Implications)
problem solving
responsibility
strategic planning
supervisory management
SWOT analysis
tactical planning
technical skills
top management

Now, listen to the chapter's Audio Key Terms List for the correct pronunciation of each term.

Exercise 1

A manager's job involves each of the activities listed in this exercise. Match each of the listed activities with one of the examples of managerial practices given below.

controlling
leading
organizing
planning

a) After consulting advisors and market research, the CEO of a major banking institution decides that the bank needs to focus more on promoting small-scale investing for the public. The CEO calls a meeting of top management in order to develop strategies to achieve this goal. This is an example of ______________________________.

b) The supervisory manager of one location of a major coffee chain participates in the monthly ground-coffee sales competition with the staff. The employees are more motivated and feel like the manager is part of their team. This is an example of ______________________________.

c) The regional manager for a national fast food chain discovers that one location has not received delivery of bread products for the week. The manager reroutes a delivery intended for a closer location and gets on the phone to ensure that another order is sent out to the closer location as soon as possible. This is an example of ______________.

d) The regional manager for a major chain of music stores collects sales figures from all locations on a monthly basis and compares them to the previous year's figures. If sales are down at any location, the regional manager schedules a visit to that location to assess the situation. This is an example of ______________________________.

Check your answers in the Answer Key.

Exercise 2

Each level of management—top, middle, and supervisory—must focus on different duties. Match the level of management with the duties in the columns below. The first one is completed for you.

supervisory management	a) putting strategies into action, supporting and implementing major decisions
middle management	b) long-term planning and goal setting, administering all major decisions, representing the company in the business world
top management	c) managing the day-to-day operations of a business

Check your answers in the Answer Key.

Exercise 3

Each level of management uses technical, human relations, and conceptual skills. However, each level relies on each skill to a different degree. Examine the pie charts below that represent the proportions to which managers rely on each skill. Label each pie chart with the correct level of management.

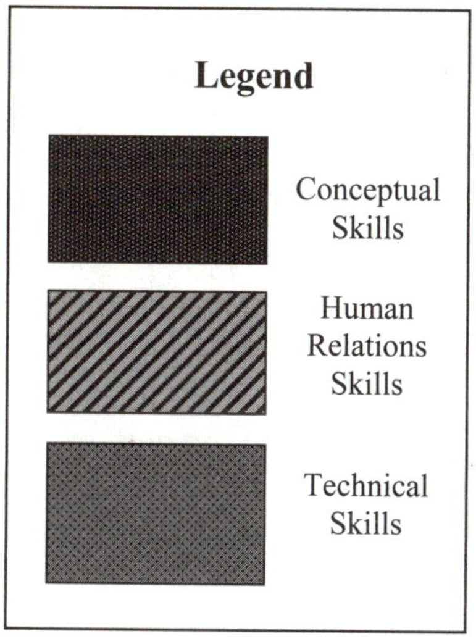

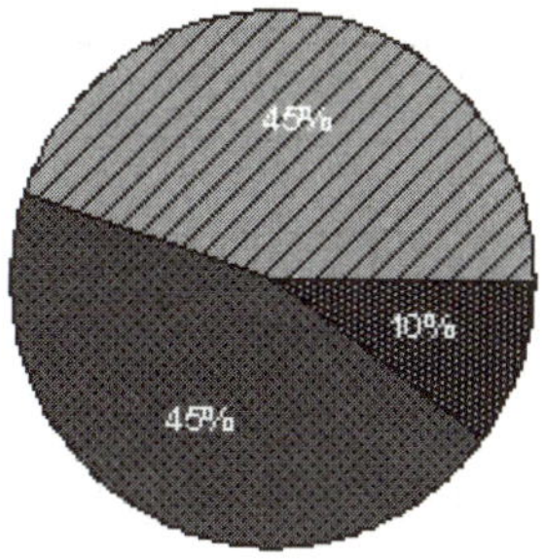

a)__________ management

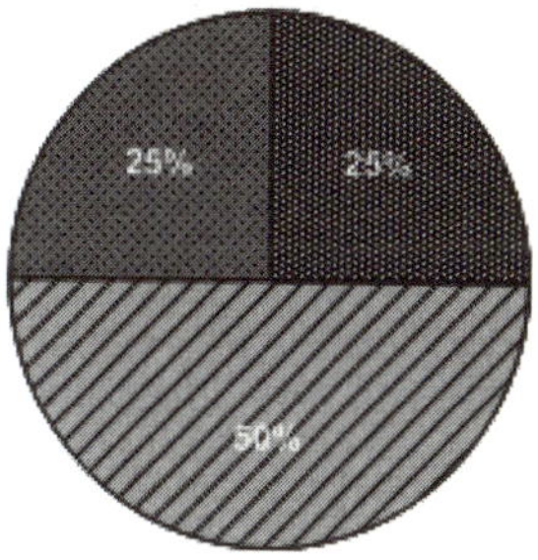

b)__________ management

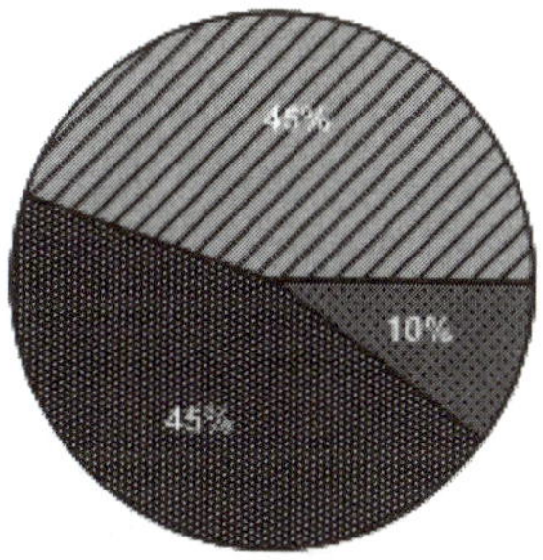

c)__________ management

Check your answers in the Answer Key.

Exercise 4

Use the terms related to organizational structure listed below to answer the clues, fill in the puzzle, and discover the Mystery Word.

accountability
authority
chain of command
delegation
departmentalization
responsibility
specialization

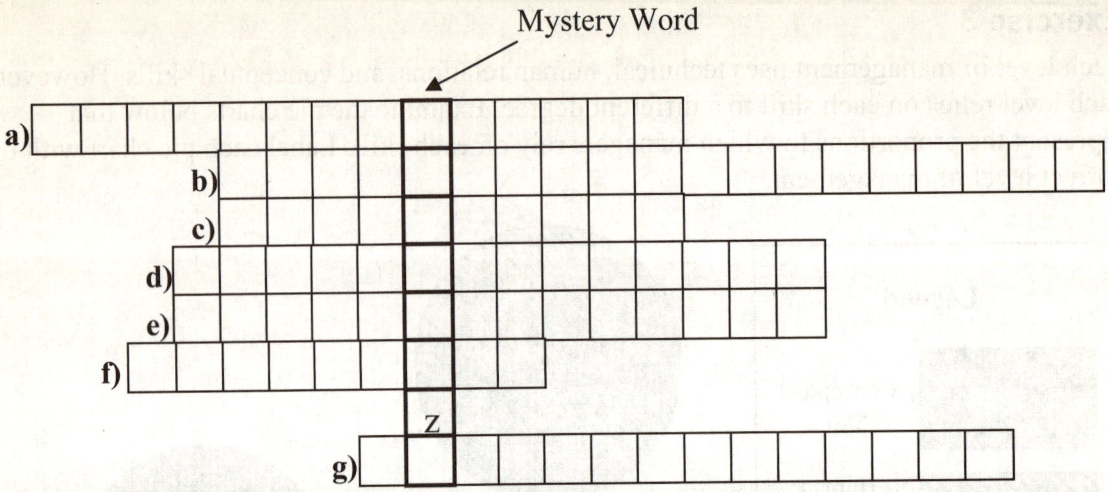

Clues

a) The decision-making authority that emanates from the top of a company to the bottom.
b) The separating of functions within an organization into separate units.
c) Placing the responsibility of completing a task or a function in the hands of a subordinate.
d) Dividing production into parts and assigning those parts to individuals.
e) The responsibility of an individual or team to complete the task assigned.
f) Responsibility for the final outcome of tasks completed by others and the right to change those outcomes.
g) The obligation to perform the task assigned.

The Mystery Word is: ______________________________.

Check your answers in the Answer Key.

Grammar Tip

Modal verbs are a kind of auxiliary (helping) verb, meaning they must be used with another verb. Different **modal verbs** have different meanings. The chart below gives the function of some of the most common modal verbs.

Function	Modal Verbs	Examples
possibility	**can, could, may, might**	English exams **can** be difficult. It **could** rain tonight. She **may** finish her project tonight. They **might** go to the party.
ability	**can, could (past tense)**	He **can** play the piano. I **could** read by the time I was four years old.
obligation	**must, has (have, had) to**	They **must** finish the test in one hour. We **have to** take the video back today.

advisability, propriety	**should, ought to**	He **should** study for the test. She **ought to** thank her guests for their gifts.

Note: There are other **modal verbs** and some of these **modal verbs** can be used in other ways.

Exercise 5

Use the modal verbs from the chart above to fill in the blanks in the labels for the road signs below.

a) You ____________ stop here.

b) You ______________ fish here.

c) Rocks _____________ fall here.

d) You _____________ check for other cars and yield to them here.

e) You _____________ not honk here.

f) You _____________ take a detour here.

Check your answers in the Answer Key.

In the News 5.1

A Doggone Shame

Zena Olijnyk

The world's biggest public relations agencies are no match for a single photo of Pebbles, the Los Angeles–area Yorkshire terrier who died after eating pet food suspected of containing contaminated wheat gluten. Take one look at the seven-year-old pooch, lying on its side with an intravenous needle attached to its paw, and it's easy to see why Menu Foods Income Fund, the Mississauga, Ont.-based manufacturer of the pet food Pebbles ate, is being cast as one of the villains in what may be the largest-ever North American consumer-product recall. The pet food crisis started with Menu, ...but it's spreading to other producers like Hill's Pet Nutrition and Del Monte.

Pebbles, who died of kidney complications on March 22, has become the "poster pet" for canine and feline victims that were fed wet pet foods made with wheat gluten imported from China. Tests conducted by the U.S. Food and Drug Administration indicate the gluten was adulterated with melamine, a chemical used in laminates for furniture. Fewer than 20 deaths have been confirmed as caused by the tainted food, but thousands of worried pet owners have called Menu or the FDA.

The situation is bad enough to prompt crisis managers to question the long-term health of Menu, which in 2006 earned $6.4 million on revenue of about $356 million, and operates in a North American pet food market worth US$10 billion....

Some communications experts suggest Menu—which makes pet food for some of the biggest consumer products companies in the world, including Procter & Gamble and Colgate-Palmolive—did not react well when alerted to trouble.... Mike Paul, president of New York public relations and crisis-management firm MGP & Associates PR, agrees that Menu, and the pet food industry in general, mishandled a problem consumers first reported on Feb. 20. The recall came on March 16—two weeks after animals used in a Menu tasting trial started to die. The lag was unacceptable, Paul says, given that pets rank second only to children when it comes to tugging at heartstrings. Companies are too concerned, he adds, about "the court of law rather than the court of public opinion."...

Companies faced with a public relations disaster should understand they can't always "win" the communications battle, Gene Grabowski [vice-president with Washington-based Levick Strategic Communications] says, but they can mitigate the impact. As examples of how to make the best of a bad situation, he points to the Tylenol package-tampering case of the 1980s—the manufacturer quickly recalled all Tylenol, then reintroduced the pain reliever with tamper-proof packaging—and the more recent "mea culpa" from discount U.S. airline JetBlue for poorly treating passengers stranded by bad winter weather. Crisis management, says Grabowski, is "not usually about winning, it's about managing the outcome."

Source: Zena Olijnyk, "A Doggone Shame," *Canadian Business Online,* April 9, 2007. Courtesy of *Canadian Business* magazine.

For the complete article, visit
www.canadianbusiness.com/shared/print.jsp?content=20070409_85396_85396

Exercise 6

a) It is suggested in the article above that Menu Foods did not react well when it was alerted to a problem with its soft pet foods. This could be attributed to the organization's lack of:

i) organizational structure
ii) brainstorming
iii) crisis planning
iv) delegation
v) conceptual skills

b) Gene Grabowski asserts that crisis management is not necessarily about winning, but about:

i) authority
ii) organizing
iii) tactical planning
iv) top management
v) managing outcomes

c) When an organization encounters the kind of problem described in the article, we would look to ________________ to take responsibility and to act quickly.

i) supervisory management
ii) top management
iii) middle management
iv) chain of command
v) none of the above

d) Which function of management would have to be re-examined in order to ensure that this type of problem does not recur?

i) planning
ii) organizing
iii) controlling
iv) leading
v) responsibility

e) Organizations often have a "Plan B" for situations that unexpectedly arise. This "Plan B" is also known as:

i) accountability
ii) contingency planning
iii) operational planning
iv) strategic planning
v) decision making

Check your answers in the Answer Key.

Exercise 7

The sentences below relate to the **In the News 5.1** article, "A Doggone Shame." Reread the article. Then, use the modal verbs from the chart in the **Grammar Tip** to fill in the blanks in the sentences.

a) Animals that ate the tainted pet food ______________ have died.

b) Public relations firms ____________ not prevent Menu Foods Income Fund from being seen as a villain.

c) The long-term health of Menu ______________ suffer greatly from this crisis.

d) According to Mike Paul, Menu Foods ____________ have recalled its products sooner.

e) Paul suggests that companies _____________ be concerned about the "court of public opinion."

f) Gene Grabowski claims that companies _____________ get past a crisis if they manage it well.

g) After a tampering problem in the 1980s, Tylenol introduced special packaging so that its product _____________ not be tampered with.

Check your answers in the Answer Key.

Exercise 8

Listen to the dialogue. Number these concepts in the order that you hear them.

a) ____ brainstorming
b) ____ SWOT analysis
c) ____ technical skills
d) ____ authority
e) ____ problem solving
f) ____ PMI
g) ____ accountability
h) ____ decision making
i) ____ human relations skills
j) ____ conceptual skills

Exercise 9

Following is a list of factors that would be relevant in a SWOT analysis for a family restaurant in a popular resort area. Read all of the factors and indicate beside each whether they would represent a Strength, Weakness, Opportunity, or Threat. Remember that strengths and weaknesses are internal and are controllable and that opportunities and threats are external and are not controllable. The first one is done for you.

a) __S__ Management are very experienced.

b) _____ Waste disposal regulations are about to become more restrictive.

c) _____ It may be difficult finding trained waitstaff in the area.

d) _____ Most accommodation in the area is geared to families.

e) _____ People on holiday eat out frequently.

f) _____ Finances are in good shape, with an adequate line of credit.

g) _____ The poor economy is causing people to stay home rather than travel.

h) _____ Management have not yet developed a comprehensive marketing plan.

i) _____ Casual, family dining will appeal to multiple market segments.

j) _____ Currently, there are only take-out restaurants and one pizzeria in the area.

Check your answers in the Answer Key.

Exercise 10

The following terms deal with task assignment within an organization. Insert each term into the scenario below that best describes it.

accountability
authority
delegation
responsibility

a) Jacques is the supervisory manager of a district office of a large office supplies company. Jacques has a small team working under him. He has assigned sales to two of his team, inventory to two others, and the accounts to the last two. Jacques is practising ______________________.

b) Eiko is a middle manager at a banking institution. The top management of her institution has demanded that her department cut 10 percent from their operating costs for the next calendar year. Eiko has passed along this demand to the supervisory managers and accountants in her department. However, if the cuts are not made by the end of the year, Eiko will be in trouble with her employer. Eiko has ______________________ for the task.

c) Tariq is a middle manager at the regional sales division of a large automaker. Every month, he must decide the sales goals for the month. Tariq has the ______________________ to set sales goals.

d) Christina is a supervisory manager for a cosmetics distributor. She has asked her assistant manager, Sam, to do a monthly inventory of products. Sam has ______________ for the inventory.

Check your answers in the Answer Key.

Exercise 11

The terms listed here refer to different forms of authority. Match the forms of authority with the correct definitions. The first one is completed for you.

line authority	a) Authority given to experts who advise based on specialized knowledge.
staff authority	b) Authority given to groups of people who work together to make decisions.
committee and team authority	c) Authority that follows a strict chain of command from the top to the bottom of the company.

Check your answers in the Answer Key.

Exercise 12

Match each term describing a type of organization with the picture that best depicts it.

divisional organization
functional organization
international organization
project organization

Paper Company

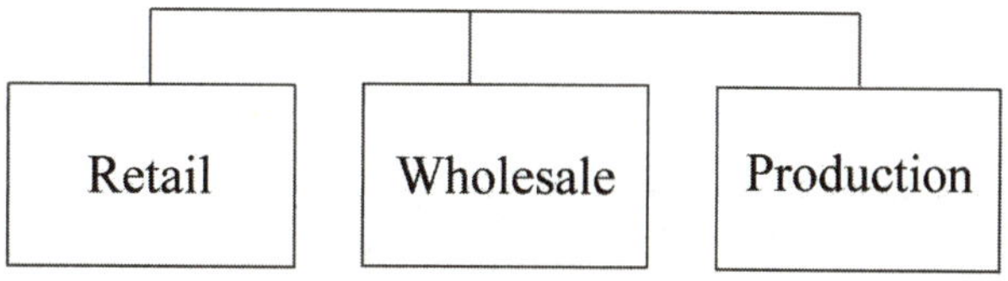

a) ____________________ organization

Housing Company

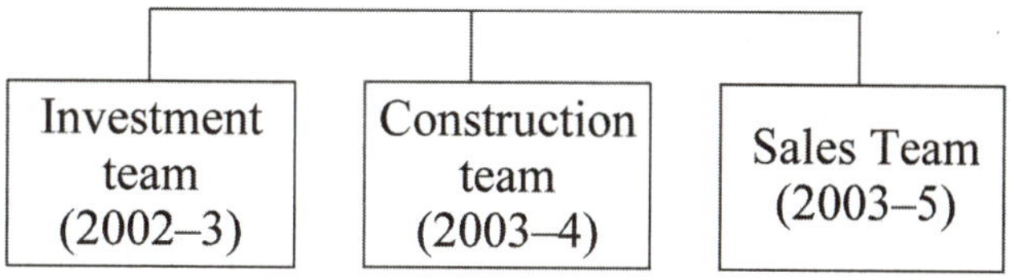

b) ____________________ organization

Plastics Company

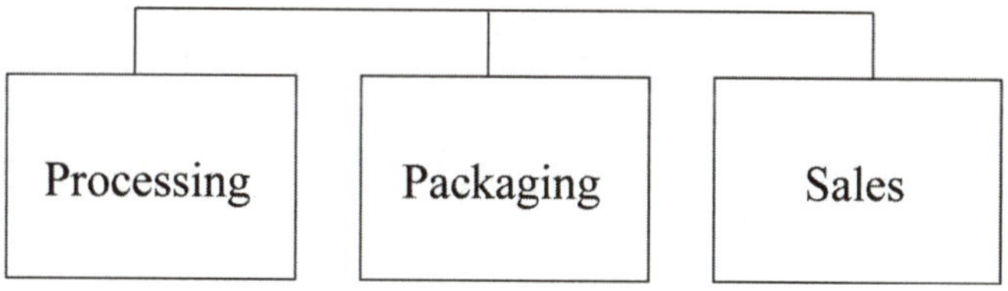

c) ____________________ organization

Telecommunications Company

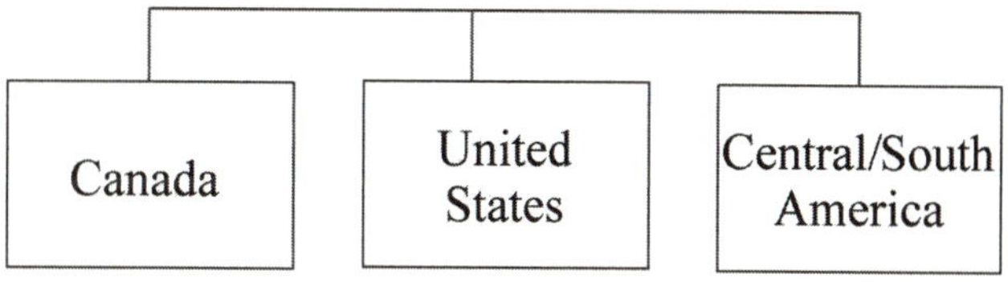

d) ____________________ organization

Check your answers in the Answer Key.

In the News 5.2

The following are five brief descriptions of firms considering strategic options. These are excerpted from *Canadian Business Online.* The search was conducted by entering "strategic planning" into their homepage search mechanism. The search yielded 68 matches. This is typically what you find on any given day. Businesses must regularly look at their options and make decisions based upon what they find. Read the following and try to determine similarities and differences among these businesses.

Wendy's Hires JP Morgan, Lehman Brothers to Help Review Strategic Options

DUBLIN, Ohio (AP)—Wendy's International Inc., the No. 3 hamburger chain, said Tuesday it has hired JP Morgan as its lead advisor to help it review strategic options, which may include selling the company.

The company's special committee of the board of directors also selected Lehman Brothers Inc. as co-advisor.

The committee, which was established April 25, is looking into a number of strategic options, including a sale, changes to capital structure and revisions to the company's strategic plan.

Source: Associated Press, "Wendy's Hires JP Morgan, Lehman Brothers to Help Review Strategic Options," Canadian Business Online, May 15, 2007.

Quanex Considers Strategic Alternatives, Include Sale, for Building Products Group

HOUSTON (AP)—Quanex Corp., which makes carbon and alloy steel bars, said Wednesday its board is reviewing strategic alternatives for the company's building products division.

Among options under consideration are a tax-free spinoff of the group to Quanex shareholders, a sale or a joint venture.

In morning trading after the announcement, Quanex shares jumped $3.30, or 7.4 percent, to $47.97. The stock has traded between $29.15 and $45.22 during the past 52 weeks.

Chairman and Chief Executive Raymond A. Jean said separating the company's vehicular products and buildings products divisions may provide greater value for shareholders due to the groups' different products, processes and end markets.

Quanex said there is no guarantee that the strategic review will result in a transaction. The board does not plan to disclose further developments until it has approved a course of action.

Source: Associated Press, "Quanex Considers Strategic Alternatives, Include Sale, for Building Products Group," Canadian Business Online, May 16, 2007.

Republic Property Trust to Evaluate Strategic Alternatives, Including a Possible Sale

HERNDON, Va. (AP)—Real estate investment trust Republic Property Trust said Monday it is going to evaluate strategic alternatives, including a possible sale of the company.

Other options include a joint venture, merger, exercising rights on one or more option properties and continuing to execute its business plan on a stand-alone basis.

Republic Property Trust formed a special committee to assess the alternatives.

The company said it received an unsolicited indication of interest from another public REIT last week that had no specific price or terms. The special committee and its advisors will take a look at the inquiry and any other expressions of interest that arise.

Republic Property Trust has not set a specific timetable for completion of its evaluation.

Source: Associated Press, "Republic Property Trust to Evaluate Strategic Alternatives, Including a Possible Sale," *Canadian Business Online*, May 14, 2007. Used with Permission of The Associated Press © 2007. All Rights Reserved.

Arrow International Forms Special Committee to Explore Strategic Alternatives

READING, Pa. (AP)—Arrow International Inc., which makes catheters used in heart surgery, on Wednesday said it plans to consider "strategic alternatives" for the business.

Strategic alternatives can include stock buybacks, acquisitions or a sale. Arrow said it will pursue alternatives "aimed at enhancing shareholder value."

A special committee of the board has hired investment banking firm Lazard Freres & Co. as an adviser.

Source: Associated Press, "Arrow International Forms Special Committee to Explore Strategic Alternatives," *Canadian Business Online*, May 9, 2007, www.canadianbusiness.com/shared/print.jsp?content=D8P0S1T00. Used with Permission of The Associated Press © 2007. All Rights Reserved.

Lamson & Sessions Creates Committee to Oversee Strategic Evaluation Process

CLEVELAND (AP)—Lamson & Sessions Co., a maker of plumbing and drainage products, on Tuesday said its board created a special committee of six independent directors to oversee the company's strategic evaluation process.

Lamson & Sessions in February said it would seek a buyer for all or part of the company.

The special committee elected James T. Bartlett as chair.

"Lamson & Sessions intends to disclose developments regarding the strategic evaluation process only if and when the board of directors has approved a specific transaction or course of action," according to a company release.

Shares of Lamson & Sessions added 46 cents to $27 in aftermarket activity, after gaining 20 cents to $26.54 during the regular trading session.

Source: Associated Press, "Lamson & Sessions Creates Committee to Oversee Strategic Evaluation Process," *Canadian Business Online*, May 8, 2007,. Used with Permission of The Associated Press © 2007. All Rights Reserved.

For these and other business insights, visit *www.canadianbusiness.com.*

Exercise 13

You were asked to notice, in your reading, similarities and differences among these companies. Answer the following questions to determine what these similarities and differences may be and why understanding them is important.

a) Identify the type of business that each of these five companies performs.

b) Each of the five companies has at least one strategic option in common. What is that option?

c) Which two companies' share prices increased as a result of the strategic planning announcement?

d) Which two companies hired consulting firms to advise them in their strategic planning?

e) To whom are these consultants accountable?

f) In each case, who within the company is looking into the strategic options?

Check your answers in the Answer Key.

Test Your Knowledge 5

Use the listed terms to fill in the spaces in the scenario below.

authority
board of directors
chain of command
contingency planning
middle managers
mission statement
operational planning
PMI (Pluses, Minuses, Implications)
strategic planning
SWOT analysis
tactical planning

Sayid has just taken an upper management position at Hexcorp Inc. In terms of the a) _______________________, Sayid reports to the b) _________________________, the group of people elected by shareholders to monitor the company. Sayid has c) _________________ over all of the d) ______________________ who manage the different departments at Hexcorp.

One of the first things that Sayid did upon assuming his new position was to conduct a e) _______________________ to assess the strengths and weaknesses of the company and the business environment in which the company is operating. Sayid has also reviewed the company's f) ________________________ in order to remind himself of the company's guiding principles. Sayid will spend the next week doing g) ___________________, to develop new strategies for taking the company closer to its organizational goals. Sayid will then sit down and share the goals with the middle managers who will do h) ______________________ and i) _________________________ in order to determine the short-term and day-to-day strategies to fulfill those goals.

Sayid and the middle managers will also decide if any new projects or initiatives need to be undertaken. In order to decide which initiative should be undertaken, the group will do a j) _______________________ for each proposed initiative in order to assess the positives and negatives of implementing them. When planning those initiatives, Sayid and the other managers will have to do k) ________________________ for each of the new initiatives in case things don't go as planned.

Check your answers in the Answer Key.

Chapter 6

Leadership and Motivation

Before You Start

Study the terms below and be sure that you understand each one. If any of the terms are unclear to you, you can find definitions in the Glossary.

Key Terms

autocratic leadership
classical theory of motivation
contingency approach
democratic leadership
distributed leadership
empowerment
equity theory
expectancy theory
extrinsic reward
free-reign leadership
goal-setting theory
hierarchy of needs theory
human relations
intrinsic reward
job satisfaction
management by objectives (MBO)
morale
motivation
participative leadership
reinforcement theory
theory X
theory Y
theory Z
turnover
two-factor theory

Now, listen to the chapter's Audio Key Terms List for the correct pronunciation of each term.

Exercise 1

The listed terms deal with human relations and related issues. Complete each scenario with the correct term.

human relations
job satisfaction
morale
turnover

a) Sarah manages a large office in a telecommunications company. Sarah spends a lot of time meeting with employees and assessing employee needs and attitudes. She includes her employees in decision-making processes so that they will be highly motivated. Sarah is using her ______________________ skills.

b) Sayid works at a company where there are few opportunities for advancement. Employees are never involved in decision-making processes and, as a result, never really feel like they are part of a team. Usually, people work there for as long as a year and then move on to something else. Sayid's office has a high ______________________ rate.

c) Everyone at Jemilla's office works together well. They like each other and feel like a part of a team. They are involved in decision-making processes and have ample opportunity to advance in the company. Everyone enjoys working there. The group Jemilla works with has high ______________________.

d) Tom is an illustrator for children's books. He works mostly from home, going into the office every once in a while for meetings and to deliver his work. He likes this arrangement very much. Tom loves drawing and can spend hours on his work without getting tired or bored. Tom has a great deal of ______________________.

Check your answers in the Answer Key.

Grammar Tip

Conditional sentences are used to talk about possible, unreal, or hypothetical situations. This chapter will review the **first conditional,** which deals with possible situations.

In **first conditional** sentences, there are two clauses. The event described in the main clause depends on the event or condition described in the **conditional clause**. The **conditional clause** is usually expressed in the present simple tense and the main clause is usually expressed in the future simple tense. Study the examples below.

Conditional Clause (condition)	**Main Clause** (possible event)
If you *go* to school,	you *will learn*.
If she *walks* too far,	she *will be* tired.

In the examples above, the **conditional clause** comes before the main clause. However, **first conditional** sentences can also be arranged in the opposite way. Notice that when the

conditional clause comes first, a comma must separate it from the main clause. When the main clause comes first, no comma is necessary. Study the examples below.

Main Clause (possible event)	**Conditional Clause** (condition)
He *will pass* the test	if he *studies*.
They *will make* money	if they *sell* their product.

Note: *If* is the most common conditional conjunction. However, it is also possible to use *unless*, *provided that*, *providing that*, *so long as*, *as long as*, and some others.

Exercise 2

Use the verbs provided to complete the following first conditional sentences.

a) If he ____________________ (go) downtown, he ______________________ (take) the subway.

b) She ______________________ (take) the position if they __________________ (offer) it to her.

c) If they ___________________ (sell) their house, they ___________________ (buy) a new one.

d) He ______________________ (complete) the project if she ________________ (take) her vacation next week.

e) If you ___________________ (get) the job, you __________________ (be) happy.

Check your answers in the Answer Key.

Exercise 3

Use the statements below to write your own first conditional sentences. Try writing some of them with the conditional clause first and others with the main clause first. Don't forget to include commas where necessary.

a) She wants the job. She needs to get her CFA.

____

b) Management treats their employees well. The employees have high morale.

____

c) He motivates his employees. His department has a low turnover rate.

____

d) They like their job because it is challenging.

____

e) Morale in our department is high, therefore turnover is low.

____

Check your answers in the Answer Key.

Exercise 4

Motivation in the workplace can come from intrinsic or extrinsic sources. Categorize the following rewards as intrinsic (*I*) or extrinsic (*E*).

a) ______ I like my work because it is challenging.

b) ______ I work hard in hope that I will get a bonus at the end of the year.

c) ______ I take pride in doing excellent work.

d) ______ I am fascinated by my work. It is so interesting!

e) ______ I love it when my boss tells me I've done a good job.

f) ______ I am working toward a promotion.

g) ______ I work hard so that I won't get fired. I need my job.

h) ______ I want to perform better than everyone else in my office.

Check your answers in the Answer Key.

In the News 6.1

Healthy Leadership: Trillium Motivates from the Ground Up

Suzanne Bowness

In what sounds like the corporate equivalent of making lemonade out of lemons, Trillium Health Centre 10 years ago turned the difficult circumstances of a forced merger (Mississauga Hospital and Queensway General) into an opportunity to create a new distributed leadership environment.

Caroline Brereton, VP of people support (she is also a registered nurse with an MBA), credits Trillium's visionary CEO Ken White with realizing that overcoming the animosity between the two hospitals would only happen by abandoning the hierarchical model usually found in healthcare organizations in favour of distributed leadership. "[Our] principles are based on the belief that people don't just come for their day jobs, they come with leadership skills from other work they do outside the organization and a passion to make a difference."

With 4200 employees, 1500 volunteers, and a $350 million operating budget to serve over a million people across Ontario's Mississauga/Etobicoke region, simply keeping track of so many workers, let alone empowering each to become leaders, is a challenge. To support individual leaders, Trillium came up with its "1001 Leaders" concept, which encourages everyone to seize leadership opportunities no matter what their position. Through a comprehensive planning process, Trillium identifies organizational and patient-centred projects in which to invest, and then offers formal secondments to put those projects into action.

For instance, Brereton describes a project in which the hospital was trying to figure out how to ease the workload on its nurses. A nurse and a porter were seconded to work on solving the problem. They were supported with project management training and the hiring of a coach to facilitate the process. Not only did the project lead to major improvements on the workload issue, but the nurse and porter also grew their professional skills; the nurse now coordinates a second patient-centred care project, and the porter has moved into a formal management leadership role.

Besides seconding individuals into leadership positions, Trillium engages employees on a collective level with its decentralized organizational structure. Each of the 10 or so divisions within the organization is responsible for setting its own vision, goals and objectives. Each is led by a worker drawn from the clinical and management levels and represents up to 600 staff members. Partnership councils, led and chaired by a staff member and supported by their manager, advise on work/life issues. Brereton points out that this structure makes it easy to ask people within a division how they would like HR issues addressed, rather than making false presumptions.

In addition to regularly surveying employees and acting on their suggestions with initiatives like benefit plans and flexible work arrangements, Brereton says Trillium—winner of a "Canada Top 100 Employer Award" from *Maclean's* magazine for four consecutive years—

is constantly scanning the environment for new ideas to bring into the organization. Brereton is now working on a program to benchmark and improve on work/life balance issues. "Organizations have to be explicit about the value of their people," she says. "It can't be words on a wall—they have to make it real."

Source: Suzanne Bowness, "Healthy Leadership: Trillium Motivates from the Ground Up," *Canadian Business Online,* January 8, 2007. Courtesy of Suzanne Bowness, freelance writer, and Caroline Brereton, Trillium Health Centre.

For the complete article, visit
www.canadianbusiness.com/innovation/article.jsp?content=20070108_125019_6168.

Exercise 5

a) What did the merger, 10 years ago, force Trillium Health Centre to create?

b) What is Caroline Brereton's position in the organization?

c) What was it that Trillium had to overcome as a result of the merger?

d) In order to support individual leadership, what concept did Trillium come up with?

e) What has Trillium done to help staff deal will work/life issues?

f) What recognition of leadership excellence has Trillium received for the past four years?

Check your answers in the Answer Key.

Exercise 6

How we deal with problems in the workplace often means the difference between success and failure. Whether we are a CEO, a project team member or work in a distributed leadership environment, it is important for us to understand how we interact with others in a problem-solving context.

The statements listed below represent different leadership approaches to problem solving. Read each carefully. Using the scale provided below, rank each statement from 1 to 5, according to how well it reflects your own response when you encounter problems. Then score your responses on the chart provided.

5 = I *always* deal with problems in this way
4 = I *frequently* deal with problems in this way
3 = I *sometimes* deal with problems in this way
2 = I *seldom* deal with problems in this way
1 = I *never* deal with problems in this way

a) _____ Consultation takes time. I just take the necessary action.

b) _____ Let's talk about this problem.

c) _____ They know how to deal with it. Just leave them alone.

d) _____ I get paid to make the big decisions and that's what I do.

e) _____ I like to get everyone's input and then make the decision.

f) _____ That's not my area of expertise. Let the engineers work it out.

g) _____ When I want your opinion, I'll ask for it.

h) _____ Is everyone in agreement that this is the solution we should take?

i) _____ She was hired as our in-house lawyer. She'll advise us.

j) _____ This is an emergency. I'll take full responsibility for the decision.

k) _____ Let's get input from all departments.

l) _____ Let them work it out. They know what they're doing.

Scorecard

Autocratic Leadership	**Participative Leadership**	**Free-rein Leadership**
a)	b)	c)
d)	e)	f)
g)	h)	i)
j)	k)	l)
Total:	Total:	Total:

The highest total score indicates your most frequent approach to leadership. The lowest indicates your least frequent approach to leadership. The thing about leadership is that we need to adjust our leadership style to deal with the various problems that arise in business. Knowing what your *dominant* style is will assist you in adjusting your style appropriately. Review what your textbook has to say about leadership.

Exercise 7

Listen to the dialogue. Number these concepts in the order that you hear them.

a) _____ intrinsic rewards

b) _____ job satisfaction

c) _____ empowerment

d) _____ distributed leadership

e) _____ turnover

f) _____ motivation

g) _____ extrinsic rewards

h) _____ goal-setting theory

i) _____ managerial style

j) _____ management by objectives

k) _____ free-reign leadership

Check your answers in the Answer Key.

Exercise 8

Good leadership is more than dealing with problems as they occur. The effective leader is responsible for motivating employees or the people with whom they work to perform at the peak of their abilities. The leader, therefore, must understand what motivates people to perform well. Match the definitions below with the appropriate motivational theory. The first one is completed for you.

hierarchy of needs theory	a) This theory assumes that people dislike work, will avoid it whenever possible, and are only motivated by fear or money.
two-factor theory	b) This theory assumes that employees weigh the amount of work they do against the compensation they receive and then compare them to what others do and receive.
equity theory	c) This theory is based on the belief that there are five levels of human needs and that basic needs must be met before people will be motivated to work toward higher-level needs.
theory X	d) This theory is based on the idea that employees are motivated to perform when goals are clear, time-based, and achievable.
theory Y	e) This theory assumes that people like work, seek responsibility, and are motivated by both extrinsic and intrinsic rewards.
theory Z	f) This theory of motivation suggests that the factors that motivate people to be productive are different from those factors that provide satisfaction.
expectancy theory	g) This theory sees the organization as a family in which co-operation and shared values are highly prized and are the factors which motivate employees.

Check your answers in the Answer Key.

Exercise 9

The following theoretical terms deal with motivation in the workplace. Match the name of each theory with the scenario below that best illustrates its meaning.

classical theory of motivation	equity theory	theory X
	expectancy theory	theory Y
contingency approach	goal-setting theory	theory Z
democratic leadership	reinforcement theory	two-factor theory

a) At Hexcorp Inc., management has implemented a system of rewards and punishments. Employees who perform well receive bonuses, while those who don't are put on probation and ultimately fired. Hexcorp management subscribes to ____________________.

b) Ridgeway Enterprises has a clearly outlined and achievable system of performance bonuses at every level of its operations. It also has a clearly established hierarchy with specific qualifications outlined for advancement. Ridgeway management believes that employees will be motivated when clear goals and rewards are placed in front of them. Ridgeway management believes in ____________________.

c) The Apex Corporation undergoes an assessment and goal-setting process every year. Management at all levels meet with employees to establish reasonable and clearly outlined goals for each department. Management believes that employees who participate in setting clear and reachable goals are more likely to achieve those goals. Apex management subscribes to ____________________.

d) Pathways College has a clearly established pay scale that ensures that people with the same qualifications and responsibilities receive the same compensation. People who come to Pathways with more qualifications receive more pay. Similarly, people who take on more responsibility are compensated for the extra work. Pathways College management believes in ____________________.

e) Foster Foods management believes in its employees. They give employees a lot of freedom and opportunities to take on more responsibility. Foster Foods management subscribes to ____________________.

f) At TimeFactor Productions, management focuses on two areas of job satisfaction for employees. First of all, management tries to ensure that the working environment is as safe and pleasant as possible. They also try to ensure that employees are recognized for achievement and have opportunities to advance in the organization and take on extra responsibility. TimeFactor management believes in ____________________.

g) Bryan Cooper of Cooper's Candy motivates his employees by giving them the highest wages in the industry. He has also implemented a system of raises based on how long an employee has been with the company. Bryan Cooper subscribes to the ____________________.

h) Cedar Springs Spa and Resort treats its employees like family. Management regularly schedules social events and has an in-house childcare service. Management encourages employees to come to them with their problems and concerns. Cedar Springs management believes in ________________________.

i) The management of Lorimer Auto Supplies pays careful attention to the motivational needs of its employees and works to adopt the best policy for any situation as it arises. Lorimer subscribes to the ________________________.

Check your answers in the Answer Key.

In the News 6.2

Dispelling the Myths about Leadership:
An Interview with Kathleen Sendall
Gordon Pitts

When they talk about future CEOs in the oil patch, Kathleen Sendall's name always sits near the top of the list. As Petro-Canada's senior vice-president for North American natural gas, she has accumulated some battle scars, losing a bidding war last year for Canada Southern Petroleum Ltd. She has also gained industry breadth, having recently completed a term as "chair chick" of the Canadian Association of Petroleum Producers. Ms. Sendall talks about the challenges of her industry, and her own life as an energy executive:

You're often mentioned as a future CEO.
Oh man, that comes up quite a lot, and I've got to say [Petro-Canada CEO] Ron Brenneman is doing a great job. He has signalled he's not going anywhere in the immediate future. I really like what I do and frankly I don't spend a lot of time thinking about whether I want to be a future CEO. That hasn't been how I have chosen to live my life. I kind of take it as it comes.

You didn't start off with a burning ambition to be the boss somewhere?
No, I always feel embarrassed when I go to those time-management seminars and when they say you're supposed to have your short-, medium- and long-term goals and you're supposed to spend time every day working on your long-term goals. I never quite managed to do that.

I've used the phrase "you have to be open to opportunities." When something comes along and you can't think of a really good reason not to do it, you should go ahead and do it, providing you're going to learn from it and develop a higher level of self-awareness and actualization.

You should also do it because there are few decisions in this life that are irreversible.

If the CEO job were offered, would you take it?
I don't know. It would depend on the job and circumstances, and where I was at in my life and my career.

Your leadership style has been described in the past as "push, push hug."
I think I will push people quite hard. My experience has been that folks will rise to that challenge, but you need to be pretty cognizant of the hug part of that equation. You need to watch as to whether or not you are pushing too hard, and when you are, the hug part is important.

Are you an unconventional type of manager, someone who goes against the grain?
The obvious surface thing is that I am a female in a generally male-dominated industry. I've taken to call it a gender-challenged environment. That would be somewhat unconventional.

Am I unconventional in my approach? Maybe a bit.

In what way?
I tend to speak my mind quite clearly, some would say to the point of bluntness. I am not ambivalent in where I stand on issues.

What aspects of management have you had to work on the most?
One thing is having appropriate expectations of folks. It's really hard because you can see the picture so clearly in your head and you expect that some folks can see it just as clearly as you can, right off the bat. Often that is not the case. Sometimes I want to go from A to D without going via B and C on the way.

I get impatient, and I have to wait because sometimes it takes some folks time to catch up. It's not that they're not bright or they're stupid. It's just that they think differently than I do. They may not think in terms of a picture nor might they think holistically. They may need to see how the components build up to that picture.

Source: Gordon Pitts, "Sendall on why she's not a hugger," *reportonbusiness.com*, April 23, 2007. Reprinted with permission from *The Globe and Mail.*

For the complete article, visit
www.reportonbusiness.com/servlet/story/RTGAM,20070423.wrsendall

Exercise 10

The following are leadership myths. Choose which of the myths are true or false about Kathleen Sendall. Indicate your choice by placing a T (true) or F (false) in the space provided.

a) _____ Leaders have a burning ambition to lead.

b) _____ Leaders tend to be impatient with others.

c) _____ Leaders have well-formulated personal and business goals.

d) _____ Leaders remain open to opportunities at all times.

e) _____ Leaders are known for having high expectations of others.

f) _____ True leaders never turn down an opportunity to lead.

g) _____ Leaders are known for speaking their minds and for being blunt.

h) _____ Leaders are known for taking the unconventional approach to situations.

i) _____ Leaders are always learning from their experiences.

j) _____ Leaders believe that if you push people they will rise to the challenge.

Check your answers in the Answer Key.

Test Your Knowledge 6

Use your new knowledge and skills to solve the puzzle below! Clues are on page 88.

Clues

Across

2. The way in which employees experience their work environment as either negative or positive.
4. _____________leadership is a style of leadership in which managers dictate outcomes and expect employees to comply without question.
5. This theory assumes that people like work, seek responsibility and are motivated by both extrinsic and intrinsic rewards.
8. The subtle influences that prompt people to behave the way they do.
10. The _____________approach is a management approach that expects each situation to require its own unique solution.

Down

1. _____________ leadership is a method of empowering employees in order to give them a say not only in how they do their job, but in how the company is run.
3. Job _____________ is the enjoyment and satisfaction derived from performing one's job.
6. An _____________reward is recognition of a job well done such as praise, pay increase, or promotion.
7. Giving employees the authority to make decisions regarding customer service and other problems that may arise within their work environment.
9. This theory assumes that people dislike work, will avoid it whenever possible, and are only motivated by fear or money.

Check your answers in the Answer Key.

Chapter 7

Managing Human Resources

Before You Start

Study the terms below and be sure that you understand each one. If any of the terms are unclear to you, you can find definitions in the Glossary.

Key Terms

360-degree feedback
apprentice programs
assessment centre
bonus plan
cafeteria-style benefits
compressed workweek
contingent workers
cross-cultural training
downsizing
employee information systems
employment equity
employment insurance
external recruiting
flextime plan
fringe benefits
gain-sharing plan
human resources management
internal recruiting
job analysis
job description
job evaluation
job sharing
job specification
knowledge-based pay
layoff
management development
mentoring
merit pay
on-the-job training
orientation
pay equity
pay survey
performance appraisal
piece-rate incentive plan
profit-sharing plan
recruiting
replacement charts
salary
selection
skill-based pay
systematic job rotations and transfers
training and development
validation
vestibule training
video assessment
wages
wellness program
worker's compensation

Now, listen to the chapter's Audio Key Terms List for the correct pronunciation of each term.

Exercise 1

Before managers can fill an organization's human resources needs, they must assess those needs and create an HR plan. The terms listed below deal with human resources planning. Use the terms to fill in the blanks in the definitions below.

employee information systems
job analysis
job description
job specification
replacement charts

a) A __________________________ is a systematic review of all the jobs within a given organization.

b) __________________________ list all of the important management positions within an organization, who fills them, the time they will likely leave the position, and possible replacements from within the organization.

c) A __________________________ lists all of the duties and responsibilities associated with a position.

d) __________________________ list the qualifications of all of the people already working for an organization.

e) A __________________________ lists all of the skills and qualifications needed to perform effectively in a given position.

Check your answers in the Answer Key.

Exercise 2

There are several steps involved in hiring new employees. Put the letters from the steps illustrated below into the correct order. *Check your answers in the answer key.*

Step 1 ______, Step 2 ______, Step 3, ______, Step 4 ______, Step 5 ______

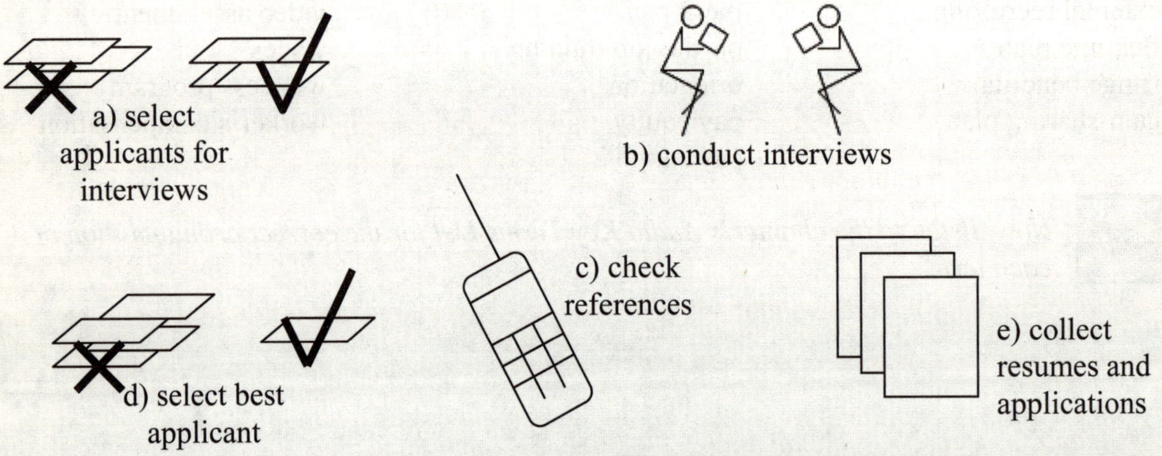

Exercise 3

There are many different processes and techniques involved in finding human resources to fill an organization's needs. You are probably already familiar with job applications, job interviews, and references, but there are some terms used by managers that may be new to you. Match the terms listed below with the correct definition. The first one is completed for you.

assessment centre

external recruiting

nternal recruiting

lection

dation

a) The process of soliciting applications for a position from qualified people outside of the organization. The process could include advertising, hiring an executive search firm, or holding a job fair, among other techniques.

b) The process of evaluating the types of information collected about job applicants according to its potential ability to forecast job performance.

c) A set of practical management tasks performed by job applicants and evaluated by management experts.

d) The process of evaluating the information collected about applicants and making equitable decisions based on the best interests of the organization.

e) The process of identifying potential job applicants from within the organization. This may include the use of employee information systems.

k your answers in the Answer Key.

xercise 4

The terms listed here deal with the processes by which an organization provides new skills and knowledge to new and current employees. Use the terms to fill in the spaces in the scenarios below.

apprentice program
cross-cultural training
management development
off-the-job training
on-the-job training
orientation
systematic job rotations and transfers
training and development
vestibule training

a) Hiro has just gotten a new job operating complex machinery at a factory that makes lenses for microscopes. The material that Hiro will be working with is quite expensive, so the company doesn't want new employees learning on the job. Instead, the company has set up a computer simulation that will train Hiro to operate the machinery correctly. Hiro is getting ____________________________ at his new job.

b) Giselle has just been hired as a middle manager by a large banking institution. In order to familiarize Giselle with the company's history, mission, goals, and policies, the company has a two-hour video that Giselle must watch. This video is part of Giselle's

____________________.

c) Raoul has just been hired as top management at a company that makes and sells paper products. As part of his training, Raoul will be given the opportunity to work in every department, including production and sales, in order to familiarize himself with all of the operations of the company. This process is called ____________________________.

d) Trish works for a telecommunications firm. Management at the firm has recently implemented a new program to train employees to be aware of and sensitive to cultural differences in the workplace. Trish will spend a day at a workshop with all of the other employees in her department. This program is an example of

______________________________.

e) The Big Drip Coffee Company trains all of its employees in its stores. Store managers an servers must spend two weeks in the store serving customers before they are considered ful employees. The Big Drip uses ____________________________.

f) Theresa just got a new job at a tool and die factory. In order to learn how to operate the new machinery involved in her position, Theresa has been paired with an experienced employee who will teach her how everything works and supervise her first few weeks of work. Theresa's training is part of an ____________________________.

g) When new management is hired at the international firm Vertical Telecommunication Inc., they are sent to a central training facility where they are taken through an extensive management training program. Only after they have been through this program are they s into their positions in the firm. Vertical uses ____________________________.

h) In order to keep its managers on the cutting edge, TopProfits Investment conducts a series of seminars and workshops every year. Topics could include everything from human resources management to orientation for new technology. TopProfits has an extensive ____________________________ program.

Check your answers in the Answer Key.

In the News 7.1

Downsize This? Cutbacks 1, Innovation 0

Jay Somerset

When profits slip, lay off employees. It's typical, if nothing else. In the auto industry, for example, DaimlerChrysler lost US$1.48 billion in 2006 and is now laying off 13 000 workers in North America.…The employee downsizing mirrors similar cuts made at Ford and GM over the last two years, and both continue to struggle. Meanwhile, Japan-based Toyota and Honda are expanding and building new plants.... How come they're doing relatively well and the Big Three are failing?

Steven H. Appelbaum, a professor of management at the John Molson School of Business in Montreal, says downsizing wasn't always the No. 1 cure-all for CEOs. "Downsizing has become a knee-jerk reaction," he says. "It's short-term thinking and the eventual loser is the company itself, because the surviving employees never invest in the company."

That's not to say downsizing is always a bad decision; sometimes cuts are necessary. However, before making any decision, especially to lay off employees, you must examine your infrastructure, says Ajar Chadha, an analyst with PricewaterhouseCoopers. He describes infrastructure as being composed of four areas: people, processes, technology, and facilities. When that's done, plan a strategy. "The key is to demonstrate decisiveness, that you're in control, and that you're being fair to those people leaving. This is how you get buy-in and, eventually, innovation."

Open communication can also breed solutions, such as employees who want to retire early, job share or work part time. "These are people who are self-selecting themselves out of the company, which means there's no lingering bad taste or rapid depletion of infrastructure," says Appelbaum. "Here downsizing doesn't have a negative connotation and innovation isn't affected. The problem is most executives aren't smart enough to ask because they don't care. This is bad management that will bite you in the end, because it's your employees who ultimately call the shots when it comes to innovation and profitability."

Downsizing can be dirty work, but some companies get it right, returning as more efficient, more focused companies.

"There are companies that made real changes instead of staying locked in an existing paradigm," says Bill Greenhalgh, CEO of Human Resources Association of Ontario (HRPAO). Greenhalgh also points to 3M and GE as companies that never face mass layoffs and—no surprise—remain innovative.

"They focus entirely on innovation, so there's never a moment when someone wakes up and says, 'Oops, we need to take a hit.' GE is like management graduate school."

Source: Jay Somerset, "Downsize This? Cutbacks 1, Innovation 0," *Canadian Business Online,* April 2, 2007. Courtesy of Jay Somerset.

For the full article, visit
www.canadianbusiness.com/shared/print.jsp?content=20070330_100807_5404

Exercise 5

Read the article, "Downsize This? Cutbacks 1, Innovation 0," above, and choose the appropriate words from the following list to fill in the blanks.

focused	efficient	job sharing
profitability	infrastructure	expanding
employees	real changes	fair
locked	innovation	downsizing
	lay off	

a) The employee __________ mirrors similar cuts at Ford and GM over the past two years.

b) Japan-based Toyota and Honda are __________ and building new plants in southern Ontario.

c) Downsizing is short-term thinking because the surviving __________ never reinvest in the company.

d) Before making any decision, especially to __________ employees, you must examine your infrastructure.

e) __________ is composed of four areas: people, processes, technology, and facilities.

f) The key is to demonstrate that you are decisive, in control, and that you are being __________ to those employees who must leave.

g) Open communication can lead to solutions, such as early retirement, __________, or working part time.

h) It's your employees who ultimately call the shots when it comes to __________ and __________ .

i) Downsizing can be dirty work, but some companies get it right, and return as more __________ and more __________ .

j) 3M and GE are companies that made __________ instead of staying __________ in an existing paradigm.

Check your answers in the Answer Key.

Grammar Tip

In the last chapter, we reviewed the first conditional, which describes possible situations that are dependent upon a condition. In this chapter, we will review the **second conditional**, which describes hypothetical or unreal situations.

In **second conditional** sentences, there are two clauses: the **conditional clause** and the main clause. The **conditional clause** is in the *past tense*, and the main clause uses *would* and the *bare infinitive form* of the verb. Study the examples below.

Conditional Clause (condition)	**Main Clause** (unreal or hypothetical event)
If she **were** rich,	she **would work** anyway.
If they **had** more time,	they **would extend** the project.

As with the first conditional, the **conditional** and main clauses in **second conditional** sentences can be arranged in the opposite way. A comma is necessary to separate the two clauses when the **conditional clause** comes first, but not when the main clause comes first. Study the examples below.

Main Clause (unreal or hypothetical event)	**Conditional Clause** (condition)
He **would be** unhappy	if he **lost** his job.
We **would approve** the proposal	if it **was** cheaper.

Exercise 6

Use the verbs provided to complete the second conditional sentences.

a) If he ______________ (like) his job, he ______________ (be) happier.

b) The managers _______________ (hire) him if he ____________ (have) more experience.

c) We ________________ (accept) the merger if the other company ______________ (give) us more guarantees.

d) If it ________________ (is) Thursday, the human resources manager ________________ (be) here by now.

e) The team ________________ (work) better if they __________________ (know) each other better.

Check your answers in the Answer Key.

Exercise 7

The following sentences are in the first conditional. Rewrite them in the second conditional. Notice the change in meaning.

a) If our company wants to expand, we will need more resources. (It is likely that our company is discussing expansion.)

____

(Our company is not discussing expansion at this time.)

b) The management will change their policies if they want to be more inclusive. (The management does want to be more inclusive.)

____

(The management is not concerned about inclusivity at the moment.)

c) Tabitha will work harder if she likes her job. (Tabitha might like her job and so may work harder.)

____

(Tabitha isn't working at a job that she likes at the moment.)

d) Chris will change his habits if management asks him to. (Management is likely to ask Chris to change his habits; they are a current concern.)

____

(Chris is unlikely to need to change his habits; management is not concerned.)

e) If Jorge and Kiko quit, the company will need to hire a few new employees. (Jorge and Kiko are thinking of quitting or will have reason to soon.)

____

(There is no indication that Jorge and Kiko are likely to quit in the near future.)

Check your answers in the Answer Key.

In the News 7.2

Human resource managers really have their work cut out for them today. With the diversity that exists in most workplaces, a manager must also be a "cross-cultural specialist" if they wish to recruit and retain the best people.

Read the following article and remind yourself of any "misunderstandings" that you have experienced as a person who is learning English as a second language.

Improving Cross-Cultural Communication

Picture it: The CEO of a pharmaceutical company is brainstorming with his staff, and the idea of gift certificates is tossed around. One employee, an accountant and a recent immigrant from Romania, has never heard of a gift certificate, because although she's fluent in English, gift certificates don't exist in Romania. She asks, "What is a gift certificate?" and everyone looks at her like it's the stupidest question they've ever heard.

Unfortunately, this is a true story. It's just one example cited in *Recruiting, Retaining and Promoting Culturally Different Employees* by Canadian cross-cultural specialists Don Rutherford and Lionel Laroche.

Although cross-cultural challenges exist in ... workplaces, entrepreneurs can employ tactics that help to minimize the difficulties to ensure they retain and capitalize on the ideas and skills that culturally diverse employees bring.

For example, you can expect some language challenges when you hire employees for whom English is their second language. Here are the authors' suggestions for how to make life easier for such employees:

- **Simplify your message** by using less complex sentence structure and vocabulary.
- **Try to slow down your delivery** and articulate each word more clearly. Avoid contractions such as "gonna" and "wanna."
- **Watch for nonverbal clues,** such as body language, that indicate your message is not getting through.
- **Use visual aids** such as PowerPoint or charts during presentations, whenever possible.
- **Do not assume an employee is uneducated or inexperienced** if she isn't familiar with acronyms or jargon that's common in Canada. She may completely understand the concepts but may be unfamiliar with the English terms. These can easily be learned.
- **Be patient and try to follow newcomers' ideas and logic.** They may be different from your own, but just as valid.
- **Consider providing ESL courses** for non-native English speakers on your team. Courses designed to help participants modify their accents can be particularly helpful, as can those that cover specific industry terminology.

Source: PROFIT-Xtra, "Improving Cross-Cultural Communication," *Canadian Business Online,* April 12, 2007. PROFITguide.com.

For this and other interesting and relevant information, visit *www.canadianbusiness.com/shared/print.jsp?content=20070411_115358_3340*

Exercise 8

Re-read the article, "Improving Cross-Cultural Communication," above and connect the split sentences. The first one is completed for you.

a) Simplify your message...

b) Use visual aids...

c) Try to slow down your delivery...

d) Consider providing ESL courses...

e) Be patient and try to follow newcomers' ideas and logic...

f) Watch for nonverbal clues...

g) Do not assume an employee is uneducated or inexperienced...

i) because even if they are different they may be useful.

ii) and pronounce each word more clearly.

iii) by using simpler sentences and easier words.

iv) for new English speakers on your team.

v) such as actions or facial expressions.

vi) if they seem unfamiliar with expressions that are used.

vii) such as slides or charts.

Check your answers in the Answer Key.

Exercise 9

Listen to the dialogue. Number these concepts in the order that you hear them.

a) ______ motivation

b) ______ cross-cultural training

c) ______ merit pay

d) ______ fringe benefits

e) ______ flex-plan benefits

f) ______ increase production

g) ______ job satisfaction

h) ______ mentoring system

i) ______ equitable approach

j) ______ human resources management

k) ______ cafeteria-style benefits

Check your answers in the Answer Key.

Exercise 10

Organizations have different ways of compensating employees for their work. The terms listed below all deal with forms of compensation and the tools for deciding on compensation. Fill each term into the correct definition for that term.

gain-sharing plan
job evaluation
knowledge-based pay
merit pay
pay survey
piece-rate incentive plan
profit-sharing plan
salary
skill-based pay
wages

a) A compensation plan that divides a fixed percentage of the organization's annual profits among all employees is called a ______________________________.

b) A ____________________ is a compensation plan that rewards employees for increasing productivity or reducing costs and thereby increasing the profits of the organization.

c) ________________________ compensates employees for higher job performance and contributions to the success of the organization, generally involving an increase in salary.

d) ________________________ rewards employees for the acquisition of new skills that will enhance their contribution to the organization.

e) A ______________________ is an assessment by an organization of the value of a certain position within the organization. This can help management to determine compensation for that position.

f) A __________________________ rewards employees for each completed unit of production.

g) An employee's ______________________ is a fixed amount of compensation rewarded at regular periods of time, often bi-weekly or monthly, for doing a job.

h) ________________________ rewards employees for the acquisition of new knowledge that will enhance their contribution to the organization.

i) An employee's ________________________ are compensation based on a fixed hourly rate for doing a job.

Check your answers in the Answer Key.

Exercise 11

Beyond compensation, many organizations also offer benefits to their employees. Some benefits must be offered and some are optional for the organization. Benefits can include scheduling flexibility that allows employees the freedom to maintain aspects of their lives outside of work. The listed terms deal with types of benefits and flexible scheduling. Fill each term into the correct definition.

cafeteria-style benefits	fringe benefits
compressed workweek	job sharing
employment insurance	worker's compensation
flextime plan	wellness program

a) ________________________ are the fixed benefits included in the package offered by the organization to employees.

b) A ________________________ allows employees to choose what hours they will work around the organization's core business hours for which all employees must be at work.

c) ________________________ consist of a "menu" of valuated benefits from which employees may choose a fixed amount.

d) In addition to health-care benefits, some companies offer a ________________________, which gives employees strategies and tools for maintaining and improving their overall health.

e) Employers pay into a ________________________ plan that covers the health-care expenses for employees who suffer a work-related injury or illness.

f) In some organizations, employees can choose to work a ________________________ in which they work longer hours for fewer days of the week.

g) ________________________ is a relatively new concept that involves two employees working together to fulfill the role of one employee, sharing hours, compensation, and limited benefits.

h) Employees and employers both pay into an ________________________ plan that provides a minimum income for employees who are in between jobs.

Check your answers in the Answer Key.

Test Your Knowledge 7

Use key terms from the chapter to fill in the blanks in the scenario below.

Manuel has just been hired as a middle manager by a new organization called Refresh Networking Solutions. Before hiring Manuel, Refresh created a a)______________________ that outlined all of the duties involved in the position. They also compiled a b)__________________________ that listed all of the qualifications that they needed the successful applicant to have. Manuel has all of the necessary qualifications and he did very well in his interview.

Before he signed the employment contract, Manuel wanted to negotiate certain benefits. Fortunately, Refresh offers c)_____________________________, which allows Manuel to choose which benefits he wants. Manuel was also interested in negotiating a d)________________________ , which would allow him to schedule his working hours, within certain limits. Refresh agreed and Manuel signed his employment contract.

In terms of compensation, Manuel was very pleased with the package Refresh offered him. Beyond his fixed e)___________________, which they would pay to him bi-weekly, Refresh also offers a f)________________________ , which offers Manuel a part of the profits from any increased production or lowered costs that he creates in his department.

When Manuel starts his new job next week, he will be given a detailed g)_______________ by one of the senior management, in which he will learn about Refresh's mission, goals, and policies. Manuel will also be expected to do a series of h)_______________________, to familiarize him with all of the organization's operations. Within the next year, Manuel will also be sent to several i)__________________ seminars, designed to keep him up to date in terms of the skills and knowledge he will need to perform well. One of the most important seminars will be j)_________________________, which will train Manuel to be sensitive to cultural difference in his management role.

This first year will be a big one for Manuel. Refresh has told him that he will be given a thorough k)_____________________________ at the end of the year to see how well he has measured up to expected norms. Afterwards, he will be given l)______________________, which will be collected from those above and below him in the organization to see how well he has done in all aspects of his work.

Good luck, Manuel!

Check your answers in the Answer Key.

Chapter 8

Managing Operations: Goods and Services

Before You Start

Study the terms below and be sure that you understand each one. If any of the terms are unclear to you, you can find definitions in the Glossary.

Key Terms

analytic process
assembly process
business process re-engineering
capacity
computer-aided design (CAD)
computer-aided manufacturing (CAM)
computer-integrated manufacturing (CIM)
continuous process
economic order quantity (EOQ)
enterprise resource planning (ERP)
facility layout
facility location
flexible manufacturing
goods production
high-contact system
holding costs
intermittent process
inventory control
ISO 14000
ISO 9000
just-in-time (JIT) inventory control
lead times
lean manufacturing
logistics
low-contact system
mass customization
material requirements planning (MRP)
operations management
process manufacturing
production management
productivity
purchasing
quality
research and development (R&D)
robotics
service operations
six sigma
statistical process control (SPC)
statistical quality control (SQC)
supplier selection
supply chain
supply chain management
synthetic process
total quality management (TQM)
transportation
warehousing

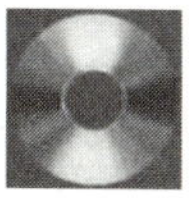

Now, listen to the chapter's Audio Key Terms List for the correct pronunciation of each term.

Exercise 1

Different types of businesses are described below. Read the descriptions and decide if each business is primarily involved in goods production, service operations, or a combination of the two. Put the letter for each description in the appropriate column in the table provided for you here.

Goods Production	Service Operations	Combination

a) A factory that makes sports equipment.

b) A high-end coffee shop.

c) An electronics repair business.

d) A dairy farm.

e) A plant nursery that is open to the public.

f) A taxi company.

g) A furniture upholstering business.

h) A local artist whose work is sold at a gallery in town.

i) A housecleaning business.

j) A bakery that is open to the public.

Check your answers in the Answer Key.

Exercise 2

The following scenario describes the different ways in which one business provides utility to its customers. Use the terms listed in this exercise to fill in the blanks and identify the different kinds of utility.

form utility
ownership utility
place utility
time utility

The Big Drip Coffee Company works hard to give its customers everything they need. In order to provide a)______________________, Big Drip has locations all over the city, usually near public transportation hubs or areas where there are a lot of offices. In the morning, at traditional coffee break times, and after work, Big Drip locations brew extra coffee and put on extra staff to ensure that customers can get their orders promptly and efficiently. In this way, Big Drip provides b)______________________ to its customers. At each Big Drip location, workers bake fresh pastries and make fresh sandwiches all day. They also have many beverages, including coffee served in a multitude of ways. This provides c)______________________ to customers. To provide d)____________________, the Big Drip offers travel mugs, T-shirts, and various other accessories with the Big Drip name and logo on them. The Big Drip Coffee Company is doing a good job of providing complete utility to its customers.

Check your answers in the Answer Key.

Exercise 3

Different types of operations are described below. Read each description and decide if the primary process involved is synthetic or analytic. Put the letter for each description in the appropriate column in the table provided for you here.

Analytic Process	Synthetic Process

a) A mill that turns wheat into flour.

b) An automobile assembly plant.

c) A florist.

d) A pulp and paper mill.

e) An interior designer.

f) A potato farm.

g) A water purification plant.

h) A sheep shearing operation.

i) A house painter.

j) A plastics recycling plant.

Check your answers in the Answer Key.

Exercise 4

Different services are described below. Read each description and decide if the service is a high-contact system or a low-contact system. Put the letter for each description in the appropriate column in the table provided for you here.

High-Contact System	Low-Contact System

a) An electric company.

b) A clothing store.

c) An internet provider.

d) An interior designer.

e) A storefront psychic.

f) A clothing designer.

g) A road maintenance crew.

h) Air traffic controllers.

i) The admissions office at a college.

j) A doctor.

Check your answers in the Answer Key.

Grammar Tip

In the last two chapters, we reviewed the first and second conditionals, which are used to talk about possible and unreal events, respectively. In this chapter we are going to review the **third conditional**, which is used to talk about things that might have happened in the past if circumstance had been different. In other words, the **third conditional** deals with unreal past events.

In third conditional sentences, there are two clauses: the main clause and the conditional clause. The **conditional clause** is in the *past perfect*, and the main clause uses *would have* and the *past participle form* of the verb. Study the examples below.

Conditional Clause (condition)	**Main Clause** (unreal past event)
If we **had finished** the report on time,	our boss **would have been** happy.
If you **had called** me earlier,	I **would have helped** you with the report.

Just as with the first and second conditional, the **conditional clause** and main clause in **third conditional** sentences can be arranged in the opposite way. A comma is necessary when the **conditional clause** comes first but not when the main clause comes first. Study the examples below.

Main Clause (unreal past event)	**Conditional Clause** (condition)
She **would have gotten** the job	if she **had applied**.
He **would have failed** the test	if he **hadn't studied**.

Exercise 5

Use the verbs provided to complete these sentences in the third conditional.

a) If I ____________________ (want) that job, I ____________________ (apply).

b) If we ____________________ (be) more aggressive, we ____________________ (make) the sale.

c) They ____________________ (approve) the proposal if he ____________________ (submit) it.

d) The company ______________________ (make) more money if the market ________________________ (improve).

e) If the factory______________________ (produce) less, there ___________________________ (be) a shortage.

Check your answers in the Answer Key.

Exercise 6

The following sentences are in the second conditional. Rewrite the sentences so that they are in the third conditional. Notice the change in meaning.

a) If he were here, he would enjoy this party. (The party is now.)

____ (The party was yesterday.)

b) They would buy these desks if they knew about the sale. (The sale is now.)

____ (The sale was last week.)

c) He would present his proposal if he came to work. (He is absent from work today.)

____ (He was absent from work yesterday.)

d) If we gave him more training, he would understand the job better. (He has just started work.)

____ (He started work in the past.)

e) If she stayed at the office for lunch, she would get tired faster. (She generally goes out for lunch.)

____ (She went out for lunch yesterday.)

Check your answers in the Answer Key.

In the News 8.1

How To: Funkify Roller-Coasters

Andy Holloway

The race for roller-coaster supremacy has always been based on who could drive riders faster, higher and harder. When that concept got tired, theme parks sent us down rides backward, upside down or spinning. So what's next? Building theme-based coasters that are less stomach churning and more interactive, like the RoboCoaster G2.

Built by AMEC Dynamic Structures Ltd., the Port Coquitlam, B.C.-based division of international infrastructure services giant AMEC, RoboCoaster is a roller-coaster with a programmable robot attached to each car. The robot can provide six degrees of motion, while the car sends riders through a series of theatres that are based on movie themes, complete with visuals, audio and props. "You can create smooth motion, so you can be flying as though you were in a hang-glider and you would absolutely believe you were there," says David Halliday, vice-president.

Doing this is trickier than just bolting a robot to a four-wheeled carriage, clamping the whole thing onto a girder and driving it along a track. For one thing, if the motion of the robot and the movie being screened in the track space is out of sync by even 1 percent, riders will get motion sickness. To address this, AMEC uses software to reference every movie frame to the robot's motions—a process called profiling. These motions are then tweaked by staff, who ride the rails and provide feedback.

In addition, while the robot is executing one move, it has to get into position for the next move without alerting the rider. Engineers play with different axes and relative positions with drive and control tools to smooth out the ride, while taking both cantilevered and dynamic loads into consideration—the robot is constantly swinging around the carriage, creating stresses on the equipment. Halliday says AMEC has developed safety nets called Golden Profiles to manage all the motions, show sets, themes, movies and robots. Exceed the defined limits, and the ride automatically shuts down.

Currently, RoboCoaster is just a prototype, but Halliday says AMEC is set to sell one, with a planned 2009 opening. It takes three years to build—twice as long and as expensive as a traditional high-end coaster—but then it's a lot easier to reinvent this ride, ensuring new thrills every summer. All together now: "Aieeeeeeee!"

Source: Andy Holloway, "How To: Funkify Roller-Coasters," *Canadian Business Online*, June 19, 2007. Courtesy of *Canadian Business* Magazine.

For the complete article, visit
www.canadianbusiness.com/shared/print.jsp?content=20060620_78926_78926

Exercise 7

In operations/manufacturing, there are a lot of acronyms used. Acronyms were explained in Chapter 2. Re-visit the definitions covered in the Key Terms section of this chapter, and decide which of the following you think would apply to the development of the RoboCoaster. Put the letter for each term in the appropriate place in table provided for you here.

Would apply	Would not apply

a) computer-altered design (CAD)

b) intermittent process

c) computer-aided design (CAD)

d) total quality management (TQM)

e) process manufacturing

f) high-contact system

g) computer-aided management (CAM)

h) research and development (R&D)

i) computer-inventory mishandling (CIM)

j) low-contact system

k) computer-aided manufacturing (CAM)

l) computer-integrated manufacturing (CIM)

Check your answers in the Answer Key.

In the News 8.2

Toot Sweet: French Train Breaks Rail Speed Record, Hitting 357.2 Mph

Ingrid Rousseau

ABOARD TRAIN V150, France (AP)—A French train with a 25 000-horsepower engine and special wheels broke thc world speed record Tuesday for conventional rail trains, reaching 357.2 mph as it zipped through the countryside to the applause of spectators. Roaring like a jet plane, with sparks flying overhead and kicking up a long trail of dust, the black-and-chrome V150 with three double-decker cars surpassed the record of 320.2 mph set in 1990 by another French train.

It fell short, however, of beating the ultimate record set by Japan's magnetically levitated train, which hit 361 mph in 2003.

The French TGV, or "train a grande vitesse," as the country's bullet train is called, had two engines on either side of the three double-decker cars for the record run, some 125 miles east of the capital on a new track linking Paris with Strasbourg.

The demonstration was meant to showcase technology that France is trying to sell to the multibillion-dollar overseas markets such as China.

People lined bridges and clapped and cheered ... as the V150 roared by.

"Everything went very well," said engineer Eric Pieczac.

"There are about 10 000 engineers who would want to be in my place," Pieczac said. "It makes me very happy, a mixed feeling of pride and honor to be able to reach this speed."

Technicians on the train had "French excellence" emblazoned on the backs of their T-shirts.

Philippe Mellier, president of Alstom Transports, the builder, had said before the test that the train would try to break the record held by the Japanese maglev train.

Normally, French TGVs travel at a cruising speed of about 186.4 mph.

The V150 was equipped with larger wheels than the usual TGV to cover more ground with each rotation and a stronger, 25 000-horsepower engine, said Alain Cuccaroni, in charge of the technical aspects of testing.

Adjustments also were made to the new track ... notably the banking on turns.... The electrical tension in the overhead cable was increased from 25 000 volts to 31 000.

It was the first time that double-decker cars were used at such a high speed, according to officials of Alstom, which makes TGVs and crawled back a year ago from the edge of bankruptcy.

The double-decker cars were transformed into a laboratory for the event so that technicians from the state-run rail company SNCF and Alstom could gather data during the run.

The goal was more than "simply breaking a record," Cuccaroni said, adding that data from the test should help improve the security and comfort of passengers.
The record gilds France's image in the expanding market for high-speed technology as countries turn to bullet trains. France competes with neighboring Germany and with Japan for contracts.

China, the biggest potential market, was to start building a high-speed line this year between Beijing and Shanghai to cut travel time from nine hours to five.

> China's state media reported last year that the government plans to build more than 7500 miles of high-speed railways in coming years at a cost of $250 billion to $310 billion.
>
> *Source:* Ingrid Rousseau, "Toot Sweet: French Train Breaks Rail Speed Record, Hitting 357.2 Mph," *Canadian Business Online*, April 3, 2007. Used with Permission of The Associated Press © 2007. All Rights Reserved.

For the complete article, visit
www.canadianbusiness.com/shared/print.jsp?content=D8096TC80

Exercise 8

Read article, "Toot Sweet: French Train Breaks Rail Speed Record, Hitting 357.2 Mph," above, and answer the following questions.

a) Which one of the following could be said to be one of the purposes of the TGV's test run?

i) mass customization
ii) continuous process
iii) business process re-engineering
iv) research and development (R&D)
v) statistical quality control (SQC)

b) Which one of the following do you think would be important for the manufacturers of this high-speed train to incorporate into their operational standards?

i) lean manufacturing
ii) low-contact system
iii) statistical quality control (SQC)
iv) inventory control
v) flexible manufacturing

c) Whenever we hear about high-speed cars or trains, we probably can't help but think about the fuel that they are burning and the pollution caused by their operation. When an organization that is interested in matching best practices for managing its impact upon the environment is interested in adopting internationally recognized performance standards, it is likely to undergo an audit for which of the following?

i) six sigma
ii) ISO 14000
iii) ISO 9000
iv) economic order quantity (EOQ)
v) supply chain management

d) If we think of the TGV as a service and that service as being the movement of people from one place to another at the right time and at an affordable cost, then we can think of the TGV as an exercise in which of the following?

i) logistics
ii) operations management
iii) flexible manufacturing

iv) mass customization
v) continuous process

e) The demonstration run of the French TGV was meant to do more than just beat the world speed record. This highly publicized event was also meant to:
i) test the tracks for their durability
ii) beat Japan in the race for speed supremacy
iii) showcase the technology in order to sell it to other nations
iv) get the Transportation Minister re-elected
v) get bragging rights to "French excellence" in train technology

f) Who are France's biggest competitors in the bullet train market?
i) China
ii) Canada's Bombardier
iii) United States
iv) Germany and Japan
v) Great Britain

g) Who would probably be France's largest customer for the TGV bullet train?
i) China
ii) Canada
iii) United States
iv) Germany and Japan
v) Great Britain

Check your answers in the Answer Key.

Exercise 9

Listen to the dialogue. Number these concepts in the order that you hear them.

a) _____ supply chain
b) _____ quality
c) _____ ISO 9000
d) _____ material requirements planning
e) _____ robotics
f) _____ capacity
g) _____ MRP II
h) _____ productivity
i) _____ total quality management
j) _____ inventory control

Check your answers in the Answer Key.

Exercise 10

Operation doesn't begin or end with production. A company has to collect raw materials for production and also, once production has finished, get the product to the supplier or customer. The following terms deal with these issues surrounding materials for, and goods from, production. Match each term with the scenario that best depicts its meaning.

holding costs	logistics	transportation
inventory control	purchasing	warehousing
lead times	supplier selection	

a) The ClearCut Paper Company contracts with national trucking company BRD Shipping to have timber shipped to its plant and to have its paper products shipped to its suppliers. BRD takes care of ClearCut's ______________________________ needs.

b) The Big Drip Coffee Company is trying to implement just-in-time (JIT) inventory control for many of its products. Big Drip has found that having a lot of product on hand continuously makes its ______________________________ too high.

c) Although Hexcorp chiefly gets its raw plastics from two different plastics firms, they keep a running list of the firms that could meet their needs in the area in case there is a problem. This list keeps track of Hexcorp's ______________________________.

d) Luigi Carrone manages the materials coming in and the product going out of Chesley Bay Seafood. He must make sure that the company has all of the fishing equipment it needs and that it is putting out enough product quickly enough to satisfy its customers. Luigi is in charge of ______________________________ at Chesley Bay.

e) Working for the Big Drip Coffee Company, Sarah Clark takes care of negotiating with growers for the raw coffee that will be processed to be consumed and sold in the Big Drip coffee shops. Her department also works on behalf of the company to get all of the paper products, food supplies, and marketing merchandise needed for the stores to operate. Sarah works in the ______________________________ department.

f) Hexcorp Inc. has two major storage areas. The first storage facility is where Hexcorp stockpiles the raw materials for production. The second storage facility is where the finished product is stored until it is shipped off to the customers. These storage areas fill Hexcorp's ______________________________ needs.

g) Tariq Surve manages Hexcorp's two storage areas. Part of his job is to keep a running count of all the raw materials and product in the storage areas. Tariq is in charge of ______________________________.

h) At Chesley Bay Seafood, one of the biggest concerns for Luigi Carrone is getting the product to the customer in good time. Over the years, he has worked to reduce the time it takes to get customers the products they have ordered. Luigi is very concerned with Chesley Bay's ______________________________.

Check your answers in the Answer Key.

Exercise 11

There are many possible choices involved in the management of manufacturing operations. The terms listed in this exercise deal with some of those choices. Match the term with the correct definition. The first one is completed for you.

process manufacturing

assembly process

continuous process

intermittent process

just-in-time (JIT) inventory control

materials requirement planning (MRP)

enterprise resource planning (ERP)

a) a computerized operations system that integrates the production of multiple firms

b) a production process that involves shorter runs and multiple products

c) a production process or part of a process that changes or refines a substance

d) a computerized production management system that predicts necessary production materials based on sales forecasts

e) a production process or part of a process that involves putting parts together to create a finished product

f) a production process that involves longer runs and usually a single product

g) a production process designed to economize on storage space by arranging for parts and supplies to arrive just in time to go on the assembly line

Check your answers in the Answer Key.

Exercise 12

Different companies choose to use different forms of production in order to meet company needs. The terms listed in this exercise deal with some of the different forms of production. Match each term with the scenario below that best depicts the process it describes.

flexible manufacturing
lean manufacturing
mass production
mass customization
competing in time

a) Hexcorp has a massive manufacturing plant. They inventory vast amounts of plastic to produce plastic lawn furniture. Because they make such an enormous quantity of lawn furniture at one time, they save money on production costs and can afford to sell their furniture at a lower price than the competition. Hexcorp uses

______________________________.

b) Chesley Bay Seafood sells shellfish to restaurants across the country. It has an extensive transportation system designed to get their shellfish to customers as quickly as possible. As a result, many large up-scale restaurants choose to get their shellfish from Chesley Bay instead of other companies. Chesley Bay is ______________________________.

c) The Off My Back Clothing Company deals in printed t-shirts and sweatshirts. They are set up so that they can readily incorporate a customer's logo and wording onto their clothing without having to make extensive changes in their production processes. They are using

______________________________.

d) ClearCut Paper Products has streamlined its production. By rearranging its operations layout and adopting automation in some areas, it was able to cut down its workforce by half. ClearCut has also developed a new technique for utilizing its raw materials more effectively so it needs less input to produce the same amount of paper. Clearcut is engaging in

______________________________.

e) A new manufacturer, Smith & Son Farm Equipment, has managed to save money on its production equipment. Instead of having different machines for all of the different equipment they produce, Smith & Son has adopted a new kind of machinery that, with a few minor adjustments, will turn out several different kinds of equipment. They have saved on space and start-up costs. Smith & Son is using ______________________________.

Check your answers in the Answer Key.

Test Your Knowledge 8

Use your new knowledge and skills to solve the clues and complete the puzzle!

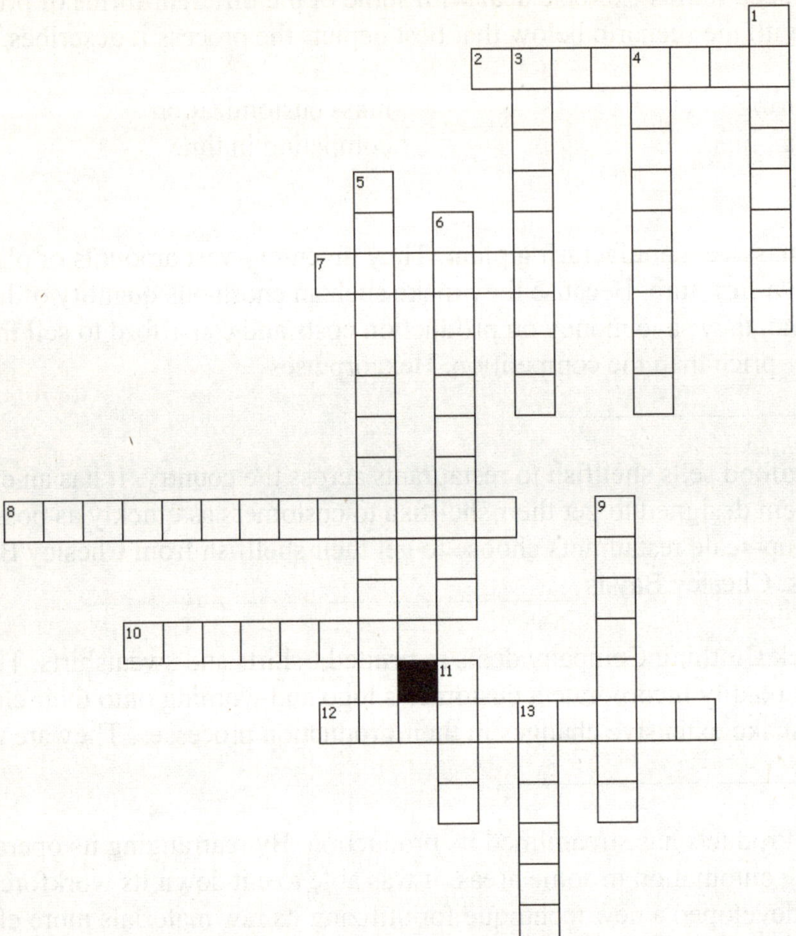

Clues

Across

2. A computerized manufacturing system that enables a single production line to produce small amounts of a range of different goods is called ____________________ manufacturing.
7. The physical organization of machinery and equipment within an operation is called facility _______________.
8. Mass _______________ is the ability of an operation to produce a large number of goods with minor adjustments according to customer specifications.

10. Processes that involve breaking down materials to obtain usable parts are called _______________ processes.
12. A computerized operations system that integrates the production of multiple firms is called _______________ resource management (ERP).

Down

1. The work undertaken by an organization in order to gain new knowledge and produce innovations in products, services, or processes is called _______________ and development (R&D).
3. The management of the quantity, location, timing, and cost of input and output materials throughout an operation is called _______________.
4. Managing and keeping track of the materials input and output of an operation is called _______________ control.
5. The way in which a company moves supplies to its operations and finished products to buyers is called _______________.
6. A production process that involves longer runs and usually a single product is called a _______________ process.
9. The geographical position of an operation is called facility _______________.
11. Manufacturing that uses minimal levels of materials and labour is called _______________ manufacturing.
13. The activities of a firm that result in tangible goods are called goods _______________.

Check your answers in the Answer Key.

Chapter 9

Technology in the Workplace

Before You Start

Study the terms below and be sure that you understand each one. If any of the terms are unclear to you, you can find definitions in the Glossary.

Key Terms

- browser
- business-to-business websites (B2B)
- computer graphics programs
- data
- database
- database management system
- desktop publishing
- directories
- electronic conferencing
- electronic spreadsheets
- extranet
- firewall
- groupware
- information
- internet
- internet service provider (ISP)
- intranet
- local area network (LAN)
- multimedia communications systems
- portable document format (PDF)
- presentation graphics software
- search engine
- teleworking/ telecommuting
- web servers
- wide area network (WAN)
- word-processing programs
- World Wide Web

Now, listen to the chapter's Audio Key Terms List for the correct pronunciation and the meaning of each term.

Exercise 1

It is easy to confuse the terms *data* and *information*. Read the following examples and categorize each as either *data* or *information*. If necessary, review the definitions of the two terms in the Glossary. Put the letter for each example into the table provided for you.

data	information

a) The sales figures from the monthly audit

b) A proposal for improved productivity that incorporates sales figures

c) Sales forecasts for the next year

d) Demographic statistics of a firm's customer base

e) Advertising strategies based on demographic statistics

f) Payroll

g) Tax records

h) An analysis of a firm's fixed costs with a focus on possible savings

Check your answers in the Answer Key.

Exercise 2

The terms listed below deal with different kinds of electronic information technologies. Some may be more familiar to you than others. Match each term with the correct definition.

electronic conferencing
electronic mail
fax machine
groupware
voice mail

a) A machine that makes a digital copy of visual information and sends it over a telephone line is called a _______________________.

b) A computerized system that receives and records telephone messages is called _______________________.

c) A system that sends computerized information electronically to other computers is called ____________________.

d) A system that allows people in multiple locations to communicate simultaneously by voice, video, or text is called ____________________.

e) A system that allows for immediate electronic communication between people on multiple microsystems or PCs is called ____________________.

Check your answers in the Answer Key.

Exercise 3

Data communication networks have changed the way business is done today. Although we use these networks every day, many of us do not understand the way they work. The terms listed here deal with the different features and options involved in data communication networks. Match each term with the correct definition.

browser	internet service provider (ISP)	the internet
directories	intranet	web servers
extranet	search engines	World Wide Web
firewall		

a) The international public data communication network linked by networks around the world and serving millions of computers is called ____________________.

b) The system of interlinked documents using a standardized method of storage and accessed through the internet is called the ____________________.

c) A firm that provides consumers with access to the internet via dial-up, DSL, or wireless connections is called an ____________________.

d) A private network set up to serve a single organization and made secure from outsiders is called an ____________________.

e) An internal network that permits outsiders limited access to specific network areas is called an ____________________.

f) A ____________________ is a large computer with software that processes requests from users for specific documents on the World Wide Web.

g) A ____________________ is a kind of software application that enables users to access documents on the World Wide Web.

h) ____________________ are web-based software applications that allow users to search for information on the World Wide Web using key words.

i) Systems that list information on the World Wide Web using categories and subcategories instead of user-inputted key words are called ____________________________.

j) A ______________________________ is a software or hardware barrier in a computer set up to prevent unauthorized access to a system.

Check your answers in the Answer Key.

Exercise 4

Many different types of software are used by organizations for different purposes. Read the scenarios below and decide which type of software would be best for each. Put the letter for each in the correct column in the table provided for you.

Type of Software	**Letters**	
word-processing programs		
electronic spreadsheets		
presentation graphics software		
desktop publishing software		
Portable Document Format (PDF)		
computer graphics programs		

a) Jane wants to present a proposal to upper management. She will make her presentation in a large, computer-enabled board room. She would like to include text, graphics, and video in her presentation.

b) Hexcorp would like to send out an electronic catalogue of its products to all of its buyers. The catalogue will include text and graphics. Because the catalogue is being sent outside of the company, Hexcorp has no idea what software the buyers will use to view the catalogue.

c) Chesley Bay Seafood wants to send out a print catalogue to all of its customers. One of the marketing team is going to put together the catalogue, get copies printed, and mail them across the country.

d) Trish wants to create a bar graph in order to view sales statistics for her division.

e) Salih is in charge of ClearCut Paper Company's human rights and ethics policies. Salih needs to create a document that will be viewed within the company, sent out to suppliers, and accessible to the public via the company's extranet.

f) Josef is creating a letter that he will mail out to a colleague at another firm.

g) Sun is a manager at one of the Big Drip Coffee Company's locations. She needs to create a document in which she can keep a running tally of the sales and costs of all of the different beverages sold at her location.

h) Prita is beginning work on a new project. She wants to create a Gantt Chart to show the schedule that she and her team worked out for the project.

i) Vertical Telecommunications is developing an orientation package that will be shown to new employees. It involves text, graphics, and video.

j) Hana is creating a proposal that she will submit to her boss textually.

k) Sheila manages a small department at a banking institution. She wants to create a document that will track the numerical results of employees' monthly performance assessments.

l) Lawrence is in charge of health and safety at one of Hexcorp's factories. There will be an extensive policy change and Lawrence needs to send out a hard-copy handbook to all employees of the company. The handbook will include text and graphics.

Check your answers in the Answer Key.

Grammar Tip

Words and phrases that are used to indicate relationships between sentences and ideas are called **linking words** or discourse markers. There are many different **linking words** that serve to indicate different relationships. Study the chart below.

Function	Linking Words/Phrases	Examples
order (logical or chronological)	first, second, next, last, finally	**First**, the new employee should undergo an orientation.
addition	also, in addition, furthermore	**Also**, the new employee should be informed of all information systems and their use.
contrast	however, although, on the other hand, in contrast	**However**, the new employee should not be overwhelmed with information right away.

alternatives	rather than, instead of	In this way, employees will be given a chance to assimilate the new information, **instead of** hearing it all at once and forgetting.
result	therefore, consequently, as a result	**Therefore**, managers should consider giving the information systems orientation at a later point.
generalizing	generally, in general, overall	**In general**, managers can anticipate spending a couple of weeks on orientation.
illustrating	for example, for instance, such as	**For instance,** a general orientation can be given on the first day, a follow-up a week later, and an information systems orientation after three weeks.
restating (used to clarify an idea)	in other words, that is	**In other words,** employees can begin work with a general orientation.
concluding	in conclusion, to conclude, in summary	**In conclusion**, new employees need a complete orientation over the first few weeks of employ.

Note: not all of the words in each category are interchangeable. If you are in doubt about how any of these are used, consult a dictionary.

Exercise 5

Use the linking words and phrases listed here to label the diagrams that best illustrate their use.

next
in addition

however
therefore

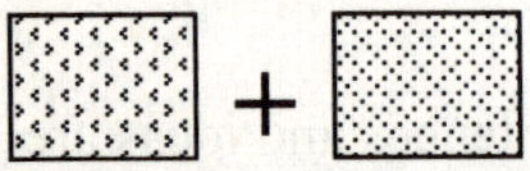

a) ______________________

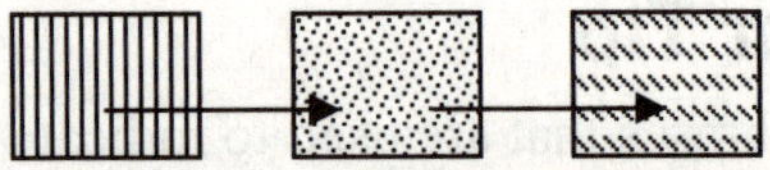

b) ______________________

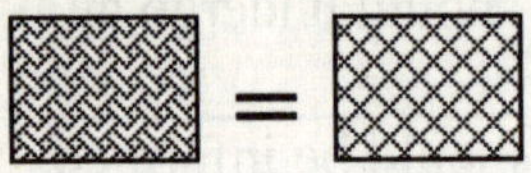

c) ______________________

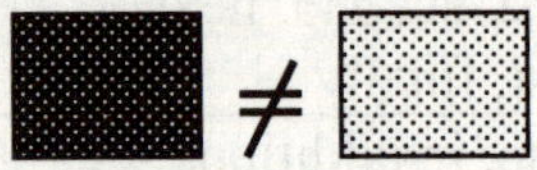

d) ______________________

Check your answers in the Answer Key.

Exercise 6

Use the linking words and phrases listed here to fill in the blanks in the scenario below.

also
first
for instance
however
in conclusion
on the other hand

Business professionals have many choices when it comes to using software to produce documents and audio-visual materials for the workplace. a) ____________________, professionals should consider what type of material they need to create. A letter will require very different software than a presentation. b) ____________________, that is not the only factor that needs to be taken into consideration. Professionals also need to consider their audience, their audience needs, and the purpose of the material. c) ____________________, a busy executive may only need a progress summary of an ongoing project and may not have time to sit though a whole presentation. Professionals d) ________________________ need to consider how the material will be read. For materials sent within an organization, professionals can be sure that the receivers will all have access to the same kinds of software for viewing the documents. e) ______________________________, materials that are being sent electronically to receivers outside of the organization should be developed using software that is common or easily translatable, such as Adobe Acrobat PDF files. f) ________ __________________, professionals need to take many factors into consideration before deciding what software to use to develop materials for business communications.

Check your answers in the Answer Key.

In the News 9.1

Ourwebsitesucks.com

Diane Peters

Business-to-business websites often present flashy animation and a well-crafted blurb on the company's history—the kind of stuff that makes the site's owner proud, but hardly inspires people to buy. Moreover, these points of pride often receive attention at the expense of things that actually do promote sales.

So, a couple of questions for you: Does your business-to-business (B2B) site make it easy for your customers to find out what they want to know? Or do you frustrate them with mystifying lingo, unhelpful information and hard-sell techniques? Look closely and you might discover your site is making mistakes that are costing you sales.

If potential customers visiting your site can't find what they want, get a bad impression of your company or feel you're wasting their time, then click!, they're gone. Website experts say they see the same mistakes on B2B sites again and again. The good news is that it's easy to fix these classic blunders and turn your site into what it's supposed to be: a business-builder.

Blunder #1: Omitting essential product information

The fix: Layer your product and service information. The top level can list the benefits and uses, while a click rewards a serious—or technically minded—buyer with details such as size and compatibility. If your prices vary, anecdotally mention what your product or service has cost previous customers doing small, medium or large installations.

Blunder #2: Making the site a chore to navigate

The fix: Simplify your site's design so everything is easy to find. Find out how your customers label your products and organize things accordingly. Convert any PDFs into HTML, and condense your written information into short chunks and bullet points.

Blunder #3: Patting yourself on the back

The fix: Clean up your site's language to peel out self-congratulatory phrases and replace them with concise, useful information about your company's products, services and policies. If you've uploaded content directly from a loquacious paper brochure, go through it and edit out the fluff.

Blunder #4: Forcing visitors to register

The fix: Open up your site, but leave opportunities for serious visitors to contact you or supply contact information as they move through the site. If you do want visitors to register, Hoa Loranger [a "user experience" specialist with Web-research firm Nielsen Norman Group in Fremont, California], suggests that you ask them to do so in exchange for something valuable, such as access to a white paper on how to save money using products in your category.

Blunder #5: Failing to speak the customer's language

The fix: Put your website under the microscope. You could hire a Web-usability consultant to conduct a usability test with a group of people. Another option is simply to have a consultant spend half a day doing an expert review of your site, comparing it with best practices. Or, for next to nothing, you could get anyone from a staffer who is not involved in your site to your 10-year-old niece to sit down and try a few tasks. Watch what they do and ask them how the experience was. Use your results to spruce up your site's language, as well as the navigation and content.

Source: Diane Peters, "Ourwebsitesucks.com," *Canadian Business Online*, PROFIT Magazine, December 2006. Courtesy of Diane Peters.

To read the entire article, visit
www.canadianbusiness.com/shared/print.jsp?content=20061201_150209_5612

Exercise 7

The following are examples of common blunders that show up on business-to-business websites. After reading the article, "Ourwebsitesucks.com," identify which blunder each of the following examples represents.

a) _____ Loaded with PDFs and industry news—I can't find anything.

b) _____ You can tell that a Webhead, who doesn't know a thing about this company's customers, developed this site.

c) _____ Product descriptions are poor, the photos are not clear, and there are no prices—I'm out of here—click!

d) _____ I don't have time to drift through your trophy room. I don't care how many awards you've won. Just get me to the business end of things.

e) _____ Look, I'm not going to give you all of the information you're requesting until I know whether your prices are reasonable and that your product specs are what I need.

Check your answers in the Answer Key.

Exercise 8

Use the linking words and phrases listed here to fill in the blanks in the statements below that deal with **In the News 9.1**. If necessary, study the **Grammar Tip** in this chapter again.

although	in other words
for example	rather than
however	in general

a) Businesses should list product information, including technical specifications, on their B2B websites. ________________________, the services and benefits should be listed first with a clickable icon to take more technically minded customers to the detailed information.

b) In order to make their sites easy to navigate, businesses should organize the information according to customer needs, ________________________ their own production methods.

c) Everything on a B2B website should be altered so that it is very easy to access and read. ________________________, PDFs should be converted to HTML documents, and long chunks of text should be broken up into bullet points or short paragraphs.

d) ________________________ businesses might be justifiably proud of their achievements, a B2B website is not the place to overwhelm customers with achievements.

e) Businesses shouldn't make it difficult for customers to access the site. ____________, it is not a good idea to require customers to register in order to use the site.

f) ____________________________, businesses should try to make everything about their site as simple and straightforward as possible. Customers will be more likely to use the site and place orders.

Check your answers in the Answer Key.

In the News 9.2

Career Guide: Work Naked

Andrew Wahl

Imagine getting up in the morning, shuffling downstairs in your slippers to grab a warm, caffeinated beverage and flicking on your computer to start work.

Sounds pretty good, doesn't it? Teleworking (a.k.a. telecommuting) seems ideal to many. They figure they will be able to maintain a better work–life balance while actually improving their productivity, because they won't have colleagues interrupting them all the time. It also frees them up from the daily commute, adding more quality time to their day. These perceived benefits are at least somewhat true. But telework suffers from several myths—the biggest of which is that the transition out of the office is easy. It often is not.

The problem isn't technology—email, instant messaging and digital collaboration are already commonly used in the corporate world. The real challenge is cultural: the relationship that exists between an employee and his boss, and the structure and style of communication within a workgroup. About 1.5 million people work from home, where they typically spend one or two days a week. "It's a balance between meeting employee requests for better work–life balance, flexibility and choice," says Bob Fortier, president of the Canadian Telework Association, "with being more competitive, reducing costs and improving the retention of employees."

Telework can be a very successful arrangement for both employees and their employers, but it has to be done right—and that's a joint responsibility. Take Pfizer Canada Inc.'s 11-person linguistic-services department in St-Laurent, Que., which started part-time teleworking four years ago. The group translates five million words a year (everything from promotional materials to ... medicine labels). Instead of co-ordinating translation requests and revising on paper, they started managing it electronically. That switch had its own benefits, because it let the company begin using database software to partially automate translations. The upshot was a 30 percent increase in productivity. Manon Genin, the department's senior manager, credits some of that improvement to teleworking. "When I'm at the office, I get interrupted because my door is always open. But when I'm at home, people will wait until I'm at the office," says Genin, who works at home one day a week. "When I'm at home, I'm a lot more productive; and when I'm at the office, I'm a lot more available."

The real key is that you are able to do your work at least as well as before. "Continually touch base to understand objectives," Fortier recommends, "and when you deliver, make sure that the delivery is received; follow up."

At Pfizer's linguistic-services department, Genin makes sure people don't disappear. She works from home on Mondays, while the others pick either Mondays and Thursdays, or Tuesdays and Fridays. On Wednesdays, everyone is in the office. "It was very important that people be at the office at least three days a week," says Genin. "And I insisted that there be a day when everybody was at the office just to maintain teamwork.... [and] to maintain our visibility, because translators are very discrete and people might forget about us."

Source: Andrew Wahl, "Career Guide: Work Naked," *Canadian Business Online*, March 12, 2007. Courtesy of *Canadian Business* Magazine.

To read the complete article, visit
www.canadianbusiness.com/shared/print.jsp?content=20070312_85363_85363

Exercise 9

Read the **In the News 9.2** article, "Career Guide: Work Naked," above. Read the partial sentences to the left and below. Re-read the article and match the partial sentences on the left with the completion of the sentence on the right. The first one is done for you.

a) People think that teleworking will...	is also a challenge.
b) Productivity will improve...	employees have self-discipline.
c) Maintaining relationships between boss and employee...	because there won't be any interruptions.
d) Maintaining communication within a work group...	makes telework a cultural challenge.
e) Telework can be successful if...	understand objectives.
f) Continually touch base to...	provide a better work–life balance.

Check your answers in the Answer Key.

Exercise 10

Use the linking words and phrases listed here to fill in the blanks in the statements below that deal with **In the News 9.2**. If necessary, study the **Grammar Tip** in this chapter again.

additionally
although
however
overall
that is

a) When they consider telecommuting, people believe that they will get more work done at home. ______________________, they look forward to avoiding the often long commute into work each day.

b) ______________________ there are benefits to telecommuting, it is not as easy as some people believe.

c) Cultural negotiations are the most difficult elements of telecommuting. ________________, people have difficulty maintaining or negotiating the traditional organizational relationships from a distance.

d) Telecommuting can benefit an organization by improving morale and job satisfaction. ________________, communication and availability must be maintained by telecommuters.

e) ____________________, the success of telecommuting is the responsibility of both the organization and the employee.

Check your answers in the Answer Key.

Exercise 11

Listen to the dialogue and number the following terms in the order in which you hear them. You may need to listen twice.

a) _____computer graphics software
b) _____electronic mail system
c) _____extranet
d) _____HTML
e) _____information
f) _____intranet
g) _____LAN
h) _____PDF

Check your answers in the Answer Key.

Exercise 12

The terms listed here deal with system architecture. Use the terms to fill in the blanks in the definitions below.

client	multimedia communications systems
client-server network	server
local area network (LAN)	wide area network (WAN)

a) A network that connects users and servers to efficiently manage database, mail, or web systems is called a________________________________.

b) An access point in a client-server network is called a ____________________________.

c) A network that covers a single building, an organization, or a small area is called a ________________________________.

d) A microcomputer that manages a client-server network is called a ________________________________.

e) A network that connects computers over a large geographic area via the telephone or satellite is called a________________________________.

f) A network that connects different types of electronics including computers, printers, fax machines, and others, is called a _____________________________________.

Check your answers in the Answer Key.

Exercise 13

Use the clues to fill in the words in the puzzle below. When you are finished, the Mystery Word will be revealed.

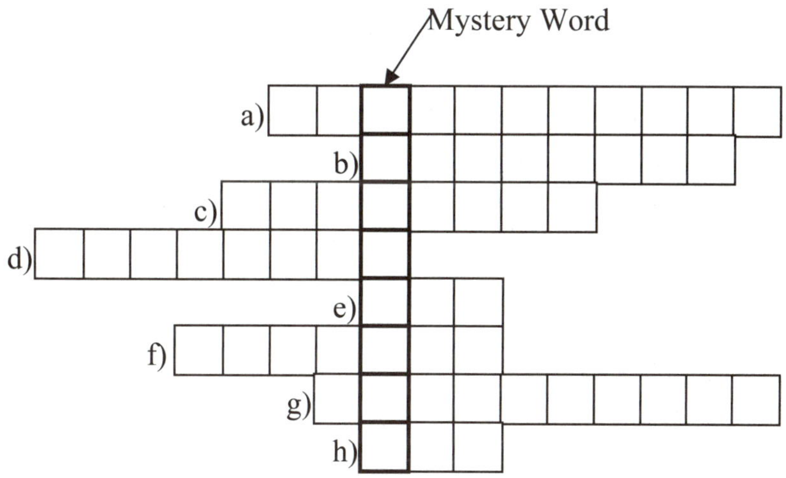

a) The analysis and interpretation of data for specific use.

b) The international public data communication network linked by networks around the world and serving millions of computers.

c) An internal network set up to serve a single organization and made secure from outsiders.

d) A ______________ management system is a large computer with software that processes requests from users for specific data, avoiding redundancy.

e) The short-form or acronym for a network that connects computers over a large geographic area via the telephone or satellite.

f) Software programs that allow users to track different types of numerical data and the relationships between those data are called ______________________ spreadsheets.

g) The short-form or acronym for a network that covers a single building, an organization, or a small area.

Check your answers in the Answer Key.

Test Your Knowledge 9

Use the terms from the chapter listed here to fill in the spaces in the scenario below.

browser
electronic conferencing
electronic spreadsheet programs
internet service provider (ISP)
local area network (LAN)
presentation graphics software
word-processing programs

Jolene is in charge of setting up the technological needs for a new travel agency. She has to get in touch with an a) __________________ in order to set up a connection in the office to the internet. She will also have to equip the office with PCs for all the employees. The PCs will need to have b) ___________________ software installed on them so that the employees can access documents on the World Wide Web. Jolene has decided that the office doesn't need a smaller private network, or c)__________________, because it isn't a very large office.

In addition to access to the internet, Jolene must ensure that the employees are equipped with all of the software that they will need for their work. In order to calculate payroll, the accountant will need d) ______________________. For writing textual documents, like letters and memos, all staff will need e) ______________________. They will also need f) ________________________ for creating text, graphics, and video for larger meetings. At some point in the future, Jolene intends to get the equipment and software necessary for g) _____________________ installed in the meeting room so that management can hold meetings with remote clients.

Check your answers in the Answer Key.

Chapter 10

A Brief Look at Accounting

Before You Start

Study the terms below and be sure that you understand each one. If any of the terms are unclear to you, you can find definitions in the Glossary.

Key Terms

accounting
accounting information system (AIS)
asset
audit
balance sheet
bankruptcy
bookkeeping
budget
cash-flow statement
certified general accountant (CGA)
certified management accountant (CMA)
chartered accountant (CA)
compliance
cost of goods sold (or manufactured)
double-entry bookkeeping
fiduciary duty
financial statement
forensic accountant
gross profit (gross margin)
income statement
liability
liquidity
malfeasance
managerial accounting
net income
operating expenses
private accountant
revenue

Now, listen to the chapter's Audio Key Terms List for the correct pronunciation of each term.

Exercise 1

Accounting is a complex area of business with many different duties involved. Use the terms listed below to fill in the spaces in the definitions.

accounting
audit
bookkeeping
chartered accountant (CA)
certified general accountant (CGA)
certified management accountant (CMA)
forensic accountant
private accountant

a) An individual who has the education and experience required and has successfully completed the licensing examination and has received the professional designation to act as accountant to outside firms is a ______________________________.

b) ___________________________ is a phase of accounting that consists of recording transactions.

c) ___________________________ is a comprehensive system for gathering, interpreting, and communicating financial information.

d) An individual who has successfully completed an educational program and examination and works within a private firm or a CGA firm is a ______________________________.

e) An ___________________ is an examination of a firm's financial records, by an accountant, to determine whether proper controls and accuracy were used in preparing its financial reports.

f) An individual who has a university degree, passed the requisite examination, and completed a program in strategic leadership, who usually works within a firm on internal management accounting is a ______________________________.

g) A ______________________ is an accountant, usually working with criminal investigators, who examines the financial records of a firm in order to uncover any illegal activities.

h) A ______________________ is an accountant working as a salaried employee of a firm to perform the company's day-to-day accounting activities.

Check your answers in the Answer Key.

Exercise 2

Accountants can focus on a broad spectrum of financial issues for organizations. Use the terms listed here to fill in the spaces in the scenarios below.

assets	financial statement
balance sheet	liabilities
cash-flow statement	liquidity
cost of goods sold (or manufactured)	

a) The Big Drip Coffee Company currently has mortgages on several of its locations and outstanding accounts with several suppliers. These are Big Drip's ____________________.

b) Tasha has prepared a ________________________ for her company that includes balance sheets, income statements, and an analysis of funds coming in and out of the company over a certain period of time.

c) Faisal is preparing an analysis of his company's ______________________, that is, an analysis of the ease and speed with which the company's assets can be converted into cash.

d) Hexcorp owns a manufacturing plant, two warehouses, and a certain amount of raw material and stock. These are Hexcorp's _____________________.

e) Sam has prepared a current_________________________ for his company. It shows his company's financial position at this time.

f) Dorothy has produced a monthly_______________________ for her company, accounting for all of the funds produced and spent this month.

Check your answers in the Answer Key.

Exercise 3

The terms listed below deal with the information contained in financial records. Match each term with the correct definition. The first one is completed for you.

cost of goods sold	a) costs that are not included in cost of goods sold.
double-entry bookkeeping	b) money coming into the firm as a result of sales, licensing fees, rent, or interest.
gross profit (gross margin)	c) a firm's gross profit after operating expenses and income taxes have been deducted.
net income	d) any expenses from the production and sale of a good or service during a specific period of time.
operating expenses	e) a system that requires that each transaction be recorded to demonstrate its impact upon assets and also its impact upon liabilities and owners' equity, providing a balanced accounting equation.
revenue	f) a firm's gross sales or revenues less cost of goods sold.

Check your answers in the Answer Key.

Grammar Tip

When we are reporting what someone has said, we can do it in two ways. First, using quotation marks, we can directly report the person's exact words. This is called *direct speech*. Study the example below.

The accountant said, "**Your** accounts are in good shape."

We can also report what the person said from our own perspective. When we report speech in this way, we do not use quotation marks. This is called *indirect speech* or **reported speech**. Study the example below.

The accountant said that **our** accounts are in good shape.

Notice particularly the change in the pronoun in the sentence. When you are using reported speech, pronouns often have to change. In most cases, you will also need to add *that* before the **reported speech**. Study the further examples below.

direct speech: Tania confirmed, "**I** have finished calculating our gross income."
reported speech: Tania confirmed *that* **she** has finished calculating our gross income.

direct speech: Solomon told me, "**My** boss wants **me** to reduce operating expenses."
reported speech: Solomon told me *that* **his** boss wants **him** to reduce operating costs.

direct speech: My boss said, "Get **me** the financial report by 4pm."
reported speech: My boss said *that* I should get **him** the financial report by 4pm.

Notice that in the last example here, we need to add a subject and modal verb. This is because the original statement was in the imperative mood in which the subject (you) is not stated but is understood.

Exercise 4

Rewrite the following examples of direct speech as reported speech. Don't forget to change the pronouns and add *that* if necessary.

a) They said, "We will have the reports done before you leave for the day."

____

b) The forensic accountants said, "We have to check your net income before we can come to any conclusions."

____

c) She told me, "I need to get my work done before I can see you."

____

d) I asked the accountants, "How long will be it until the next financial statement?"

____

e) The top managers said, "Our revenues for this quarter haven't been as high as we would like."

____

Check your answers in the Answer Key.

Exercise 5a

Use the terms listed here to fill in the blanks in the scenario below.

bankruptcy
cash-flow statement
compliance
fiduciary duty
forensic accountant
malfeasance
private accountant

In order to prevent their creditors from taking control of their business in a a) ______________ proceeding, Dare to Dream Cruiselines got creative. It fudged its most recent b) ______________, showing that more money was coming into the firm and less going out than was actually the case. However, an employee leaked this example of c) ______________ to the media and an investigation was called for by the firm's shareholders and creditors. A d) ______________ was called in to investigate the firm's accounting practices. The firm's own e) ______________ was unavailable for comment. The fudged numbers were tracked down and the firm's true financial situation assessed. In a statement to the public, the firm's CEO said, "On behalf of Dare to Dream, I would like to apologize to our shareholders, creditors, and the public, for this gross breach of our f)______________." The detective in charge of the investigation said, "Our investigation is completed and it is likely that those responsible will go to trial." In a press conference on Monday, Prime Minister Stutsky said, "I feel that corporate heads carry a great deal of responsibility in modern society. It is vital that they exhibit fair play and g) ______________ in all of their activities. This kind of scandal is unacceptable."

Exercise 5b

Now, rewrite the direct speech from the scenario above as reported speech. Use the spaces below.

a) The firm's CEO said, "On behalf of Dare to Dream, I would like to apologize to our shareholders, creditors, and the public."

____

____

b) The detective in charge of the investigation said, "Our investigation is completed and it is likely that those responsible will go to trial."

____

____

c) Prime Minister Stutsky said, "I feel that corporate heads carry a great deal of responsibility in modern society."

___

___

Check your answers in the Answer Key.

In the News 10.1

Conduct Unbecoming

John Gray

Accountants were in the spotlight over the weekend. At the Academy Awards, the tuxedo-clad auditors from PriceWaterhouseCoopers marched up the red carpet in Hollywood to deliver those famous envelopes containing the names of the actors, scriptwriters and set designers who would bring home an Oscar that night. Canadian accountants were in the spotlight too, but for a much less distinguished reason. Earlier this month the Institute of Chartered Accountants of Ontario [ICAO] quietly found three senior Deloitte & Touche LLP auditors who worked on the books of Livent Inc. guilty of professional misconduct.

The damning 72-page report slams the partners at Deloitte for violating both professional standards and accounting rules during their work on the financial statements of the now infamous theatre company behind such Broadway shows as *Phantom of the Opera* and *Ragtime*. That is before Livent collapsed into bankruptcy amid allegations of widespread accounting fraud. Deloitte—and others affiliated with the firm—are now defendants in a raft of shareholder lawsuits while Livent's executives also face criminal fraud charges.

The accountants breached the ICAO's policies when they approved the accounting treatment of millions of dollars worth of questionable transactions by Livent—some with little or no supporting documentation. The report also criticizes the accountants for failing to follow their own procedures in dealing with Livent ... and for putting too much trust in the representations of Livent's management despite mounting evidence at the time that company executives were lying to the auditors. "Given the seriousness of the issues, skeptical auditors owed it to themselves, the shareholders and the public to collectively analyze the evidence as a whole and they did not," reads the report.

Since the collapse of Livent in 1999, there have been a lot of changes in the way accounting firms approach high-risk clients—especially given the other recent high-profile financial disasters at such companies as Enron, WorldCom, Adelphia and Nortel.

There are inherent weaknesses in relying on accounting firms who are paid by public companies to uncover fraud or other malfeasance in their books, says Chris Knapp, an accounting professor at the University of Oklahoma who has written extensively about Livent.... "To stand toe-to-toe with a strong CEO and accuse him of wrongdoing takes a lot of backbone and a certain set of skills," he says. "Those are skills that not a lot of accountants have."

[One] solution is being tested in South Africa, which has had to overcome many homegrown accounting scandals. Legislation passed late last year now forces auditors to report to government regulators, police or tax authorities any fraud, theft or "material breach of any fiduciary duty" discovered in the course of their duties ... within three days. Bringing in the police or government regulators takes the pressure off accountants, who might otherwise have to fight with a CEO trying to cover up fraud or sweep some breach of fiduciary duty under the rug. There is little wiggle room for the accountants when it comes to reporting: Failure to report a financial transgression could result in a fine of up to 10 million Rand (about $1.6 million) and/or 10 years in prison.

That's a lot more than the Deloitte accountants face for breaching the professional conduct rules of the ICAO. Sanctions against the three men are expected to be as little as a reprimand, a fine or—the ultimate punishment—expulsion from the institute.... Who knows? Maybe it will take the threat of doing hard time in jail for some accountants to finally take fraud as seriously as many shareholders.

Source: John Gray, "Conduct Unbecoming," *Canadian Business Online*, February 27, 2007. Courtesy of *Canadian Business* Magazine.

For the full article, visit *www.canadianbusiness.com/columnists/john_gray/article.jsp?content=20070227_104838_5056*

Exercise 6

Read the article, "Conduct Unbecoming," above, and answer the following questions.

a) What does the acronym ICAO stand for and what is its function?

b) Who did they find guilty of professional misconduct?

c) What is the company, Livent, known for?

d) Why is it unrealistic to rely on accounting firms to report fraud or other malfeasance in the books of firms for whom they are working?

e) What is the recent South African legislation demanding of its auditors?

f) What does the author believe it will take for accountants to take fraud seriously?

Check your answers in the Answer Key.

In the News 10.2

Wild West Accounting
Al Rosen

If you steal a Canadian's wallet, you could end up in jail. But if you steal a Canadian's retirement savings, little is usually said or done about it. Unlike in the United States, we are not seeing any exemplary prosecutions for securities fraud in Canada. And without any widely perceived deterrent, we are virtually encouraging the scam artists to continue taking advantage of Canadian investors. Worse, we are spooking foreign investors who continue to see Canada as the "Wild West," to use the words of Bank of Canada governor David Dodge.

Canada needs to act quickly to clamp down on accounting problems. Stagnant or long-dormant proceedings are tantamount to no prosecution at all. Thus, it's shocking to examine the current state of investigations concerning certain former executives at Philip Services, Livent, Nortel and Royal Group Technologies, to name just a few. Suspicions surrounding Philip Services and Livent both surfaced in 1998—come on, you remember: the year of Monica Lewinsky, Mark McGwire and Calista Flockhart. Well, it seems that the investigation files have been gathering dust alongside the infamous blue dress, home run ball No. 61 and those *Ally McBeal* episodes.

Canada does not lack for cases of financial chicanery, but where are our tough jail sentences like those recently handed down to former executives of WorldCom, Adelphia and Enron in the United States? ... David Brown, the recently departed chairman of the Ontario Securities Commission, believed that his organization's mandate wasn't "to bring lawbreakers to justice," but rather to "promote the integrity of the capital markets and foster confidence in them." But that seems to be a bit of a strange strategy: to ignore the problems in the hopes that collective Canadian denial will "promote" confidence.

Our politicians need to be pushed into action, and we have to start with three important steps. First, traditional power structures have to be eliminated: Canada's accounting and auditing practitioners have to be separated from the rule setters, to keep them from setting deliberately weak investor protection hurdles. Second, an independent Canada-wide enforcement (not regulatory) agency has to be set up to initiate proceedings against corporate scam artists. Simply put, the crooks are light years ahead of the provincial commissions in carrying out financial fleecings. And third, penalties for abusers have to be stiff enough to change behaviour. Many of the current penalties handed out are routinely treated as a mere cost of doing business.

Investors have no choice but to send a loud message that they've been scammed enough and that recent token reforms are not enough. The reality is that our current Canadian investor protection system is badly broken, and continuing silence from investors is not the solution.

Source: Al Rosen, "Wild West Accounting," *Canadian Business Online,* August 15, 2005. Courtesy of the author.

For the full article, visit
www.canadianbusiness.com/opinion/article.jsp?content=20050815_69943_69943

Exercise 7

a) How is Canada encouraging scam artists to continue taking advantage of Canadian investors?

b) According to the Bank of Canada's governor, David Dodge, how do foreign investors see Canada?

c) What is the current state of many investigations regarding accounting practices?

d) What does David Brown, former chair of the Ontario Securities Commission, believe about the mandate of the OSC?

e) What are the three steps that need to be taken to remedy the current situation?

Check your answers in the Answer Key.

Exercise 8

Listen to the dialogue and number the following terms in the order in which you hear them. You may need to listen twice.

a) _____ private accountant

b) _____ liquidity

c) _____ audit

d) _____ forensic accountants

e) _____ revenues

f) _____ double-entry bookkeeping

g) _____ financial statements

h) _____ malfeasance

i) _____ fiduciary duty

Check your answers in the Answer Key.

Exercise 9

Hexcorp wants you to begin its accounting procedures. The first thing they want you to do is to categorize each of the following examples as either assets or liabilities. Put the letter for each example in the table provided for you here.

assets	liabilities

a) warehoused raw materials

b) mortgage on the factory

c) accounts receivable

d) warehoused finished, unsold product

e) accounts payable

f) the factory

g) Hexcorp shares purchased by shareholders

h) the production machinery

i) leased office space

j) Hexcorp's shares in one of its supplier's companies

k) outstanding taxes

l) leased warehouse

Check your answers in the Answer Key.

Exercise 10

Solve the clues to fill in the squares and find the Mystery Word!

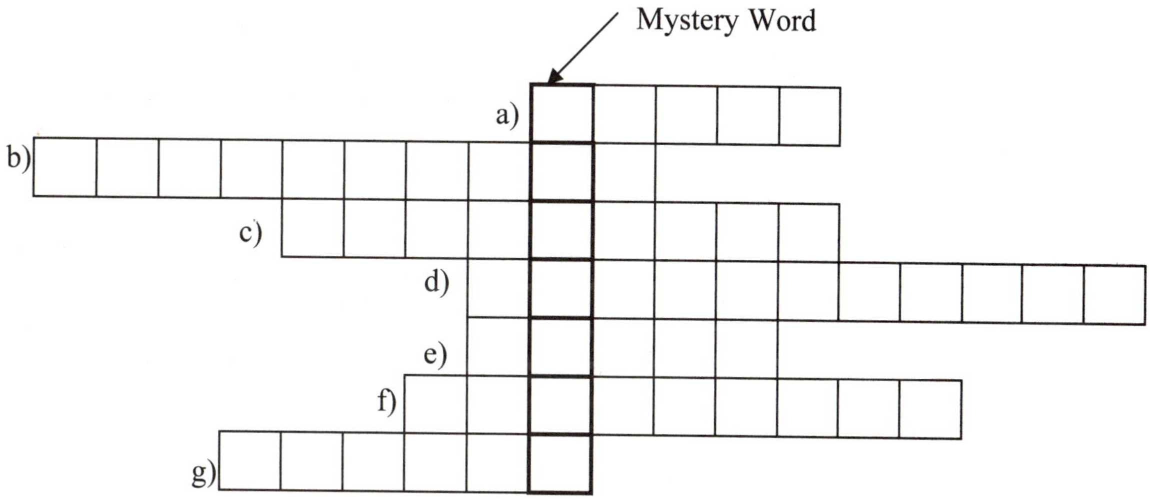

Clues

a) Anything of financial value that is owned by an individual or a firm.
b) The status of a firm in which the financial situation has deteriorated to the point where creditors are entitled by law to administer the firm; insolvency.
c) _______________ duty is a responsibility to behave in a legal and trustworthy manner and in the best interests of the firm.
d) A phase of accounting that consists of recording transactions.
e) An examination of a firm's financial records, by an accountant, to determine whether proper controls and accuracy were used in preparing its financial reports.
f) _______________ statement reports such as a balance sheet, cash-flow statement, or income statement that reflects a firm's financial status.
g) A plan that forecasts revenues and expenditures over the coming year.

The Mystery Word is ______________________________.

Check your answers in the Answer Key.

Test Your Knowledge 10

Use these terms from the chapter to fill in the spaces in the scenario below.

balance sheets	fiduciary duty
bookkeeping	financial statement
budget	gross profit (gross margin)
certified general accountant (CGA)	liabilities
double-entry bookkeeping	liquidity

Sharon has just been taken on as a manager in the accounting department of Hexcorp Inc. Sharon has excellent credentials, including qualification as a a) _______________ Sharon's first task will be to review Hexcorp's b) __________________, including c) _________________, cash-flow statements, and income statements, in order to gain an understanding of the firm's financial standing.

Once she has settled into the job, Sharon will monitor the d) _______________ practices, or the recording of financial data, of the junior accountants. Hexcorp uses a e) _________________ system in order to provide balanced accounts at all times. Sharon will assess the firm's f) ________________, or cash available, and its g) _________________, or money owed, in order to be ready to advise management at all times.

In time, Sharon will be expected to sit down and consult with upper management in their preparation of the h) ________________ for the following year. Sharon will have to ensure that Hexcorp meets it goals and achieves a satisfactory i) _______________ level. Sharon will also have to make sure that Hexcorp fulfils its ethical responsibilities or its j) _________________.

Check your answers in the Answer Key.

Chapter 11

A Brief Look at Finance

Before You Start

Study the terms below and be sure that you understand each one. If any of the terms are unclear to you, you can find definitions in the Glossary.

Key Terms

acquisition
bear market
budget (*see* Ch. 10)
bull market
capital structure
capitalization
cash-flow forecast
collateral
commercial paper
debt financing
dividends
equity financing
finance
financial control
financial management (*see* Ch.10)
financial plan
initial public offering (IPO)
insider trading
interest
line of credit
loan (secured, unsecured)
owner's equity
promissory note
prospectus
risk/return trade-off
stock (common, preferred)
trade credit
venture capital

Now, listen to the chapter's Audio Key Terms List for the correct pronunciation of each term.

Exercise 1

There are many different ways of financing an operation. Use the following terms to fill in the spaces in the scenarios below.

commercial paper	line of credit	promissory note
debt financing	loan (secured unsecured)	venture capital
interest		

a) BigBucks Equity is making a loan to a promising new IT firm called @Work Inc. BigBucks will charge @Work very high interest for this loan of ____________________.

b) Hexcorp, an established and profitable plastics company, wants to purchase a new production plant. It doesn't have the cash to do that now, but it is asking for a loan from BigBucks to finance the mortgage for the new production plant. Hexcorp is getting ________________________ from BigBucks.

c) The Big Drip Coffee Company suspects that the price of coffee is about to rise dramatically. It wants to buy large quantities of coffee beans to warehouse, but it doesn't have a large amount of liquid assets at the moment. The Big Drip sells __________________________ to insurance companies and banks through its broker at lower than face value, with the standard understanding that they will be paid within 270 days at face value.

d) The Doll Face Beauty Salon has a $5000_________________________ with its bank. This means that Doll Face can take out money, up to $5000 when it needs it, instead of taking out a loan all at once. This way, Doll Face will only pay interest on the money that it uses.

e) When it first started out, Past Away Antiques took out a loan to outfit its store. Every month, Past Away must pay ______________________, a certain percentage on top of the amount of the loan, to its bank.

f) Cheap Eats Café is asking the bank for a __________________ of $5000 to help finance its latest renovation.

g) Hexcorp has negotiated with its supplier of raw plastic to accept payment at a later time. In order to confirm this arrangement, Hexcorp has had to sign a ______________________ sent by the supplier in which they commit to make the payment within a specified time.

Check your answers in the Answer Key.

Exercise 2

Use the terms listed here to fill in the spaces in the scenario below.

acquisition
finance
financial control
financial management
financial plan

Lenka is in charge of a)___________________________ for Hexcorp. She carefully watches how the company is spending and making money. Recently, she sat down with upper management to prepare a b) _______________________, setting goals for the next year, five years, and ten years. Over the years, Lenka will have to exercise c) ____________ __________, comparing how the company is doing financially with its financial plan. One of the goals that Hexcorp has is the d) _______________________ of a raw plastic–processing plant. Upper management has asked Lenka to figure out how Hexcorp should e) __________ this goal.

Check your answers in the Answer Key.

Exercise 3

Use the listed terms to label the images below.

budget
collateral
owner's equity

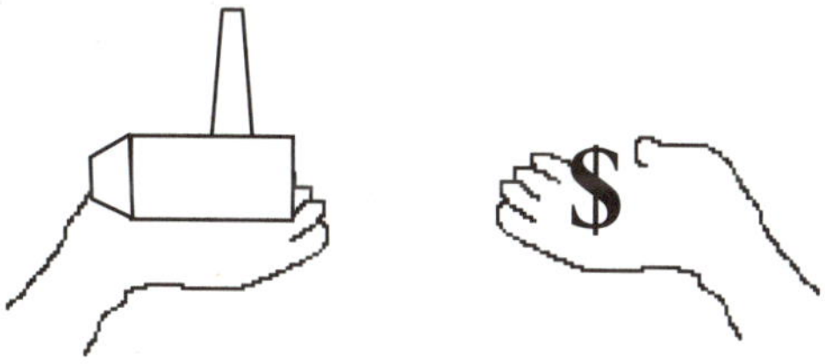

a)________________________

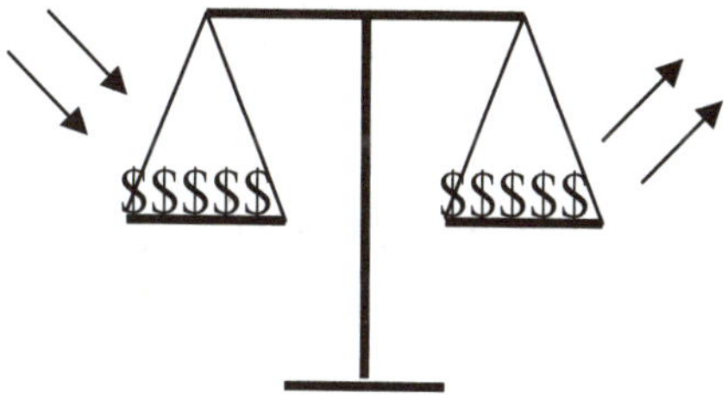

b)_________________________

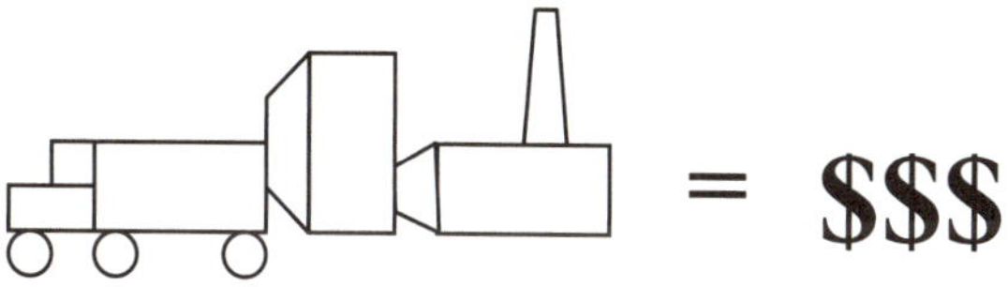

c)________________________

Check your answers in the Answer Key.

Exercise 4

Use the terms listed below to fill in the spaces in the definitions.

bear market	dividends	preferred stock
bull market	equity financing	prospectus
capitalization	initial public offering	
common stock	insider trading	

a) ______________________ is profiting on the stock market by using knowledge that is not available to others.

b) A ______________________ is a document required for registration with a securities exchange. This is a detailed statement including information about the firm, its management, its operations, and the purpose of the initial public offering.

c) A ______________________ is a period of time during which investors believe that stock prices will fall and act on that belief.

d) Issuing stock or retaining earnings in order to cover long-term expenditures is called ______________________.

e) A firm's dollar or market price per share on a specific day multiplied by the number of common shares is its ______________________.

f) People who have ______________________ have voting rights, but in terms of claim on assets are last in line.

g) An ______________________ is the first time that stock in a particular company is available for sale to the general public.

h) ______________________ are pro-rated distributions of profits to stockholders.

i) People who have ______________________ have no voting rights, but have first claim on a firm's assets and profits.

j) A ______________________ is a period of time during which investors believe that stock prices are on the rise and act upon that belief.

Check your answers in the Answer Key.

Grammar Tip

All clauses can be **active** or **passive**. In the **active construction**, the action and the thing or person doing the action come first in the clause. Study the examples below.

> *The public* **bought** some stock in the company.
> *Fanny* **drafted** the company's prospectus yesterday.
> *The customers* **received** the dividends on time.

In the **passive construction**, the thing or person receiving the action comes first and the verb must be "helped" by an auxiliary or helping verb. The most common auxiliary verbs in the **passive construction** are *to be*, *to have*, and *to get*. The **passive construction** is formed by combining the auxiliary verb with the past participle of the main verb. Study the same examples below rewritten in the passive.

> Some stock in the company **was bought** *by the public*.
> The company's prospectus **was drafted** yesterday.
> The dividends **were received** on time.

Notice that in the last two **passive construction** examples, the thing/person/people doing the action are not even included. Also, notice how much further along in the sentence the verb is in the **passive construction**. For these reasons, the **active construction** is preferable in most cases. The subject and the verb are often regarded as the most important parts of a clause or sentence. In all writing, but in business writing in particular, it is desirable to give the most important information first in order to communicate more effectively.

There are a few instances in which the **passive construction** can be useful. First of all, if you want to give more importance to the object, you can use the **passive construction**. This can usually be judged by the context surrounding the clause. Study the example below.

> We bought shares in a new company. It **was run** by *a couple of young computer nerds*.

In this case, the company has already been mentioned, so it makes sense to begin the next sentence with the same main idea.

You can also use the **passive construction** to avoid assigning blame or responsibility to an individual. This can be desirable if you are speaking to a customer or superior. Study the examples below.

active:	Jim **didn't finish** the report on time.
passive:	The report **wasn't finished** on time.
active:	Sherry **filled** your order incorrectly.
passive:	Your order **was filled** incorrectly.

Exercise 5

Rewrite the following active sentences as passive sentences. Leave the subject of the active sentence out of your passive version.

a) Management didn't approve the acquisition of the smaller company.

____

b) The authorities disapprove of insider trading.

____

c) Jamil drew up the new budget yesterday.

____

d) Giselle analyzed the company's capitalization.

____

e) Big Bucks gave a lot of venture capital to @Work.

____

Check your answers in the Answer Key.

Exercise 6

Rewrite the following passive sentences as active sentences. If no subject is provided, make up your own.

a) Most of the shares were bought by Hexcorp.

____

b) A promissory note was given to the supplier by Doll Face Beauty Salon.

____

c) The bear market was caused by a scandal in the finance industry.

____

d) A cash-flow forecast was developed for the company.

____

e) Steve was given a $5000 line of credit.

____

Check your answers in the Answer Key.

In the News 11.1

Read the following Initial Public Offering (IPO) announcements.

Israeli Lab Info Systems Firm Starlims Prices U.S. IPO at $13.50 Per Share

HOLLYWOOD, Fla. (AP)—Starlims Technologies Ltd., which provides laboratory information management systems, said Thursday its initial public offering of 2.1 million shares priced at $13.50 per share, the low end of the anticipated range.

The Tel Aviv, Israel-based company expected the offering to price between $13.50 and $15.50 per share. Starlims expects to raise about $25.5 million from the offering.

Starlims plans to use proceeds for general corporate purposes, including working capital and capital expenditures. The company may also use some of the proceeds for acquisitions or investments.

In addition to its headquarters in Tel Aviv, Starlims has operations in Florida, Canada, Great Britain and Hong Kong.

Oppenheimer is serving as lead underwriter for the offering. JMP Securities LLC is also underwriting the offering.

Starlims shares began trading on the NASDAQ Stock Market under the symbol "LIMS," and rose 15 cents to $13.65 in morning trading.

Source: Associated Press, "Israeli Lab Info Systems Firm Starlims Prices U.S. IPO at $13.50 Per Share," *Canadian Business Online,* May 24, 2007.

Blackstone Initial Public Offering Could Raise Up to $4.75 Billion
Joe Bel Bruno

NEW YORK (AP)—Blackstone Group LP, the second-largest U.S. private equity firm, said Monday it plans to raise between US$3.87 billion and US$4.13 billion in an initial public offering later this year.

In a filing with the Securities and Exchange Commission, the New York-based firm said it will value its common units at between $29 and $31 each. The terms come one day after

Blackstone announced that China would invest $3 billion in the firm alongside its public offering.

Underwriters—which include Morgan Stanley, Citigroup Inc., Merrill Lynch & Co., Lehman Brothers Holdings Inc., and Deutsche Bank AG—have the option to float an additional 20 million units. This could raise the size of the IPO to $4.75 billion.
Blackstone plans to list on the New York Stock Exchange under the symbol "BX."
With the investment by China, Blackstone could raise as much as $7.75 billion once its management side becomes publicly traded. The investment from China marks the first time that the Chinese have made a direct investment in a U.S. private equity fund.

The Blackstone agreement, announced over the weekend, marks China's long-anticipated attempt to diversify how it invests its almost $1 trillion in foreign exchange reserves.

The firm, which has racked up some $400 billion in deals and announced its public offering in March, operates a $15.6 billion fund, and its holdings include everything from Madame Tussaud's wax museums to real estate company Equity Office Properties Trust.

The IPO will also help it tap new sources of capital for multibillion-dollar acquisitions. The deal with China will allow Blackstone to directly buy into Chinese companies as that country becomes more receptive to foreign investments.

Source: Joe Bel Bruno, "Blackstone Initial Public Offering Could Raise Up to $4.75 Billion," *Canadian Business Online*, May 21, 2007.

Starent Networks Expects to Raise $81.9M in Initial Public Offering of 10.5M Shares

NEW YORK (AP)—Starent Networks Corp., which sells hardware and software that allows wireless networks to offer multimedia services to subscribers, expects to raise $81.9 million in an initial public offering of 10.5 million shares, according to a regulatory filing with the Securities and Exchange Commission.

The Tewksbury, Mass.-based company estimates that the offering will price between $9 and $11 per share. The expected net proceeds assume an offering price of $10, the midpoint of the expected price range.

Starent plans to use the net proceeds for working capital and other general corporate purposes, including developing new products, sales and marketing activities and capital expenditures. The company said it also may use some of the proceeds for acquisitions.

Starent Networks plans to offer 9 million shares.
Goldman Sachs and Lehman Brothers are the lead underwriters for the offering. JP Morgan Securities and Thomas Weisel Partners are also helping to sell shares to investors.

Starent has applied to list its shares on the NASDAQ Stock Market under the symbol "STAR."

Source: Associated Press, "Starent Networks Expects to Raise $81.9M in Initial Public Offering of 10.5M Shares," *Canadian Business Online*, May 18, 2007. Used with Permission of The Associated Press © 2007. All Rights Reserved.

For the complete articles, visit
www.canadianbusiness.com/shared/print.jsp?content=D8PAQI5O0
www.canadianbusiness.com/shared/print.jsp?content=b052115A
www.canadianbusiness.com/shared/print.jsp?content=D8P6V9NO0

Exercise 7

Reread each announcement, then fill in the blanks provided with the appropriate information.

a) Starlims Technologies Ltd.

i) What type of business is Starlims? ______________________________

ii) How many shares are being offered? ______________________________

iii) What is the price per share? ______________________________

iv) Where is the company based? ______________________________

v) How much money do they expect to raise? ______________________________

vi) How will they use the proceeds? ______________________________

vii) Who is underwriting this IPO? ______________________________

viii) Under what symbol will they be trading? ______________________________

b) Blackstone Group LP

i) What type of business is Blackstone Group? ______________________________

ii) How many shares are being offered? ______________________________

iii) What is the price per share? ______________________________

iv) Where is the company based? ______________________________

v) How much money do they expect to raise? ______________________________

vi) How will they use the proceeds? ______________________________

vii) Who is underwriting this IPO? ______________________________

viii) Under what symbol will they be trading? ______________________________

c) Starent Networks Corp.

i) What type of business is Starent Networks? ______________________________

ii) How many shares are being offered? ______________________________

iii) What is the price per share? ______________________________

iv) Where is the company based? ______________________________

v) How much money do they expect to raise? ______________________________

vi) How will they use the proceeds? ______________________________

vii) Who is underwriting this IPO? ______________________________

viii) Under what symbol will they be trading? ______________________________

Check your answers in the Answer Key.

In the News 11.2

Microsoft to Buy Online Ad Firm aQuantive for $6 Billion, in Company's Largest Acquisition

REDMOND, Wash. (AP)—Microsoft Corp. said Friday it will buy online advertising firm aQuantive Inc. for about $6 billion in cash, paying a premium to catch up with major ad deals by its competitors over the last six weeks. Shares of aQuantive soared more than 77 percent.

It is the largest acquisition in the software company's history, said Kevin Johnson, president of Microsoft's platforms and services division, in a conference call following the announcement.

The $66.50-per-share purchase price represents an 85 percent premium to aQuantive's Thursday closing price of $35.87.

Acknowledging that paying such a substantial premium is something Microsoft has avoided in the past, Chief Financial Officer Chris Liddell said the company believes aQuantive is "exactly the right company to buy" to help position it in a growing market.

Estimates put the online advertising market at $40 billion, and it is expected to grow at a rate of 20 percent a year, Liddell said.

The two companies have "very complementary" technologies, Johnson said, adding that by bringing them together, there is "significant value" to be unlocked.

The company is still far behind Google Inc. and Yahoo in search traffic and thus, search advertising revenue.

Last month Google Inc. agreed to buy online advertising company DoubleClick Inc. for $3.1 billion, and Yahoo Inc. struck a deal to buy the privately held online ad exchange Right Media Inc. for $680 million. Microsoft had expressed interest in buying DoubleClick before being trumped by Google.

"Today's announcement represents the next step in the evolution of our ad network from our initial investment in MSN, to the broader Microsoft network including Xbox Live, Windows Live and Office Live, and now to the full capacity of the Internet," said Microsoft Chief Executive Steve Ballmer in a statement.

The deal is expected to close in the first half of Microsoft's fiscal 2008. The acquisition is not expected to significantly affect the company's prior financial guidance. In fiscal 2008, it will "clearly" add revenue, but will not affect earnings per share or operating income, Liddell said.

The purchase price represents about 2 percent of Microsoft's market capitalization.

With about 2600 employees, aQuantive will continue to operate from its Seattle headquarters as part of Microsoft's online services business. The company, which operates marketing services firm Avenue A/Razorfish, reported 2006 profit of $54 million on sales of $442.2 million.

Shares of aQuantive rose $27.68 to $63.55 in morning trading, while Microsoft shares fell 35 cents to $30.63.

Source: Associated Press, "Microsoft to Buy Online Ad Firm AQuantive for $6 Billion, in Company's Largest Acquisition," *Canadian Business Online,* May 18, 2007. Used with Permission of The Associated Press © 2007. All Rights Reserved.

For the complete article, visit
www.canadianbusiness.com/shared/print.jsp?content=D8P6QVKG0

Exercise 8

Read the article, "Microsoft to Buy Online Ad Firm aQuantive for $6 Billion, in Company's Largest Acquisition," above. Fill in the blanks with the appropriate information. Be as precise as possible. You may need to read the article again and check the meanings of some of the terms used. Many of the terms can be found in the Glossary.

a) The cost of aQuantive Inc. to Microsoft Corp. will be _______________.

b) The firm aQuantive is in the _________________ business.

c) In order to catch up with its competitors, Microsoft is paying a ______________ for aQuantive.

d) In Microsoft's history, the purchase of aQuantive will be its largest ______________.

e) The online advertising market is worth ______________ and its annual growth is expected to be ______________.

f) ____________ and ____________ are far ahead of Microsoft in terms of __________________ revenue.

g) Microsoft expects the deal to close in the ______________ of fiscal 2008.

h) About two percent of Microsoft's ____________________ is represented by this purchase price.

Check your answers in the Answer Key.

Exercise 9

Listen carefully to the dialogue. Number these concepts in the order that you hear them. You may have to listen twice.

a) _____ bull market

b) _____ equity financing

c) _____ acquisition

d) _____ IPO

e) _____ capitalization

f) _____ risk/return trade-off

g) _____ financial control

h) _____ commercial paper

i) _____ prospectus

j) _____ stock

Check your answers in the Answer Key.

Exercise 10

Use the listed terms to fill in the spaces in the scenario below.

budget	interest	stock
collateral	line of credit	venture capital
initial public offering (IPO)	loan	
	prospectus	

Klaus Steiger is starting up a new IT firm. A couple of months ago, he drew up a a) ____________________ and realized that he needed substantial funds for his enterprise. In order to get funds for his company, he has done a number of things. First of all, a big financial firm has decided to take a risk in funding his new enterprise and offered him some b) ________________________. The c) ________________________ will be high, but he has faith in his idea, so he has decided to accept. He also has used his home as d) ________________________ to get a substantial e) ________________________ from his primary banking institution. He is trying to get a f) ___________________________ for emergencies from a second institution, but they are asking him for a g) ________________, detailing the management, operations, and financial planning for his company. He is working on that right now, knowing that he will be able to use it when he goes public next year, when he plans to make his h) ____________________________. He hopes to sell a decent amount of i) _________________________ in his company so that he can fund an expansion. Klaus is very ambitious.

Check your answers in the Answer Key.

Test Your Knowledge 11

Use your new knowledge to solve the clues and fill in the puzzle below.

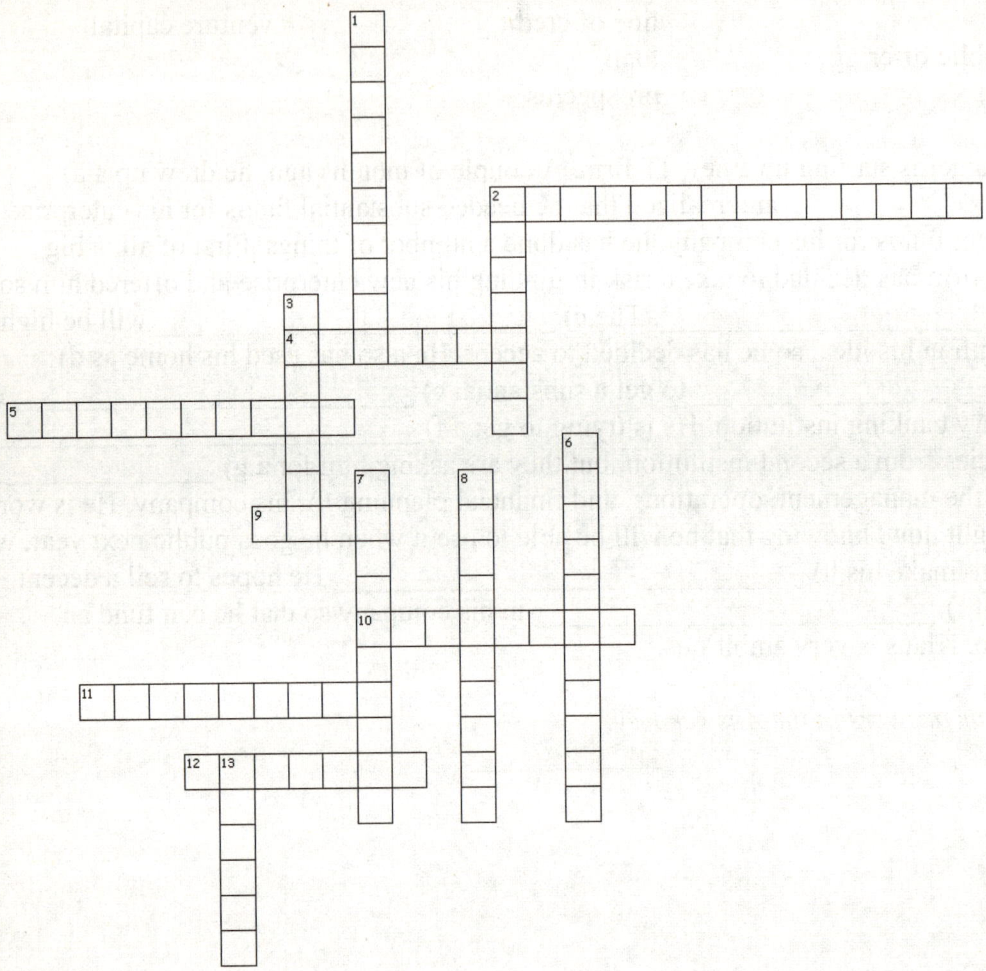

Clues

Across

2. ________________ is a firm's dollar or market price per share on a specific day multiplied by the number of common shares.
4. Profiting on the stock market by using knowledge that is not available to others is called ________________ trading.
5. Giving ________________ means committing an asset that can be seized by the lender for non-payment of the loan.
9. A ________________ market is a period of time during which investors believe that stock prices will fall and act on that belief.
10. ________________ is the cost of borrowing money.
11. ________________ are pro-rated distributions of profits to stockholders.

12. A loan granted on the potential of a new or expanding firm is called ______________ capital.

Down

1. A ______________ is required for registration with a securities exchange; this is a detailed statement including information about a firm, its management, its operations, and the purpose of the initial public offering.
2. Comparing a firm's actual financial performance with the financial plan is called financial ______________.
3. That area of business practice in which decisions are made regarding long-term investments and the funds to secure them is called ______________.
6. The purchase and assimilation of a smaller firm is called ______________.
7. A ________________ note is a form of trade credit in which buyers sign an agreement of repayment before receiving the merchandise.
8. ______________ paper is a method of acquiring short-term funds by selling unsecured notes for less than face value to be repurchased within 270 days of issue.
13. Owner's ______________ is the net proceeds if a firm were to sell all of its assets and pay all of its debt.

Check your answers in the Answer Key.

Chapter 12

Managing Marketing and Understanding Consumer Behaviour

Before You Start

Study the terms below and be sure that you understand each one. If any of the terms are unclear to you, you can find definitions in the Glossary.

Key Terms

brand
brand loyalty
consumer behaviour
consumer goods
demographics
early adopters
emotional motives
industrial goods
market research
market segmentation
marketing
marketing concept
marketing mix
marketing plan
place (distribution)
price
primary data
product
product differentiation
promotion
rational motives
relationship marketing
secondary data
services
target market
utility
value

Now, listen to the chapter's Audio Key Terms List for the correct pronunciation of each term.

Exercise 1

The terms listed below deal with basic concepts in marketing. Use the terms to fill in the spaces in the definitions below.

consumer goods	place (distribution)	services
industrial goods	price	utility
marketing concept	product	value
marketing mix	promotion	

a) The _______________ is that part of the marketing mix that involves creating a good, service, or idea that leads to the needs satisfaction of customers.

b) _______________ is that part of the marketing mix that designs ways by which to gain the consumers' attention and prompt them to buy.

c) The part of the marketing mix that involves determining a value for a product that serves the client's profit needs and the customer's purchasing needs is called _______________.

d) Products purchased for personal use are called _______________.

e) The _______________ refers to the adoption, by an entire firm, of the goal to satisfy both current and future customers' needs at a profit.

f) _______________ is the ability of a product or service to satisfy a want or need.

g) The strategic use of product, price, promotion, and distribution in the marketing of a product or service is called the _______________.

h) A comparison of a product's or service's benefits versus its costs determines a product's _______________.

i) _______________ is the part of the marketing mix that involves movement of the product from where it is produced to where the consumer can purchase it.

j) Intangibles that can be purchased are called _______________.

k) _______________ are products purchased to use directly or indirectly to produce other goods.

Check your answers in the Answer Key.

Exercise 2

The terms listed here deal with marketing strategies. Use the terms to fill in the spaces in the scenarios below.

demographics	marketing plan	relationship marketing
market research	primary data	secondary data
market segmentation	product differentiation	target market

a) Susan is working with her agency to market a new brand of make-up. They have done the research and determined that the product will be most appealing to unmarried women aged 15–25 years old, with some disposable income. That group will be the ________________ for the marketing campaign designed by Susan and her team.

b) ShowMe Marketing is trying to determine how best to market a new product. They have conducted several focus groups on the product over the past few months. They have compiled the results of those focus groups and this will be the ________________ that will be used in developing their marketing plan.

c) Hexcorp is working with its marketing division to try to promote the plastic lawn furniture that it produces. The problem is that there are many other firms that offer similar products. Hexcorp is trying to create ads that show the features of its furniture that might make it more appealing to consumers than similar furniture produced by other companies. Hexcorp is trying to establish ________________.

d) The Big Drip Coffee Company is thinking of developing some new products or changing some of its existing products. Its marketing department is investigating the newest trends and the changing needs of customers in order to determine what would be most appealing to existing and new customers. The Big Drip is doing ________________.

e) The Scrubby Soap Company has been around for years and consumers have used their products for generations. Scrubby's new television ad is a sentimental look at the meaning that Scrubby Soap products have taken on for customers over the years. This new ad focuses on ________________.

f) In order to prepare for developing a marketing plan for Dare to Dream Cruiselines, Michel is looking at recent studies done on the vacationing habits of consumers. Michel is looking at ________________.

g) In order to better understand the habits of consumers, Mind Marketing Company is studying the traits of those consumers, and dividing the pool of consumers into easily identifiable groups. Mind Marketing is engaging in ________________.

h) ShowMe Marketing is ready to begin marketing a product for one of its clients. ShowMe has done a situation analysis, developed objectives, identified target markets, and developed a plan of action. ShowMe has a ________________ for this product.

i) Mind Marketing Company has just been hired to market a product for a new client. In order to prepare a marketing plan, Mind Marketing is looking at the current consumer base for this product. It is analyzing that consumer base in terms of age, income, ethnic background, and a number of other characteristics. Mind Marketing is analyzing the ________________ of the consumer base.

Check your answers in the Answer Key.

Exercise 3

The following terms deal with consumer behaviour, an important consideration in marketing. Match each term with the picture that best depicts it.

brand loyalty

a)

early adopters

b)

emotional motives

c)

rational motives

d)

Check your answers in the Answer Key.

Grammar Tip

Appositives are a kind of non-defining clause that consists of a noun or pronoun, often with modifiers, that serves to re-name or clarify a noun or pronoun beside it. Study the example below.

> *Hexcorp*, **a company that manufactures plastic lawn furniture,** is doing well this year.

The noun *Hexcorp* is re-named or clarified by the **appositive:** *a company that manufactures plastic lawn furniture*. The **appositive** tells you what the noun Hexcorp is.

An **appositive** must be separated from the rest of the sentence. If it comes in the middle of the sentence, it must be separated by a comma at the beginning and the end.

> *Smithsville***, a city in Ontario,** is home to Hexcorp's manufacturing plant.

If the **appositive** comes at the end of a sentence, only one comma is needed at the beginning of the **appositive**.

> The team working on The Big Drip's new ad campaign includes *Abdul***, a specialist in youth culture**.

Exercise 4

Use the information in each set of two sentences provided for you below to create one sentence with an appositive in it. Remember to include correct punctuation.

a) Mind Marketing uses market research to develop its strategies. Market research is a study of consumer needs.

____

b) ShowMe Marketing markets products and services for various companies. Services are intangibles that can be purchased.

____

c) Consumers often buy products for emotional motives. Emotional motives are motives based on feelings or impulses.

____

d) Marketers often use secondary data in their development of marketing plans. Secondary data is information obtained through previous research.

____

e) Some marketing campaigns focus on utility. Utility is the ability of a product or service to satisfy a want or need.

____

Check your answers in the Answer Key.

In the News 12.1

Real Sales in a Fake World

Kim Shiffman

Question: Who would pay actual money for a virtual product? Answer: Hundreds of thousands of active users of Second Life, the much-hyped computer-generated world created by San Francisco-based Linden Lab Inc.

Second Life "residents" create a computer-generated representation of themselves (called an "avatar") and spend time almost as they would in the real world: exploring, connecting with others, creating things and—of most interest to entrepreneurs—buying stuff.

Second Life (www.secondlife.com) costs nothing to join. Yet users spend almost $1 million every day in the in-world currency, Linden dollars, which they buy using real dollars ($1 = L$266). And they generate most of the content, designing then selling or trading their creations—anything from furniture to high fashion. What's more, they own the intellectual property rights.

That's partly why real-world companies have begun throwing money into creating a presence and hawking their wares in Second Life. Retailer American Apparel opened a store selling digital renderings of its T-shirts that players' avatars can wear. Telus sells mobile phones, complete with in-world features. Although the items sell—curious, considering your avatar comes with clothes and has no real need for a cellphone—revenue isn't what's drawing the corporate crowd. Instead, they're keen to reach a young, tech-forward demographic in a unique environment. According to Joshua Fairfield, an Indiana University law professor who studies the economics of virtual worlds, "People's attachment to places and objects in the virtual world can transfer to purchases in the real world."

But to be successful in Second Life, you have to translate your brand in a way that works there, says Reuben Steiger, president of Millions of Us Inc., a Sausalito, Calif.-based firm that helps companies market in virtual worlds. He points to news agency Reuters as a firm that gets it: "Instead of building a chest-thumping monument to Reuters, they asked themselves, 'What can we do to add value to Second Life?'" The result: Reuters assigned a full-time employee to cover Second Life goings-on, which residents can access for free.

If you've been itching for an innovative way to expose a small but exclusive group of global, tech-savvy early adopters to your brand—and you're confident your marketing staff can figure out how to truly engage those prospects, not repel them—then Second Life may be worth a second glance.

Source: Kim Shiffman, "Real Sales in a Fake World," *Profit Magazine,* March 2007. Courtesy of *Canadian Business* Magazine.

For the full article, visit *www.canadianbusiness.com/entrepreneur/sales_marketing/article.jsp?content=20070212_142819_4792*

Exercise 5

Read the above article, "Real Sales in a Fake World." Read the following questions. Now, read the article again, in order to find the answers to the questions below.

a) What is Second Life?

b) What do Second Life residents create?

c) Why would entrepreneurs in the real world be interested in this computer-generated world?

d) What kind of demographic would be attracted to this unique environment?

e) In order for real-world companies to be successful in the virtual Second Life, what must they do?

f) In addition to the demographic described previously, what else do we know about those people who are attracted to Second Life?

Check your answers in the Answer Key.

Exercise 6

Use information from **In the News 12.1**, above, to create appositives for the nouns in **bold font** in the sentences below. Rewrite the entire sentence with the appositive in it. Remember to include correct punctuation.

a) **Second Life** is popular with users.

____

b) Second Life "residents" create an **avatar** and spend time almost as they would in the real world.

____

c) Users spend almost one million **Linden dollars** every day.

____

d) **Reuters** assigned a full-time employee to cover Second Life goings-on.

____

e) Users generate most of the **content**, designing then selling or trading their creations.

____

Check your answers in the Answer Key.

In the News 12.2

A Sports Extravaganza—to Go

Andy Holloway

Even if you're not a soccer fan, it's hard to avoid getting swept up in the patriotic fervor that surrounds the FIFA World Cup, the 2006 version of which began on June 9. There's the impromptu neighbourhood parties, the pubs packed with absentee employees crowded around a 50-inch screen, the oft-bellowed phrase "Gooaaaallll!" And then there's the technology.

Want to get a glimpse of the mobile future of electronic information delivery? The World Cup is the place to be.

Download highlights onto a cellphone; stream all of the games through the web; get short message service (SMS) alerts the second your team scores. To make sure that happens without a hitch, World Cup organizers set up a network containing 30 000 devices and 45 000 connections to kick out roughly 15 terabytes of data. Consider that one terabyte is enough to hold 300 feature-length movies, or 240 000 MP3 files, and you begin to understand the mass of information flowing out of the tournament.

But it's not really the technology that makes the World Cup—or Wimbledon, or the NCAA's March Madness—special. Most of it is fairly routine, although its sheer scope is impressive. No, the business model behind the tech makes those events watersheds in the development of mobile communications. Indeed, when it comes to paying for extra content, sports fans are some of the earliest adopters. It's easy to see why. Start with a defined hard-core audience that is always willing to pony up a few extra bucks for even the slightest bits of information.

"With sports, there is content that is not only valuable but also has timeliness to it," says Rick Singer, director of worldwide sponsorship marketing at IBM, and a sports technology expert.

There's no doubt Canadians want mobile video. Leading the content charge were NHL highlights, followed by movie trailers, music videos and comedy bits. The link between them is they are all short hits that are quickly downloaded and absorbed—a consumer behaviour known as content snacking. A recent study by accounting giant KPMG concludes consumers have already picked the cellphone as their preferred converged media device, and they are open to accessing a variety of information and services.

For example, the preliminary rounds of this year's NCAA basketball tournament were streamed live and, for the first time, free on the NCAA's website, with broadcast partner CBS's full participation. March Madness on Demand was supported by ad sales. But Singer, for one, believes advertising-driven viewing won't be the only outlet. "With IPTV [Internet Protocol television], people get the ability not just to watch a tennis match, basketball game or soccer match, but also to pull up the information they want and get different angles," Singer says. "That's true value-add and goes well beyond what people are used to seeing at home."

In the United States and Canada—and to some extent other countries—sports fans are already willing to pay for certain things, such as statistics that give them an extra edge in their sports fantasy leagues. Streaming video, however, has yet to be proven to either consumers or existing broadcast partners, who have been loath to siphon even more viewers away from their primary media distribution. In a few years, all this stuff will be completely routine. We'll be fractions of a second away from accessing all of the information we need or—perhaps more importantly, from a revenue-generation standpoint—want. Only then will business bean-counters be able to yell "Gooaaaallll!"

Source: Andy Holloway, "A Sports Extravaganza—to Go," *Canadian Business Magazine,* June 19-July 17, 2006. Courtesy of *Canadian Business* Magazine.

For the full article, visit
www.canadianbusiness.com/shared/print.jsp?content=20060620_79184_79184

Exercise 7

Read the article, "A Sports Extravaganza—to Go," above. Read the partial sentences to the left and below. Reread the article and match the partial sentences on the left with the completion of the sentence on the right. The first one is done for you.

a) Soccer fans…	type of consumer behaviour.
b) "Gooaalll!" is…	have a patriotic fervor.
c) The sheer scope is impressive…	of consumers.
d) Some of the earliest adopters…	are sports fans.
e) Content snacking is a…	although most of it is fairly routine.
f) The cellphone is the preferred converged media device…	an oft-bellowed phrase.

Check your answers in the Answer Key.

Exercise 8

Use information from **In the News 12.2**, above, to create appositives for the nouns in **bold font** in the following sentences. Rewrite the entire sentence. Remember to add the correct punctuation.

a) **Rick Singer** claims that sports content has a timeliness to it.

____

b) Canadians like **content snacks**.

____

c) **KPMG** has decided that consumers have already picked the cellphone as their preferred converged media device.

____

d) This year, the NCAA and **CBS** streamed the NCAA's basketball tournament for free on the association's website.

____

Check your answers in the Answer Key.

Exercise 9

Listen to the dialogue. Number these concepts in the order that you hear them.

a) _____ utility

b) _____ primary data

c) _____ brand

d) _____ early adopters

e) _____ value

f) _____ consumer goods

g) _____ market research

h) _____ target market

i) _____ secondary data

j) _____ industrial goods

Check your answers in the Answer Key.

In the News 12.3

Our Peculiar Daily Rituals

David Graham

Do you schedule sex? When do you shower, morning or night? And while we're in the bathroom anyway, at the risk of sounding impertinent, what do you read on the john?

Over nine months last year, global advertising and marketing company BBDO got up close and extremely personal with 5000 people in 26 countries to create "The Ritual Master," an exhaustive compilation of all those minuscule, repeated details that add up to a day in our lives.

Last month, executives unveiled their findings, an enormous survey of human behaviour compiled to help their clients sell us stuff.

They poked their nose into everything from when Brazilians wake up in the morning and when the Chinese have sex to what Canadians read in the bathroom. The study focused on rituals, the small steps we take from morning till night: our waking rituals, eating rituals, sex rituals, "returning to camp" rituals and finally the evening's "protecting yourself for the future" ritual.

"Emotionally, rituals are critical to people everywhere in the world. They help transform us from one emotional state to another," says Tracy Lovatt, director of behavioural planning for BBDO, New York, and one of the architects of the study.

"What we found is that people are more alike than different, which is great news for marketers," says Lovatt.

For example, while 78 percent of people around the world say they like their sex spontaneous, at least 33 percent reveal that they get that lovin' feeling pretty regularly, between 10 p.m. and midnight. And more than 50 percent say they wait until the weekend.

The Chinese, however, embrace the notion of "appointment sex." More than 41 percent of Chinese people schedule times for sex, whether they're in the mood or not. The global average is 9 percent. The men and women of Brazil are in the same boat. BBDO learned that in these densely populated countries where extended families live together in cramped quarters, for the sake of privacy, it's not uncommon for couples to rent a room for conjugal visits.

"The idea here is to look at rituals as an important behaviour in consumers' lives, to understand what they are, how they work and how to work our clients' brands into them," said Andrew Robertson, president and CEO, BBDO Worldwide.

The survey's results allow the company to become more emotionally connected with consumers. The results of the study have implications for packaging, positioning, advertising, promotions and product development.

The website AdRANTS is unsure if it should be impressed or not. "Don't you love big research studies that nicely categorize the entire world's population into five, easy-to-define behavioural patterns?"

Source: David Graham, "Our Peculiar Daily Rituals," *Toronto Star*, May 28, 2007. Reprinted with permission - Torstar Syndication Services.

For the full article, visit *www.thestar.com/printArticle/218238*

Exercise 10

Read the article, "Our Peculiar Daily Rituals," above, carefully. Match the following segments of the article with the key term that is most closely related. You may have to check the Glossary and reread the article for a complete understanding. The first one is done for you.

a) an exhaustive compilation of details that add up to a day in our lives	product differentiation
b) findings about behaviour to help their clients sell us stuff	consumer behaviour
c) got up close and personal with 5000 people in 26 countries	emotional motives
d) rituals help transform us from one state to another	market research
e) the results will help in packaging, position, advertising, promotions, and product development	primary data

Check your answers in the Answer Key.

Exercise 11

Use information from **In the News 12.3** to create appositives for the nouns in **bold font**. Rewrite the entire sentence. Remember to add the correct punctuation.

a) "**The Ritual Master**" was created last year.

____

b) Last month, BBDO executives unveiled their **findings**.

____

c) Our **rituals** were the focus of the study.

____

d) The Chinese, however, embrace the notion of "**appointment sex**."

____

e) **Andrew Robertson** says that the study will be used to see how client brands can be fit into consumers' lives.

____

Check your answers in the Answer Key.

Exercise 12

Use the listed terms to fill in the spaces in the scenario below.

brand loyalty	market research	rational motives
early adopters	primary data	secondary data
emotional motives	products	services
marketing plan	product differentiation	

The Big Drip Coffee Company's sales have been down recently. It has decided to hire a new marketing agency, Mind Marketing, to help increase its sales. First, the marketing team must sit down with Big Drip executives and find out what they want to sell and how much money they need to get for it. The Big Drip has a number of goods or a) ________________ and intangibles or b) ________________ that it might focus on to increase sales.

Next, Mind Marketing needs to do some c) ________________ to study customer needs, so that Mind Marketing can begin to look at how The Big Drip might meet some of those needs. Through surveys, Mind Marketing will collect d) ________________. It will also collect e) ________________ from previous related studies. Using the information they get from these sources, the Mind Marketing team will analyze consumer behaviour, including the feelings, or f) ________________, and thoughts, or g) ________________, that make people choose to buy coffee and related products and services.

After analyzing the data, the marketing team will develop a h) ________________, incorporating all of the information they have from research and Big Drip executives. Because The Big Drip is an established company, with a well-recognized logo, the campaign is likely to use i) ________________ as a tactic to increase sales. The team will also have to figure out a way to distinguish Big Drip's goods from other similar goods offered by other companies. This will create j) ________________. Mind Marketing will also work with The Big Drip to create an exciting new product that will appeal to k) ________________ and, hopefully, get sales up as quickly as possible.

Check your answers in the Answer Key.

Test Your Knowledge 12

Use your new knowledge and skills to solve the clues and complete the puzzle!

Clues

Across

4. Intangibles that can be purchased.
6. A comparison of a product's or service's benefits versus its costs.

7. Brand ____________ is consumer satisfaction demonstrated through repeated purchases.
8. That part of the marketing mix that involves creating a good, service, or idea that leads to the needs satisfaction of customers.
10. ____________ goods are products purchased to use directly or indirectly to produce other goods.
11. A ____________ market is a group of people with similar wants and needs that can be expected to react to marketing efforts in a similar way.
12. The reputation or image of a product or service that consumers have come to identify with a name or symbol representing the reputation or image.

Down

1. The identification of groups through observation and analysis of characteristics such as age, income, ethnic background, race, gender, marital status, and religion for the purposes of segmentation.
2. The function in business of planning, pricing, promoting, and distributing products or services to satisfy consumer wants and needs.
3. The part of the marketing mix that involves determining a value for a product that serves the client's profit needs and the customer's purchasing needs.
5. ____________ marketing is a marketing strategy that focuses on long-term relationships with both customers and suppliers.
8. That part of the marketing mix that designs ways by which to gain the consumers' attention and prompt them to buy.
9. The ability of a product or service to satisfy a want or need.

Check your answers in the Answer Key.

Chapter 13

Creating and Promoting Goods and Services

Before You Start

Study the terms below and be sure that you understand each one. If any of the terms are unclear to you, you can find definitions in the Glossary.

Key Terms

advertising
brand equity
brand loyalty
branding
convenience goods
decline stage
growth stage
introduction stage
market test/test market
maturity stage
personal selling
point of differentiation
product
product life cycle
product line
product mix
product positioning
promotional mix
public relations
publicity
sales promotion
shopping goods
specialty goods
trade shows
viral marketing
word of mouth

Now, listen to the chapter's Audio Key Terms List for the correct pronunciation of each term.

Exercise 1

The terms listed here deal with some sales basics. Use the listed terms to fill in the spaces in the following definitions.

publicity
public relations
sales promotion
trade shows
viral marketing
word of mouth

a) _______________ is a promotional strategy that uses the internet to create product awareness.

b) A _______________ is a short-term incentive offered in order to promote sales.

c) Information about a product, service, cause, or firm that is made available to the public through a communication medium is called _____________________.

d) _______________ is recommendations and opinions about product value through casual conversation.

e) _______________ are a promotional tool, used widely in B2B, to display and demonstrate new technologies and products for sale.

f) _______________ consists of news releases created by a firm to enhance their own image with the public.

Check your answers in the Answer Key.

In the News 13.1

No one knows how to build a business better than the entrepreneurs behind some of Canada's most successful companies. These are their most powerful lessons. They know all about creating and promoting goods and services.

The Golden Rules of Growth (Part 1)

Peter van Stolk, President and CEO, Jones Soda Co., Seattle, Washington
Embrace the Unconventional

When Peter van Stolk, founder, president and CEO of the little soda company with attitude, introduced a Thanksgiving dinner pack of soda featuring flavours such as turkey and gravy, Brussels sprouts with prosciutto, and pumpkin pie, people thought he was nuts. "They'd say, 'Oh, ho ho. How funny is this turkey?'" laughs van Stolk. "What they don't know is that I'm generating millions in free publicity with it."

Indeed, the quirky flavours are meant to get people talking and build awareness for Jones Soda, which relocated from Vancouver to Seattle in 2000. While rivals such as Coke and Pepsi spend millions promoting their soft drinks during the peak summer months, van Stolk opts to spend in the off-season. "When you spend money during a competitor's peak spending time," says van Stolk, "you're pitting yourself against them, dollar for dollar."

Van Stolk has taken the road less travelled ever since he launched Jones Soda in 1994. Instead of selling soft drinks in grocery stores, van Stolk markets Jones Soda through small surf and skateboard shops. And instead of creating a standard label, he uses photos sent in by loyal consumers. "In business, you have an opportunity to lead and you have an opportunity to follow," says van Stolk. "Companies and entrepreneurs that are successful tend to lead."

Source: Kara Aaserud, Camilla Cornell, Jim McElgunn, Kim Shiffman, Richard Wright, "The Golden Rules of Growth," *Profit Magazine,* May, 2007, *Canadian Business Online.* Courtesy of Camilla Cornell.

Exercise 2

Read the article, "The Golden Rules of Growth (Part 1)," above. Fill in the blanks with the appropriate key term. Check the Glossary for the meanings of key terms if you are unsure. You may have to read the article again.

a) By developing weird flavours such as "turkey and gravy," van Stolk is generating a lot of free _____________.

b) Since the quirky flavours get people talking, ____________ __________ ___________ advertising is another free promotional tool that van Stolk uses to his advantage.

c) Using small surf and skateboard shops to distribute his product, van Stolk has used "cool" as part of his ____________ ____________.

Check your answers in the Answer Key.

Exercise 3

Use the terms listed here to fill in the spaces in the scenarios below.

brand equity	market test	product mix
brand loyalty	point of differentiation	product positioning
branding	product line	

a) In their ads, Hexcorp is careful to depict happy, wholesome families using its plastic lawn furniture. Hexcorp is working to create an association between happy family life and its product in consumers' minds. Hexcorp is focusing on _________________.

b) In the ads for The Big Drip Coffee Company, marketers are careful to point out that its coffee is picked, processed, and packed within days of reaching ripeness, and then shipped quickly to stores, unlike the coffee at other stores, which sometimes sits on the shelf for months. The Big Drip is trying to establish a _________________.

c) Sarah needs some dishwashing detergent. At the store, there is a no-name detergent for $1.67. However, Sarah decides to buy the Scrubby brand detergent because she considers it worthwhile to buy something from a known manufacturer. For Sarah, the Scrubby detergent has _______________.

d) When Evan shops for bread, he always buys Fluffy Stuff bread. Even when other companies come out with new, fortified, and healthier kinds of bread, Evan always sticks with Fluffy Stuff. Evan has _______________.

e) Edgeline Incorporated sells hockey sticks and pucks, baseball equipment, and tennis equipment. It also sells institutional equipment like professional basketball hoops, hockey nets, and soccer nets that wouldn't be of interest to the average consumer. These constitute Edgeline's __________________.

f) Smooch cosmetics sells lipstick, blush, nail polish, foundation, eye shadow, and mascara, all in complementary colour schemes. This is Smooch's _______________.

g) Hexcorp is developing a new line of upscale patio furniture. In order to determine how the product is likely to sell, Hexcorp marketers are taking the line into a few chain stores in selected upscale neighbourhoods. Hexcorp is running a ________________ on its new line.

h) In order to differentiate its products from those of other manufacturers, Smooch cosmetics uses a large image of pursed red lips on all of its products. Smooch is ______________ its products.

Check your answers in the Answer Key.

In the News 13.2

The Golden Rules of Growth (Part 2)

Ron Joyce, Partner, Jetport; Co-Founder, Tim Hortons; Chairman Emeritus, Tim Hortons Children's Foundation, Hamilton
Your brand is in the basics

When Ron Joyce joined NHL legend Tim Horton in 1964 to help run a small coffee and donut shop in Hamilton, Joyce insisted on replacing the restaurant sign, which featured Horton in his Toronto Maple Leafs jersey. "He was using hockey stardom as a method of marketing," says Joyce, who is widely credited today for building Tim Hortons, one of Canada's most cherished brands. "I always believed the name 'Tim Horton' was great enough to stand on its own. Athletes are traded and the Maple Leafs uniform didn't have a lot of depth, in my opinion."
Indeed, the name on the door didn't matter, says Joyce, if the food and coffee didn't match customer expectations.

"Initial execution and focus is so important," he says. "Our brand stands out because we integrated basic fundamentals from the very beginning. Instead of associating the name with the player, the name became associated with quality of product, service, delivery, cleanliness and so on. I don't think other coffee chains focused as well on the model as we did. We quickly became a leader in the industry."

Source: Kara Aaserud, Camilla Cornell, Jim McElgunn, Kim Shiffman, Richard Wright, "The Golden Rules of Growth," *Profit Magazine,* May, 2007. *Canadian Business Online*. Courtesy of Kara Aaserud.

Exercise 4

Read the article, "The Golden Rules of Growth (Part 2)," above. Fill in the blanks with the appropriate key term. Check the Glossary for the meanings of key terms if you are unsure. You may have to read the article again.

a) Removing the hockey uniform and letting the name "Tim Horton" stand on its own was an exercise in _____________.

b) Tim Hortons' patrons have a high degree of ____________ ____________ because they can count on the quality of the product, excellent service, delivery, and cleanliness.

c) Ron Joyce turned a product line that we normally would consider convenience goods into ____________ ____________.

Check your answers in the Answer Key.

Grammar Review

Exercise 5

In **Chapter 1**, you studied and practised using **coordinating conjunctions**. The exercise below is designed to refresh your memory and give you extra practice. If you need to, review the **Grammar Tip** in **Chapter 1**. (See page 8.)

Use the coordinating conjunctions listed to fill in the spaces in the sentences below. Use each conjunction once. Don't forget to add punctuation where it is needed.

and	or
but	nor
so	for

a) The company didn't use branding successfully ________ they didn't have a logo.

b) The department store offered shopping goods ________ specialty goods.

c) The firm began experimenting with viral marketing ________ its chief method of publicity was still word of mouth.

d) The marketers wanted the company to get more exposure ________ they suggested the company start attending trade shows.

e) The new brand had neither brand equity __________ brand loyalty working for it.

f) Most shoppers buy either convenience goods ________ shopping goods.

Check your answers in the Answer Key.

Exercise 6

In **Chapter 2**, you studied and practised using **relative pronouns**. The exercise below is designed to refresh your memory and give you extra practice. If necessary, review the **Grammar Tip** in **Chapter 2**. (See page 18.)

Use each of the **relative pronouns** listed here to fill in the spaces in the sentences below. Remember to add the correct punctuation where necessary.

that	where
which	when
who	why
what	

a) The management reviewed the brochure ___________ they use at trade shows.

b) The company developed prototypes of its new products ____________ they then used for test marketing.

c) The executive wanted to know _____________ the new sales promotion wasn't working.

d) The manager stopped into the franchise ____________ the trade show was located.

e) Bill talked to the marketing executive ____________ was in charge of their campaign.

f) My boss asked me to see _____________ has been done so far in the development project.

g) We will have to work very hard ___________ we are at the introduction stage of this project.

Check your answers in the Answer Key.

Exercise 7

In **Chapter 3**, you studied and practised using **prepositions**. The exercise below is designed to refresh your memory and give you additional practice. If necessary, review the **Grammar Tip** in **Chapter 3**. (See page 31.)

Use each of the listed **prepositions** once to fill in the spaces in the sentences below.

before	to
after	for
about	with

a) Hexcorp did a market test ___________ its broader marketing campaign.

b) Scrubby needed to reach a new market ___________ its new product line.

c) The Big Drip offered discounts ___________ its employees.

d) The growth stage of any product comes ___________ its introduction stage.

e) Hexcorp used a higher grade of plastic ___________ its new product.

f) The Doll Face Beauty Salon is asking its marketing agent __________ marketing specialty goods like high-end salon products.

Check your answers in the Answer Key.

Exercise 8

In **Chapter 4**, you studied and practised using **subordinating conjunctions**. The exercise below is designed to refresh your memory and give you additional practice. If necessary, review the **Grammar Tip** in **Chapter 4**. (See page 52.)

Use each of the listed **subordinating conjunctions** once to fill in the spaces in the sentences below.

because	while
if	until
although	after

a) ______________ a new product is in the introduction stage, it must be promoted aggressively.

b) The company used consumer surveys to gauge the response ______________ it ran its new ad campaign for a few months.

c) @Work used viral marketing ________________ most of its clients were computer savvy.

d) _______________ word of mouth for the product was good, The Big Drip Coffee Company wanted to reach a wider audience.

e) They won't be sure of the product's success ________________ they reach the maturity stage.

f) ________________ they want to get serious about branding, they should put their logo on every product.

Check your answers in the Answer Key.

In the News 13.3

The Golden Rules of Growth (Part 3)

Chip Wilson, Founder and Chairman, Lululemon Athletica Inc., Vancouver

Focus on your customer, not the competition

Ever since Chip Wilson introduced his fashionable, high performing yoga wear in 1999, competitors have been tripping over themselves to emulate it. Through it all, the founder of Lululemon Athletica has maintained yogi-like serenity.

"You are far better off worrying about how to improve your product than thinking about the competition," Wilson advises. "We're always asking ourselves, 'What problem can we solve for athletes?'"

To find the answers, the company holds frequent focus groups and solicits feedback from selected yoga instructors and athletes who receive free yoga wear in return for reporting on its performance. As well, senior managers stay in touch with what's working and what's not by spending one day a week in a retail store. "A million things come out of that," says Wilson.

Such first-hand knowledge helps Lululemon stay on the leading edge of innovation. As a result, it has scored a number of industry firsts: flat seams that eliminate chafing, and using microfabrics that wick away moisture. Recently, the firm began using fabrics that incorporate woven silver (i.e., metal) thread for its antimicrobial properties. Up next: completely seamless garments that are knit like a sock.

Source: Kara Aaserud, Camilla Cornell, Jim McElgunn, Kim Shiffman, Richard Wright, "The Golden Rules of Growth," *Profit Magazine,* May, 2007. Courtesy of Camilla Cornell.

Exercise 9

Read the article, "The Golden Rules of Growth (Part 3)," above. Fill in the blanks with the appropriate key term. Check the Glossary for the meanings of key terms if you are unsure. You may have to read the article again.

a) Always attempting to solve problems for athletes keeps Lululemon's ____________ ____________ out in front of the competition.

b) Staying at the leading edge of innovation keeps the company's products in the introduction or growth stages in their __________ __________ __________.

c) Testing out products on yoga instructors and athletes is the best kind of __________.

Check your answers in the Answer Key.

In the News 13.4

The Golden Rules of Growth (Part 4)

Ronnen Harary, Co-CEO, Spin Master Ltd., Toronto
If you're not failing, you're not pushing the envelope

"We launched Tengamo, a collectible magnetic trading game, off the success of Mighty Beans, which was a huge product line for our company—we probably did $60 million in sales on that one product line. We were under the impression that there was a marketplace for collectible novelties for kids. But at the end of the day, the product didn't sell well. And then you're faced with things like markdowns and selling for below cost. It was a costly exercise.

"But product failure is not a bad thing. It can tell you what categories not to be in. It can identify weaknesses in your firm. And if you're not having failures, you're not pushing the envelope. As long as you're not betting the farm on any one product line, then it's okay.

"We still take risks—we just try to mitigate them as much as possible through different things. For instance, we'll do a one-city market test before we roll out something nationally.

"We're constantly trying. If you want to grow 10 percent a year, then you can just expand in the categories you're in. But if you want to grow more than that, then you have to try."

Source: Kara Aaserud, Camilla Cornell, Jim McElgunn, Kim Shiffman, Richard Wright, "The Golden Rules of Growth," *Profit Magazine,* May, 2007. Courtesy of Kim Shiffman.

Exercise 10

Read the article, "The Golden Rules of Growth (Part 4)," above. Fill in the blanks with the appropriate key term. Check the Glossary for the meanings of key terms if you are unsure. You may have to read the article again.

a) The Mighty Beans __________ __________ was worth $60 million in sales.

b) To minimize risks, Spin Master will do a __________ __________ before introducing the product nationally.

Check your answers in the Answer Key.

In the News 13.5

The Golden Rules of Growth (Part 5)

Jay Gould, President and CEO, New York Fries, Brantford, Ontario
You can't be all things to all people

Keeping his eyes on fries has worked well for Gould, whose burgerless New York Fries chain boasts 185 locations in Canada, Australia, South Korea and the United Arab Emirates. "Our aim from the start was to make the best fries around," says Gould, "and we have stayed very focused on just that thing."

It took 21 years for Gould to add burgers to his business menu. However, they're offered by a separate operation with a different brand: South St. Burger Co., launched in 2005. And there's an intense focus within South St. as well: homestyle beef burgers.

"The temptation for entrepreneurs to have something for everybody can be overwhelming," says Jay Gould. "[Customers] will tell you they like veal burgers. While there might actually be a market for veal burgers, it's a different concept. You can't be all things to all people."

Source: Kara Aaserud, Camilla Cornell, Jim McElgunn, Kim Shiffman, Richard Wright, "The Golden Rules of Growth," *Profit Magazine,* May, 2007. Courtesy of Camilla Cornell.

Exercise 11

Read the article, "The Golden Rules of Growth (Part 5)," above. Fill in the blanks with the appropriate key term. Check the Glossary for the meanings of key terms if you are unsure. You may have to read the article again.

a) The __________ __________ for New York Fries was to make the best fries around.

b) Jay Gould's unique ____________ strategy for New York Fries has allowed him to expand to 185 locations in Canada, Australia, South Korea, and the United Arab Emirates.

c) Despite New York Fries' limited __________ __________, they seem to be thriving because of their adaptability in terms of garnishes.

Check your answers in the Answer Key.

In the News 13.6

The Golden Rules of Growth (Part 6)

Isadore Sharp, Chairman and CEO, Four Seasons Hotels Inc., Toronto
Make customer service everybody's business

"A number of hotel companies today provide the very best furniture, linens and bath fixtures, but it's really the quality of the experience that matters most to our guests. The front-line staff represent our product to our customers. So, to win the service battles, customer satisfaction must be everybody's business.

"At Four Seasons, every employee—whether a housekeeper or a general manager—goes through a series of four or five interviews. We are most interested in whether they have the right attitude and if they would make a good fit with their peers. To enable them to put themselves in the guests' shoes, as part of their training they spend a night in one of our hotels as a guest.

"We treat employees as we would like to be treated ourselves. We create opportunities by establishing career paths and promotion from within, and we pay as much attention to employee complaints as to guest complaints. We upgrade employee facilities whenever we upgrade a hotel, and there are no reserved parking spots and no separate tables in the staff cafeteria.

"We have been able to create an atmosphere of trust and respect. We have far lower turnover than is typical in the hotel industry, and 30 000 employees who are always thinking of new ways to make our guest experience more rewarding."

Source: Kara Aaserud, Camilla Cornell, Jim McElgunn, Kim Shiffman, Richard Wright, "The Golden Rules of Growth," *Profit Magazine,* May, 2007. Courtesy of Camilla Cornell.

Exercise 12

Read the article, "The Golden Rules of Growth (Part 4)," above. Fill in the blanks with the appropriate key term. Check the Glossary for the meanings of key terms if you are unsure. You may have to read the article again.

a) Isadore Sharp has taken his Four Seasons hotel chain to the pinnacle of ____________ ____________. Once you've stayed at Four Seasons, you will never want to stay anywhere else.

b) His ____________ ____________ is luxury-class hotel accommodation with unsurpassed customer service.

c) Every employee is involved in the ____________ ____________ process because they are committed to making the guest experience more rewarding.

Check your answers in the Answer Key.

In the News 13.7

The Golden Rules of Growth (Part 7)

Michael Budman, Co-founder, Roots Canada Ltd., Toronto
Cultivate creativity

Michael Budman was in one of his Toronto stores on Boxing Day last year and noticed the huge number of Asian customers lined up at the cash. "Immediately, I said, 'Why don't we do something to give back to the Asian community?'" recalls Budman. "'We're really focused on our leather bags, so let's create a Chinese prosperity bag and we'll celebrate Chinese New Year.' So, that's what we did." The bags jumped off the shelves. "It was our idea," he says, "and we didn't chase anybody. We did it all on our own."

That, says Budman, is the secret to Roots' success: constant renewal, freshness, passion for innovation and an aversion to following the crowd. "The minute you're chasing somebody else, you've already failed."

Creativity is all about thinking differently and seeing possibilities that others haven't seen. To keep new ideas flowing, Budman has perfected the art of studying people. "I'm constantly aware of lifestyles and environment. I'm conscious of the people around me, what they're doing."

Kids are another source of inspiration. "I love their energy, their health and wellness, their youthfulness and how they dress," says Budman. His son was behind one of Roots' best-selling products, the poor-boy cap, which was worn by Canada's Olympic athletes in Nagano in 1998. "At his 11th birthday, in February 1997, my son, who should have been wearing a helmet to play hockey, was wearing a Roots poor-boy hat. It looked so great that in 1998 Roots rolled it out on a larger scale. That hat did really well for us."

Source: Kara Aaserud, Camilla Cornell, Jim McElgunn, Kim Shiffman, Richard Wright, "The Golden Rules of Growth," *Profit Magazine,* May, 2007. Courtesy of Richard Wright.

Exercise 13

Read the article, "The Golden Rules of Growth (Part 7)," above. Fill in the blanks with the appropriate key term. Check the Glossary for the meanings of key terms if you are unsure. You may have to read the article again.

a) The Chinese community heard about the prosperity bags, and because of ____________ ____________ in that community, the bags flew off the shelves.

b) The quality and uniqueness of Roots products has always been their ____________ ____________ ____________.

c) The ___________ generated by the Nagano games brought Roots several big Olympic contracts.

Check your answers in the Answer Key.

In the News 13.8

The Golden Rules of Growth (Part 8)

Frank Buckley, President, W.K. Buckley Investments Ltd., Toronto
Find your point of differentiation

"I came by my bad taste honestly," gibes Frank Buckley. "I inherited it from my father." That quip was first featured on advertising placards in buses and streetcars in 1986, along with Buckley's picture and the now famous slogan: "It tastes awful. And it works."

The ad was risky on two fronts: it put Buckley's face in front of his products, while drawing attention to the cough mixture's negative aspects. But Buckley says he never really worried much about the downside of the concept. "At that time, we were competing with the giants and we weren't doing very well," says Buckley. "I thought it might be worthwhile taking a chance."

Defying conventional marketing wisdom made the ads distinctive and memorable, which helped differentiate Buckley's within the traditionally banal cough-remedy category and burn it into the minds of consumers. The ads used the product's bad taste to communicate proof that it worked. And consumers appreciated the straight talk about the product's weaker aspects.

From the moment the bad-taste ads were launched, W.K. Buckley Ltd.'s fiscal health steadily improved. By the time pharma giant Novartis acquired the firm in 2002, Buckley's share of the country's $300-million cough-and-cold medicine market had grown from 3 percent to 18 percent. Boasts Buckley: "We were second in sales across the country — first, if you leave out Quebec."

Source: Kara Aaserud, Camilla Cornell, Jim McElgunn, Kim Shiffman, Richard Wright, "The Golden Rules of Growth," *Profit Magazine,* May, 2007. Courtesy of Richard Wright.

For the complete article, visit
www.canadianbusiness.com/shared/print.jsp?content=20070419_100910_5528

Exercise 14

Read the article, "The Golden Rules of Growth (Part 8)," above. Fill in the blanks with the appropriate key term. Check the Glossary for the meanings of key terms if you are unsure. You may have to read the article again.

a) Buckley's ______________ ______________ ______________ is represented by the statement, "It tastes awful. And it works."

b) _______________ that was distinctive and memorable defied conventional marketing wisdom.

c) Buckley's developed a ____________ ____________ that helped the company to grow from 3 percent of the $300 million cough-and-cold medicine market to 18 percent.

Check your answers in the Answer Key.

Exercise 15

The graph below illustrates the stages of the product life cycle. Use the stages listed here to label the points on the graph on the lines provided below.

decline stage	introduction stage
growth stage	maturity stage

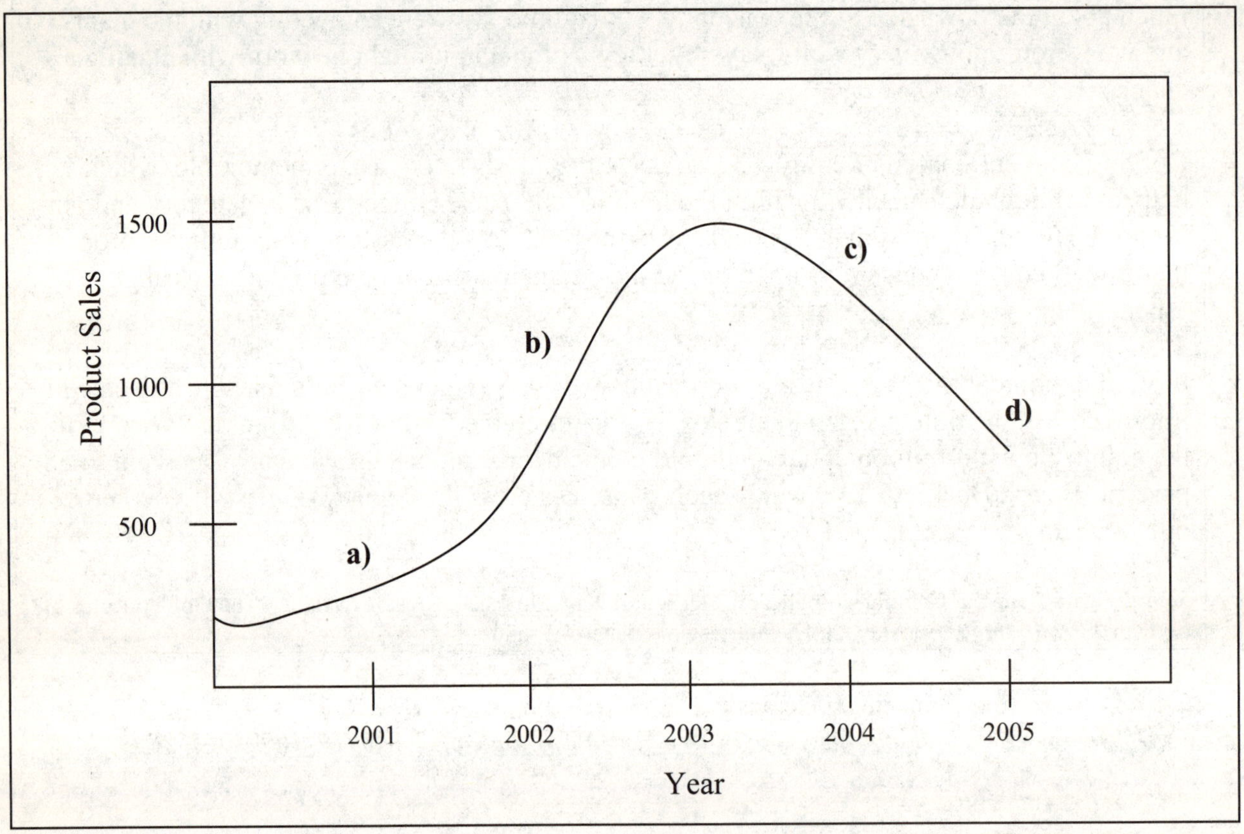

a) ______________________________ c) ______________________________

b) ______________________________ d) ______________________________

Check your answers in the Answer Key.

Exercise 16

Listen to the dialogue. Number these concepts in the order that you hear them. You may need to listen more than once.

a) _____ product positioning

b) _____ decline stage

c) _____ sales promotion

d) _____ advertising

e) _____ growth stage

f) _____ promotional mix

g) _____ branding

h) _____ introduction stage

i) _____ product life cycle

j) _____ maturity stage

Check your answers in the Answer Key.

In the News 13.9

Keeping One Step Ahead of a Shoe Craze

Tara Perkins

Many companies go to outrageous lengths and expense to have their wares endorsed by a celebrity. If a picture is worth a thousand words, one image of a Hollywood starlet eating or driving or wearing a product can be worth a thousand ads.

But those images are something that Ron Snyder, the 50-year-old chief executive officer of Crocs Inc., has tried to avoid. Shots of fashionistas donning the company's clog-like shoes just add to his headaches.

He's happy that the garish footwear has been a runaway success. But ever since Crocs pulled off the biggest initial public offering in shoe history early last year, Mr. Snyder has been keenly aware of critics who say the colourful shoes are a fad doomed to follow tie-dyed shirts and Cabbage Patch Kids down the path to near-extinction.
"Any company that has a product that's very popular and very hot with the consumers and retailers is always susceptible to be a one-hit wonder," Mr. Snyder said in an interview from Scottsdale, Ariz., where he has a second home.

Don't misunderstand—he loves to see people wearing Crocs. He just likes it better when those people are, well, not trendsetters.

"We think there's a better foundation in comfort and function than there is in style and fashion" for the brand, he said. The shoes are made out of the company's closed-cell resin, called Croslite, which makes for soft, comfortable, lightweight shoes that grip slippery surfaces but don't stink on sweaty feet. Crocs have become a staple for nurses, teachers and gardeners and a sizable chunk of the mainstream market.

Whatever the use, there's no denying the shoes are hot. Crocs' profit jumped to $64.4-million (U.S.) last year, from $17-million the year before....

Crocs are sold in more than 80 countries and the company has facilities ranging from a factory in Quebec City to a distribution centre in Shenzhen, China.

The secret of Crocs' success, as Mr. Snyder tells it, is that "our demographic is the largest of any shoe ever." There are Crocs for everyone from toddlers to grandmas. "When we went into Israel, for example, we got every demographic," he said. "I was over there, probably nine months ago, and there's literally a guy with a machine gun walking down the street, one of the military there, he's got Crocs on. And then I walk into a square, and there's an Orthodox Jew speaking on a podium and he's got Crocs on. I couldn't believe it."

Mr. Snyder's goal is to diversify. He has made a handful of recent acquisitions to that end. Crocs paid $1.5-million for Fury Inc.... Crocs is now making hockey and lacrosse equipment featuring Croslite....

Crocs paid about $7.5-million for EXO Italia, a footwear designer in Padova, Italy.... The fruit of that partnership will be more traditionally shaped shoes made with Croslite.

Crocs scooped up Jibbitz LLC for $13.5-million. Jibbitz are described by one blogger as "bling for your Crocs."

The shopping spree continued this year, with Crocs buying sandal maker Ocean Minded LLC for $1.75-million in February.

Crocs has poached a designer from Under Armour, Dawn Barbour, "and we will be launching an apparel line later this year," Mr. Snyder said.

"They will be your casual, comfortable, go-to clothing, just like your Crocs are," he said. "We'll launch larger lines for kids, men and women in spring of 2008."
While Mr. Snyder does all he can to expand into new markets, he believes there's room left for the basic shoe line to grow.

"I still think there's 40 percent of the people, or maybe 50 percent of the people, who say 'Wait a minute, those are just too ugly, I'm not going to try them,'" he said. "But, when their friends say 'Wait a minute, just trust me and try them on,' we get another convert."

Source: Tara Perkins, "Keeping One Step Ahead of a Shoe Craze," *Report on Business,* April 14, 2007R. Reprinted with permission from *The Globe and Mail.*

For the complete article, visit *www.theglobeandmail.com/servlet/story/RTGAM.20070414.wrdecision14/BNStory /robNews/*

Exercise 17

Read the article, "Keeping One Step Ahead of a Shoe Craze," above, then answer the questions below. You may have to read the article again.

a) What product does Ron Snyder's Crocs Inc. produce?

____

b) What is Ron Snyder's main concern about the business?

____

c) What are three benefits that consumers enjoy when wearing Snyder's Crocs?

____

d) Who is the target market for Crocs; who wears these things?

____

e) What are two reasons why you would consider Crocs to be a successful company?

____

f) At what stage in the product life cycle is Crocs, and what is Snyder's goal?

____

g) How has Snyder decided to achieve his goal for the company?

____

Check your answers in the Answer Key.

Test Your Knowledge 13

Use the clues to solve the puzzle and find the Mystery Word!

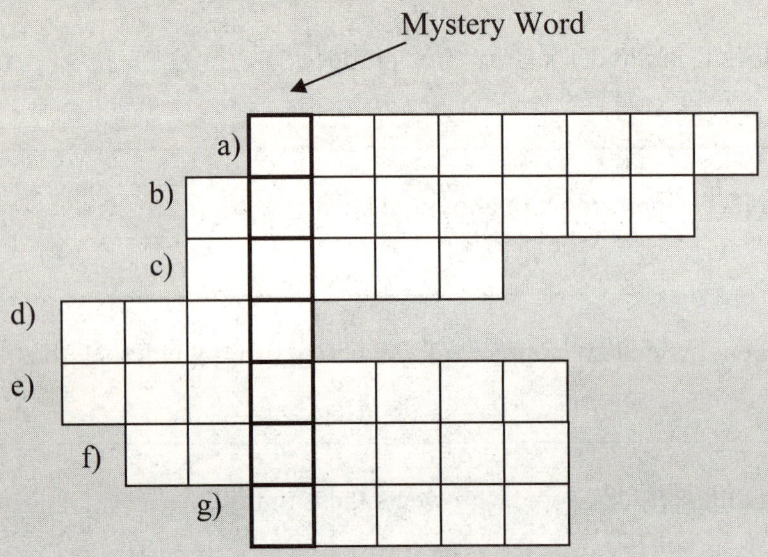

Clues

a) _______________ selling is one-on-one communication between a salesperson and a potential customer.
b) Using a device, such as a symbol, phrase, name, or design, to distinguish a firm's products from those of the competition.
c) ____________ of differentiation is how a firm's product or service differs significantly and beneficially from that of the competition.
d) ____________ of mouth is recommendations and opinions about product value through casual conversation.
e) ____________ stage is the stage in the product life cycle when sales begin to slow while profits are at their highest levels. By this point, competition has begun to eat away at sales and eventually causes sales, and therefore profit, to begin to fall.
f) ____________ stage is the final stage of the product life cycle, where sales continue to fall and where decisions must be made about whether to remove the product from the market or at least to reduce or discontinue promotional support.
g) ____________ shows are a promotional tool, used widely in B2B, to display and demonstrate new technologies and products for sale.

The Mystery Word is ____________________________.

Check your answers in the Answer Key.

Chapter 14

Pricing Goods and Services

Before You Start

Study the terms below and be sure that you understand each one. If any of the terms are unclear to you, you can find definitions in the Glossary.

Key Terms

break-even analysis
break-even point
cash discount
discount
everyday low pricing (EDLP)
fixed costs
high–low pricing strategy
market share
non-price strategy
odd–even pricing
penetration pricing strategy
price leadership
price lining
price-skimming strategy
pricing
psychological pricing
quantity discount
seasonal discount
target costing
trade discount
value pricing
variable costs

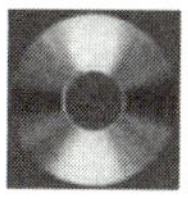

Now, listen to the chapter's Audio Key Terms List for the correct pronunciation of each term.

Exercise 1

The following terms deal with pricing goods and services, an important element of business management. Match each of the terms with one of the scenarios below.

everyday low pricing (EDLP)
non-price strategy
odd–even pricing
penetration pricing strategy
price leadership
price lining
price-skimming strategy

a) The Big Drip Coffee Company has developed a new product. Its marketing department has decided that they should price the new product at the highest price that consumers will pay in order to capitalize on the novelty of the new product. The Big Drip is using a __________ __________________ with its new product.

b) Hexcorp's products are priced at just less than a dollar amount. For instance, Hexcorp's lawn chairs are $14.99 instead of $15.00. This makes customers feel that its products are cheaper than they actually are. This strategy is called ____________________.

c) Scrubby is introducing a new line of dry cloths designed for dusting. It is worried that customers might not take a chance on this new product; it is pricing the product as low as possible in order to encourage people to become familiar with the new product. Scrubby is engaging in a ____________________.

d) The budget department store CheapMart has a line of its own brand of products that it keeps priced below the average cost of its competitors' prices. It maintains these prices constantly. CheapMart has ____________________.

e) ClearCut Paper Company is a leader in the industry, selling more paper products than all of its competitors combined. As such, most paper companies tend to price their product close to ClearCut's prices. ClearCut has ____________________ in its industry.

f) Hexcorp has several different styles of lawn furniture in its line. In order to create a separation among the different styles, Hexcorp prices theses styles more widely than is necessary, considering customary mark-ups. Hexcorp's strategy is called

____________________.

g) Smooch brand cosmetics wants to increase its sales. Instead of pricing its products lower, Smooch is offering a free lipstick with all purchases of its products. Smooch is using a ____________________ to increase its sales.

Check your answers in the Answer Key.

Exercise 2a

The terms below deal with some of the considerations businesses have to take into account when deciding how to price a product. Use the terms to fill in the spaces in the sentences below.

break-even analysis	fixed costs
break-even point	variable costs

a) ____________________ are the expenses that are unchanged with the quantity of products that are produced and sold.

b) A __________________ is an evaluation of the relationship between total revenues and total costs to determine the profitability at various output levels.

c) __________________ are the expenses that change with the quantity of products that are produced and sold.

d) The _________________ is the precise number of units that must be sold at a given price before the firm covers both its fixed and variable costs.

Check your answers in the Answer Key.

Exercise 2b

Now, use the terms from **Exercise 2a** to label the figures below that best illustrate each term.

a)________________________

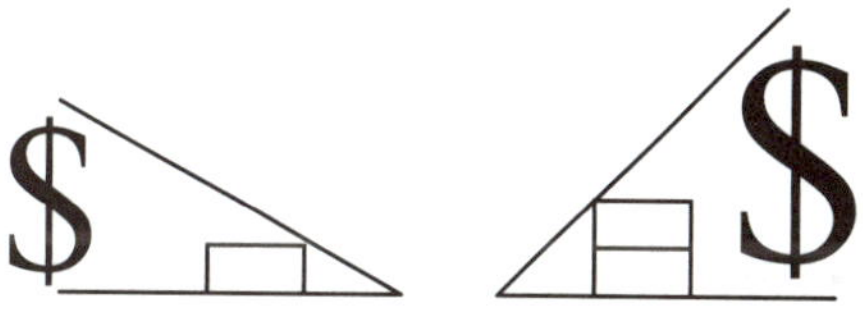

b)_________________________

c)___________________________

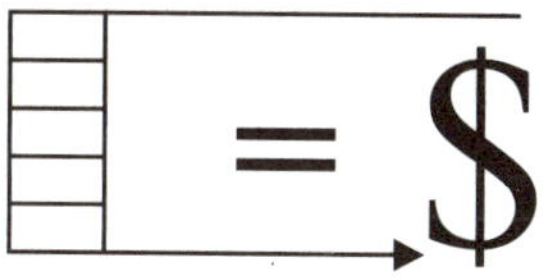

d)___________________________

Check your answers in the Answer Key.

Exercise 3

The terms listed here deal with pricing discounts. Use the terms to fill in the spaces in the scenarios below.

cash discount
discount
quantity discount
seasonal discount
trade discount

a) Alice is a senior citizen. Every Tuesday, she can buy things at her local pharmacy for lower prices if she shows her identification. On Tuesdays, Alice gets a ________________.

b) Every fall, Smooch reduces the prices on its lighter-coloured cosmetics. Smooch knows that women will buy fewer of these colours in cooler weather. In the fall, Smooch offers a ________________.

c) Listen Up Electronics offers lower prices to customers who pay with cash rather than cheques, credit cards, or debit cards. Listen Up offers a ______________________.

d) ClearCut Paper Products runs a stationery division that provides personalized stationery, wedding invitations, and other fine stationery supplies. The price for these items gets lower when customers order larger amounts. ClearCut offers a ______________________.

e) ClearCut sells paper at a reduced price to other stationery suppliers. ClearCut gives a ______________________.

Check your answers in the Answer Key.

In the News 14.1

Beating the Lofty Loonie (Part 1)
Laura Pratt

The Canadian dollar's dramatic runup has been disastrous for many entrepreneurs who rely heavily on sales to the U.S. The Cdn. dollar current value of more than 93¢ is nearly 47 percent higher than the 63¢ it traded at just two years ago. Never in our history have businesses had to adjust so quickly to such a massive currency swing.

Yet many companies are finding solutions. See how five CEOs rose to the challenge:

Jeffrey Klein, president, Honeybee Technology Inc., Pointe Claire, Que.

Founded in 1997, Honeybee delivers customer relationship management software via the Web. More than 85 percent of its revenue—over $4.6 million—is from the U.S.

"We saw this coming, so about two years ago we engaged a financial consulting firm to review our cost structure," says Klein. "We knew our margins would be squeezed. We make our money based on volume, and we had to figure out ways to increase it. They helped us identify bottlenecks in our systems.

"We've spent the past year and a half rewriting our software to increase our capacity, re-engineering the database so it can handle many more transactions, which is how we're remunerated. We have the capacity now to quadruple our volumes over two years ago with only a marginal cost increase—maybe a 10 percent to 15 percent increase in staffing. It's as simple as that. We didn't change our price; we increased our capacity. And the increased volume protected our margins. We could have lost somewhere between half a million and a million a year, but we will more than offset that with increased volumes.

"In business, you have to react to the environment. This forced us to really examine our cost structure and way of doing business. Canadian dollar aside, we really benefited from the scrutiny we put our company under. From every bad emerges a good."

Source: Laura Pratt, "Beating the Lofty Loonie," *Canadian Business Online*, February 10, 2005. Reprinted with permission of Laura Pratt, freelance writer.

Exercise 4

a) What kind of service does Honeybee Technology Inc. provide its customers?

b) From where does most of its revenue come?

c) Was Honeybee expecting the quick rise in the dollar and, if so, how did they prepare?

d) Did they change their pricing as a result of the rising value of the dollar?

e) What was Honeybee's solution to the problem of the rising dollar?

Check your answers in the Answer Key.

In the News 14.2

Beating the Lofty Loonie (Part 2)
Laura Pratt

Kathryn From, CEO, Bravado Designs Inc., Toronto

This 13-year-old manufacturer of maternity and nursing lingerie had 2004 sales of almost $5.5 million. About 85 percent are exports, principally to the U.S., and it prices all its exports in American dollars.

"Most people, if they were paying attention, realized the dollar was undervalued," says From. "So we never based our profitability on a 65¢ or even a 70¢ dollar. We operated with the idea that the dollar is probably better valued in the high-70s or 80¢ range. We would bear that in mind when we looked at product pricing and things like that, so we were somewhat prepared.

"We've had some really good years, and were able to stockpile cash reserves. That really helps a lot. In the past, we were able to say, 'Here's a new marketing opportunity that costs $30 000. Let's do it.' Now we have to be more analytical in calculating what a cost–benefit would be.

"We don't have room to raise our prices in the end-user market, so we have had to look at other ways to maximize our margin. About 20 percent of our sales come from online, so we're looking at how we can maximize that revenue stream without upsetting our wholesale customer base. After all, you get a lot more dollars per bra that way. Instead of selling a bra for $16, we're selling it for $32, and still making it for $8.

"We're also looking into forging bigger and better relationships with really important customers, to turn $250 000 accounts into $500 000 accounts. We hope the volume of business would increase as we focus more actively on developing relationships with customers.

"We also have a very active new-product-development stream, which is relatively new for us. We relied on one product for the last 12 years. We have a new product that's been launched to rave reviews, and another new collection coming out in the fall. Selling more products to the same customer base is another way of growing our revenues.

"But it's not all bad. This is what, in some ways, an entrepreneur dreams of, because it forces you to make tough decisions—to weigh the benefits, risks and rewards. My partner and I haven't had to go to the bank for years, but we don't have as much cash coming in, so we've had to do that now. But, frankly, that's what gets me up in the morning. It's fun. It's a challenge. It separates the men from the boys."

Source: Laura Pratt, "Beating the Lofty Loonie," *Canadian Business Online,* February 10, 2005. Reprinted with permission of Laura Pratt, freelance writer.

Exercise 5

a) What kind of product does Bravado Designs Inc. manufacture?

b) To where does Bravado export the majority of its manufactured goods?

c) Was Bravado expecting the quick rise in the dollar and, if so, how did they prepare?

d) Did they change their pricing as a result of the rising value of the dollar?

e) What was Bravado's solution to the problem of the rising dollar?

Check your answers in the Answer Key.

In the News 14.3

Beating the Lofty Loonie (Part 3)

Laura Pratt

Mark Redmond, president and CEO, Ceapro Inc., Edmonton

This eight-year-old biotech firm does 98 percent of its business in U.S. dollars. That includes the 40 percent of its business from direct sales to the U.S., plus sales to Japan and Europe.

"Our business has continued to grow, year after year, but the exchange rate is masking our performance when we record our earnings in Canadian dollars," says Redmond. "We've grown our markets by about 20 percent over the past year, but investors don't see that. That certainly has taken some momentum away from us. The SME world is all about capital. People perceive that you're not growing as fast as you expected, and the shine comes off the investment. So we've had to work harder on investor relations.

"Our general administrative costs in Canada have stayed the same in the face of our [declining] ability to bring dollars in. So we've worked to improve our efficiencies and margin rates. We've gotten new equipment that operates at a higher efficiency rate. In the last year, we've invested probably half a million dollars in equipment, so our growth will be more readily visible to investors. We're redoubling our efforts in terms of sales, despite the fact that, as we report them in Canadian dollars, the sales look smaller.

"Beyond that, there's actually been a positive. We may be based in Canada, and manufacture in Canada, but we buy plastic bottles and chemicals from the States. They've become cheaper, so when we look at our overall business, the margin rates have remained the same. And in Japan and Europe, their currencies' buying power has increased against the U.S. dollar, so the cost of our goods is cheaper there. That's the silver lining."

Source: Laura Pratt, "Beating the Lofty Loonie," *Canadian Business Online*, February 10, 2005. Reprinted with permission of Laura Pratt, freelance writer.

Exercise 6

a) What kind of business is Ceapro in?

b) In what currency is most of its business transacted?

c) Did Ceapro change their pricing as a result of the rising dollar?

d) What has Ceapro's solution been to the rise in the dollar?

Check your answers in the Answer Key.

In the News 14.4

Beating the Lofty Loonie (Part 4)

Laura Pratt

Bruce Batchelor, publisher and CEO, Trafford Publishing, Victoria

Last year, exports comprised more than 85 percent of the on-demand publishing house's sales of $6.6 million.

"We are doing some hedging to protect against an extreme drop," says Batchelor. "And we have diversified away from our great reliance on U.S.-dollar clients by opening subsidiaries in England and Ireland to cater to authors and book buyers paying in pounds sterling and euros, as well as boosting our presence in Central and Eastern Canada, particularly with the francophone market.

"We've ramped up our marketing to authors who pay us in other currencies. We've translated our marketing materials and hired bilingual-francophone and bilingual-Hispanic staff. We've begun promoting in Quebec at the salons du livre [book fairs] and in some publications. We're also making more intensive follow-ups with prospective authors in English-speaking Canada, and have boosted our Canadian print advertising.

"We haven't really switched our sales away from the U.S.—those are still increasing steadily. Rather, we've grown our non-U.S.-dollar sales at a faster pace.

"Some of our expenses have gone down. Most of our marketing costs are paid in U.S. dollars, even if the media coverage extends to Canada, Europe and beyond. And our paper supply comes from Xerox, which buys from Washington state paper mills. We've been able to switch from paper with no post-consumer content to 30 percent post-consumer recycled paper with only a small change in price when calculated in Canadian dollars.

"Beyond this, we are continually re-engineering our processes to improve efficiencies and enhance the service we provide to authors from over 80 countries. It is important to us to maintain the profit levels we achieved last year, so we can again issue dividends to shareholders. Keeping comfortably profitable in the face of currency fluctuations will only happen if we can both steadily grow our revenues and simultaneously widen our margins.

"And we're thinking about changing our pricing for U.S. customers, though if/when we do this it will be in combination with a tangible increase in the value of our publishing packages. But our latest thinking is that we'll be able to increase our margins enough, through re-engineering, automation and economies of scale, to not need any price boost. The drop in the U.S. dollar has forced/encouraged us to expedite the process for gaining that efficiency. We'll end up stronger, since these efficiencies apply for clients' work in all currencies."

Source: Laura Pratt, "Beating the Lofty Loonie," *Canadian Business Online*, February 10, 2005. Reprinted with permission of Laura Pratt, freelance writer.

Exercise 7

a) What kind of business is Trafford in?

b) From where does most of its revenue come?

c) Was Trafford prepared for the fast rise in the dollar?

d) Did they change their pricing as a result of the rising value of the dollar?

e) What has been Trafford's solution to the problem of the rising dollar?

Check your answers in the Answer Key.

In the News 14.5

Beating the Lofty Loonie (Part 5)

Laura Pratt

Gary Darychuk, CEO, Directors' Choice and CliniCall Patient Recruitment Inc., Saint John, N.B.

A full 95 percent of sales are in U.S. dollars for Directors' Choice, a customer-contact centre for the funeral industry, and its small startup CliniCall, which provides the same service for the clinical-research industry. The drop in the U.S. dollar cost Directors' Choice $280 000 in profit last year.

"We have just completed a client-by-client analysis of profitability and have found that, with a weak U.S. dollar, some clients barely cover our overhead, let alone contribute to distributable profit," says Darychuk. "We haven't had a price increase for a couple of years, because we had technology problems that affected our level of service, and we didn't feel comfortable having price increases last year. That's going to be one strategy, and we'll be able to get away with that because we have a very high level of service. People don't have the risk of losing a death call, because we can answer their phones better than the other options available to them. We don't know how much we'll raise prices by—maybe 10 percent.

"Secondly, we are going to selectively use a time-based billing system, as opposed to our current transaction-based pricing. In our analysis, we found that many of our clients spend more time talking with our agents than necessary, due to the relationships they have developed over the years. We believe a time-based system will put the responsibility of effectively using our staff on the shoulders of our clients.

"Finally, we are pushing for growth in our top line. With overheads covered, revenue beyond our direct costs will flow to the bottom line. We have increased our client base by 45 percent since last May, and we expect that growth rate to continue for another 18 months. Hopefully, by then the U.S. dollar will have strengthened."

Source: Laura Pratt, "Beating the Lofty Loonie," *Canadian Business Online*, February 10, 2005. Reprinted with permission of Laura Pratt, freelance writer.

For the complete article, visit
www.canadianbusiness.com/shared/print.jsp?content=20050207_105450_4756

Exercise 8

a) What kinds of services do Director's Choice and CliniCall Patient Recruitment Inc. provide to its customers?

b) From where does most of its revenue come?

c) Were Director's Choice and CliniCall prepared for the fast rise of the dollar?

d) Did they change their pricing as a result of the rising value of the dollar?

e) What solutions to the rising dollar problem has this group implemented?

Check your answers in the Answer Key.

In the News 14.6

For Big Brands, a Different Kind of Face Time

Keith McArthur

Whether they love the Sony PlayStation or hate it, there's no shortage of discussion groups for gamers on Facebook, the online social networking sensation taking Canada and the world at breakneck speed.

Among the 500-plus groups Facebook members can join, there's the functionally named "Playstation 3" group (three members), the hostile "DEATH TO PLAYSTATION 3" group (48 members) and the girlfriend-dominated "PlayStation 3 has ruined my sex life" group (nine members).

Then there's the "PlayStation Canada" group, paid for by Sony Corp.'s Canadian marketing team, at a whopping 27 335 members and growing.

It's an early Canadian example of the strategy Facebook Inc. is betting on in an effort to turn its unfathomable growth in users—up 3 to 5 percent a week—into a similar growth in revenue and profit.

"We decided from a revenue perspective that banners were the best way to monetize the site as we were growing," said Mike Murphy, vice-president of media sales at Palo Alto, Calif.-based Facebook Inc.

"What we found is that in order to allow marketers to leverage the benefits that a social network can deliver, we needed to include integration and sponsored content as part of that so that marketers could create a daily dialogue with their most passionate users and have a feedback loop about how they engage."

The social networking site is betting that sponsored brand content will be the biggest driver of future revenue growth, but Mr. Murphy says there are no guarantees.

Facebook works by allowing users to set up personal pages. They can post pictures, join interest groups, link to friends' pages and post messages on other pages.

Marketers pay for the ability to advertise their groups in "news feeds" alongside user updates on what's going on with their friends. Pricing is based on how many consumers see the newsfeed item, irrespective of how many users actually join a sponsored group. Marketers can also define the parameters about who gets their message—male university and high school students living in Canada, for example.

Marketers behind sponsored groups also have the ability to delete posts or discussion topics they don't like, though Mr. Murphy says they're often better off leaving negative comments on the board.

"If you have some user who makes a comment that 'Nintendo is better than PlayStation,' typically that passionate group who has joined the Sony PlayStation group protects and defends that brand vigorously," Mr. Murphy said.

"It almost turns that one negative comment into 20 positive ones."

Source: Keith McArthur, "For Big Brands, a Different Kind of Face Time," *Report on Business,* April 28, 2007. Reprinted with permission from *The Globe and Mail.*

For the complete article, visit *www.theglobeandmail.com/servlet/story/RTGAM.20070427.wexecutive0426/BNStory/robExecutive*

Exercise 9

1. What is Facebook's product or service? Be careful—think about this. Re-read the article to be sure that you understand what is being sold.

2. For marketers using Facebook, what is the pricing unit on which their costs will be based?

3. Would these costs represent fixed costs or variable costs to the marketer?

4. What determines the costs to the marketer?

5. At this stage, with what you know about Facebook, would you be able to do a break-even analysis?

Check your answers in the Answer Key.

Exercise 10

Listen to the dialogue. Number these concepts in the order that you hear them.

a) _____ odd–even pricing

b) _____ mark-up

c) _____ pricing

d) _____ seasonal discounts

e) _____ price lining

f) _____ break-even point

g) _____ fixed costs

h) _____ unit price

i) _____ variable costs

Check your answers in the Answer Key.

Grammar Review

Exercise 11

In **Chapter 5**, you studied and practised using **modal verbs**. This exercise is designed to refresh your memory and give you extra practice. If you need to, review the **Grammar Tip** in **Chapter 5**. (See page 62.)

can
might
must
should

Use the listed modal verbs to fill in the spaces in the sentences below.

a) We don't know if we are going to have the meeting tomorrow because the manager said that it ________________ be cancelled.

b) People buy less ice cream in the winter so retailers ________________ try giving a seasonal discount.

c) We need to calculate our break-even point so that we ________________ cover our costs.

d) Our sales are low so we ________________ re-think our pricing strategy.

Check your answers in the Answer Key.

Exercise 12

In **Chapter 6**, you studied and practised using **first conditional** sentences. This exercise is designed to refresh your memory and give you extra practice. If you need to, review the **Grammar Tip** in **Chapter 6**. (See page 76.)

Use the statements below to write first conditional sentences. Try writing some of them with the conditional clause first and others with the main clause first. Don't forget to include commas where necessary.

a) She is a senior. She gets a discount.

____

b) We buy 12 dozen muffins. We get a quantity discount.

____

c) His variable costs are low. His break-even point is low.

____

d) She pays cash. She gets a cash discount.

____

e) They work in the industry. They get an industry discount.

____

Check your answers in the Answer Key.

Exercise 13

In **Chapter 7**, you studied and practised using **second conditional** sentences. This exercise is designed to refresh your memory and give you extra practice. If you need to, review the **Grammar Tip** in **Chapter 7**. (See page 95.)

Rewrite the first conditional sentences from **Exercise 12** in the second conditional. Notice the change in meaning.

a) ____

b) ____

c) ____

d) ____

e) ____

Check your answers in the Answer Key.

Exercise 14

In **Chapter 8**, you studied and practised using **third conditional** sentences. This exercise is designed to refresh your memory and give you extra practice. If you need to, review the **Grammar Tip** in **Chapter 8**. (See page 108.)

Use the verbs provided to complete these sentences in the third conditional.

a) If we _____________ (use) a non-pricing strategy, our sales _________________ (increase).

b) Our variable costs _______________ (be) lower if we _________________ (use) a cheaper supplier.

c) We ________________ (launch) the new product if we ______________ (have) a larger market share.

d) If we ______________ (price) it better, it ____________________ (sell).

e) If we _______________ (be) a price leader, we ___________________ (price) products higher.

Check your answers in the Answer Key.

Test Your Knowledge 14

Use your new knowledge and skills to solve the clues and complete the puzzle!

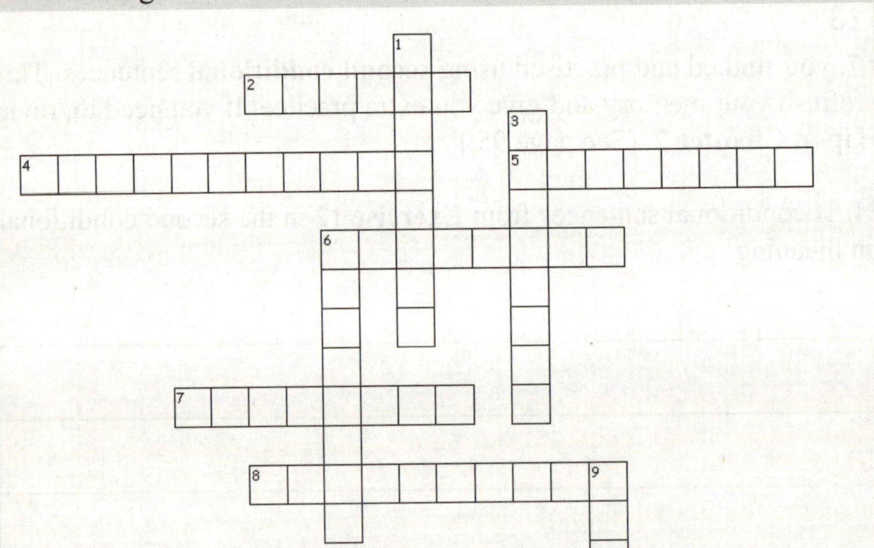

Clues

Across

2. The amount, usually a percentage, added to the cost of goods sold to determine selling price.
4. _______________ pricing strategy involves the decision to set the initial price very low in order to sell as many units as possible.
5. A break-even _______________ is an evaluation of the relationship between total revenues and total costs to determine the profitability at various output levels.
6. A price _______________ strategy is the decision to set the initial price at the highest point that people would be willing to pay in order to maximize profit.
7. A reduction in the price by the seller in order to persuade the customer to purchase.
8. Price _______________ is exhibited by the firm that establishes industry prices which other companies follow.

Down

1. A _______________ discount is when buying in large quantities means a lower price for the purchaser.
3. _______________ costs are the expenses that change with the quantity of products that are produced and sold.
6. A _______________ discount is when lower prices are offered for off-season merchandise.
9. The amount of money or other consideration exchanged for use or ownership of a good or service.

Check your answers in the Answer Key.

Chapter 15

Distributing Goods and Services

Before You Start

Study the terms below and be sure that you understand each one. If any of the terms are unclear to you, you can find definitions in the Glossary.

Key Terms

channel conflict
containerization
direct channel
direct selling
distribution channel
distribution mix
e-catalogues
e-intermediaries
electronic order
electronic storefront
exclusive distribution
global positioning system (GPS)
hub
intensive distribution
intermediary
intermodal
internet-based retailing
inventory control
logistics visibility
materials handling
multiple channels
retailers
sales agent/broker
selective distribution
transportation
vertical marketing system (VMS)
wholesalers

Now, listen to the chapter's Audio Key Terms List for the correct pronunciation of each term.

Exercise 1

The terms listed here deal with virtual distribution. Use the terms to fill in the spaces in the scenarios below.

e-catalogue
e-intermediary
electronic order
electronic storefront
internet-based retailing

a) The website www.shopalot.com connects online consumers with firms that offer products for order over the internet. It is a searchable database of clothing and accessories that combines the products of about 20 different firms. www.shopalot.com is an

____________________.

b) Legally Binding Inc., a firm that produces hand-made, leather-bound notebooks, journals, and other stationery, offers its goods through their website. Customers choose the product, Legally Binding produces it, and ships it to the customer. Legally Binding makes most of its sales through ____________________.

c) Savory Seeds does most of its business through mail order. In the past, this chiefly involved the ground-based postal system and print-based marketing. However, Savory now offers a website with a listing of all of its products and their details. Savory now uses an ____________________ to promote and retail its products.

d) In order to get their product, customers of Legally Binding Inc. must place an ____________________.

e) Mrs. Dress Up Clothing Company has all of its products displayed, priced, and available for order on its website. Mrs. Dress Up has an ____________________.

Check your answers in the Answer Key.

Exercise 2

The following terms deal with the physical aspects of distribution. Use each term to label the picture that best depicts it.

containerization
global positioning system (GPS)
intermodal
logistics visibility
transportation

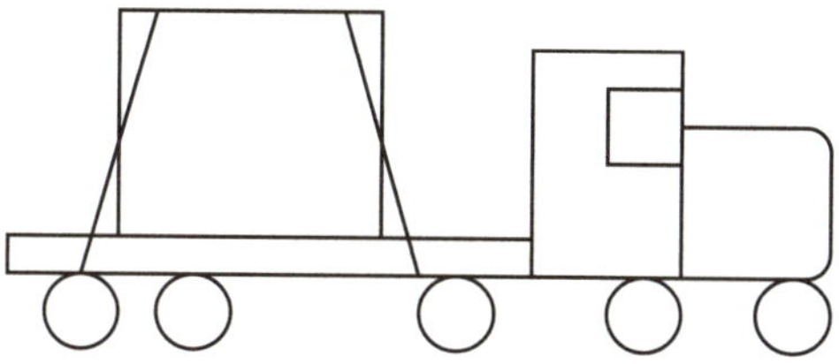

a)________________________

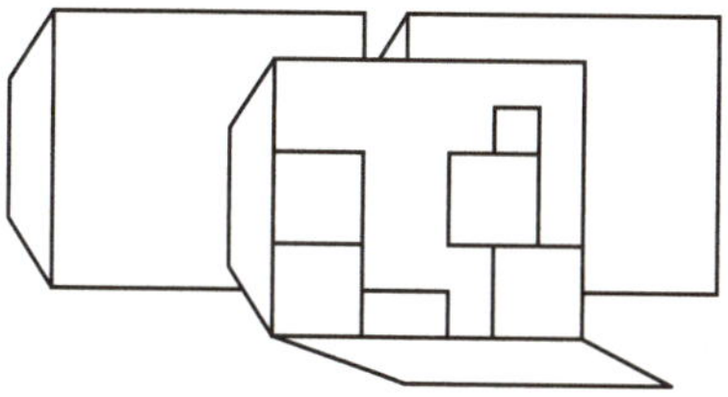

b)________________________

c)________________________

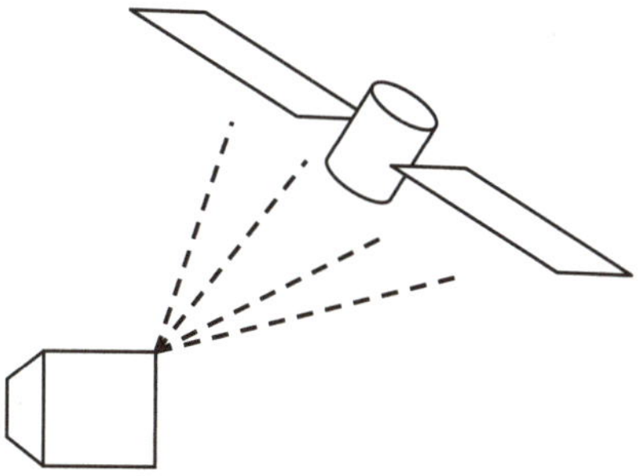

d)________________________

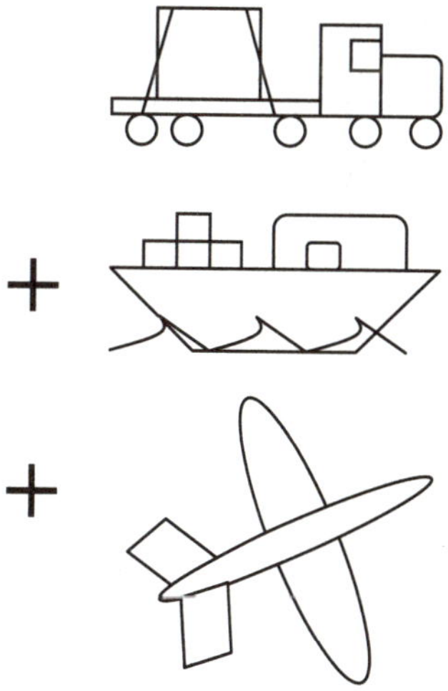

e) ________________________

Check your answers in the Answer Key.

Exercise 3

The following terms deal with kinds of distribution. Match each term with the correct definition. The first one is completed for you.

exclusive distribution	a) The situation in which the distribution of a product involves many channels and many intermediaries for maximum exposure.
hub	b) The situation in which the distribution of a product involves a limited number of intermediaries and channels.
intensive distribution	c) A central place from which all or most of a company's products are distributed.
selective distribution	d) The situation in which the distribution of a product involves only one intermediary.

Check your answers in the Answer Key.

In the News 15.1

Don't Let Channel Conflict Eat Away at Your Sales

Dominic Rubino

My parents stole $100 000 from me and gave it to my brother. Who cares, right? What does that have to do with sales?

Actually, it wasn't my parents who stole the money; it was the company I was working for. They didn't steal it from me; they stole it from one of our sales agents. And it wasn't my brother they gave it to; it was the direct sales channel. Yet the anger that my team of agents and I felt—and the damage this theft did to the company—were as bad as if my parents had stolen something from one child and given it to another.

How would you feel if that happened in your family? I'm sure family dinners would be rather tense! That's exactly how the members of a sales team feel when they lose a deal internally.

If your company sells its products or services through multiple channels, then you're at risk of this kind of damage. It's called channel conflict, and it can be political cancer for your business. If you don't deal with it properly, everyone will be alienated.

Channel conflict can become an issue for any company, big or small, that's looking for opportunities to expand. It might occur because your sales agreements are vague or outdated, or because the internet, by blurring borders, has left your reps and agents selling in the same territory. Or the problem might arise from something as simple as creating a toll-free number that, although it gives your customers a new way to reach you, leaves your contact-centre staff scrapping with your reps and agents over who gets recognized for the sale.

Here are some warning signs that your firm is suffering from this ailment:

Your customers complain that they've seen different prices for the same product.

Your distributors complain to you about your predatory pricing, or stepping on their toes.

Sales from your distributors are dropping off quickly.

Fortunately, channel conflict isn't inevitable. There are ways to minimize or even eliminate it:

Minimizing channel conflict requires setting clear policies on who does and gets what, and clearly communicating them. That might be tough to implement while you're growing the channel, but it's worth the effort. You should spell out who gets paid for what, when, where and for how much before you contract with a third-party sales team. I've seen it done based on dollar volume, head-office location or product mix. The simple test of "where, geographically, is the decision-maker?" is great as a first step.

Eliminating channel conflict requires the wisdom of Solomon. If conflict already exists in your company, I'd suggest you publicly announce some new rules (see above) and then treat everything on a case-by-case basis to show your commitment. To really impress your possibly mutinous agents, why not ask them how to approach the situation? Of course, do the same thing with your direct sales team. Somewhere in the middle will be a reasonable solution. The crucial thing is get input from all sides to show that you're serious about the issue, and that their input is valued.

As you deal with channel conflict, think about the analogy with parents who play favourites among their children. Never lose sight of the fact that this isn't just about business, it's an emotional issue as well. Give channel conflict the time and attention it deserves, so all your channel teams can focus on sales instead of family politics.

Source: Dominic Rubino, "Don't Let Channel Conflict Eat Away at Your Sales," *Canadian Business Online,* September 28, 2007. Courtesy of Dominic Rubino, Certified FocalPoint Business Coach.

For the complete article, visit
www.canadianbusiness.com/shared/print.jsp?content=20060927_110232_4536

Exercise 4

a) Under what conditions is there a risk of channel conflict?

b) If not dealt with quickly and properly, what can result?

c) Identify three causes of channel conflict.

d) Identify three warning signs that your company is experiencing channel conflict.

e) How does a company minimize channel conflict?

f) How does a company eliminate channel conflict?

Check your answers in the Answer Key.

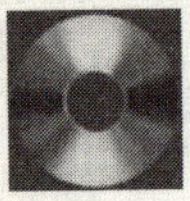

Exercise 5

Listen to the dialogue. Number these concepts in the order that you hear them. You may need to listen more than once.

a) _____ electronic order

b) _____ e-intermediaries

c) _____ retailers

d) _____ electronic storefront

e) _____ internet-based retailing

f) _____ inventory control

g) _____ distribution channel

h) _____ vertical marketing system

i) _____ e-catalogue

j) _____ materials handling

Check your answers in the Answer Key.

Exercise 6

The terms listed here deal with distribution management. Use the terms to fill in the spaces in the scenarios below.

intermediary
inventory control
materials handling
retailers
wholesaler

a) Beaver Lodge Lumber is a major producer of building products. Beaver Lodge sells to contractors and retailers, but not directly to consumers. Beaver Lodge is a

__________________________.

b) Smooch Cosmetics doesn't sell directly to customers. Smooch sells its products to __________________________ who then sell directly to the consumer.

c) Solutions Inc. directs products from manufacturers to retailers. Solutions doesn't actually produce anything or sell anything directly to the consumer. Solutions is an

__________________________.

d) Seth works in a warehouse at ClearCut Paper Products. His job is to track and manage the stock of products in the warehouse, ensuring that the flow of product out to retailers and in from the factory are roughly equal. Seth's job is an example of

__________________________.

e) Emile works for a hardware store. His job is to monitor the stock in the store and the warehouse and order more product if necessary. Emile's job is an example of

__________________________.

Check your answers in the Answer Key.

Grammar Review

Exercise 7

In **Chapter 9**, you studied and practised using **linking words and phrases.** This exercise is designed to refresh your memory and give you extra practice. If you need to, review the **Grammar Tip** in **Chapter 9**. (See page 123.)

Use the linking words and phrases listed here to fill in the spaces in the sentences below.

consequently
for example
furthermore
generally
however
instead of

a) ClearCut uses e-catalogues to inform customers of its products. ____________________, customers can purchase through an electronic order system.

b) Our inventory control processes kept us supplied through the busy season. ____________________, we had trouble with staffing.

c) Legally Binding Inc. chooses to sell directly to the customer ______________ going through an intermediary.

d) Hexcorp has a good logistics visibility system. ________________, shipments are rarely lost and customers are always satisfied.

e) ________________, Hexcorp uses trucking as its primary mode of transportation.

f) ClearCut Paper Products distributes through multiple channels. ________________, a broker negotiates their wholesale contracts, while various retailers carry their paper products.

Check your answers in the Answer Key.

Exercise 8

In **Chapter 10**, you studied and practised using **reported speech**. This exercise is designed to refresh your memory and give you extra practice. If you need to, review the **Grammar Tip** in **Chapter 10**. (See page 136.)

Rewrite the following direct speech sentences as reported speech.

a) The exporter said, "I am going to have to use an intermodal transportation system."

____

b) The sales agent said, "You should start using a global positioning system (GPS) with your transportation system."

____

c) Our transportation manager protested, "I didn't forget to send the shipment."

____

d) The message with the electronic order said, "Your products are really great!"

____

e) Her broker told her, "You need to rethink your distribution mix."

____

f) The man whispered, "I don't know how to do this."

____

g) I asked her, "Do you think he will help with your distribution problem?"

____

Check your answers in the Answer Key.

Exercise 9

In **Chapter 11**, you studied and practised using the **active construction**. This exercise is designed to refresh your memory and give you extra practice. If you need to, review the **Grammar Tip** in **Chapter 11**. (See page 148.)

Rewrite the following passive sentences as active sentences. If necessary, make up a subject for your sentence.

a) The distribution mix was established by management.

____

b) The electronic order was submitted by the customer.

____

c) The intermediary was contacted by the manufacturer.

____

d) The channel conflict at Hexcorp was created by overproduction.

____

e) The e-catalogues were formatted by the marketing team.

____

f) The wholesalers were contacted by the retailers.

____

g) My e-intermediaries were chosen by my business partner.

____

Check your answers in the Answer Key.

Exercise 10

In **Chapter 12**, you studied and practised using **appositives**. This exercise is designed to refresh your memory and give you extra practice. If you need to, review the **Grammar Tip** in **Chapter 12**. (See page 165.)

Use the information in the two sentences provided for you to create one sentence with an appositive in it. Remember to include correct punctuation.

a) The exporter has an intermodal transportation system. An intermodal transportation system is one that involves multiple modes of travel.

____

b) The trucking industry was experiencing a channel conflict. A channel conflict is an overload of distribution channels.

____

c) The Big Drip engages in direct selling. The Big Drip is a popular chain of coffee shops.

____

d) Legally Binding uses an electronic storefront to sell its goods. Legally Binding is a producer of handmade books.

____

e) www.shopalot.com works as an e-intermediary for multiple manufacturers. An e-intermediary is a electronic distributor.

____

f) Salih decided that intensive distribution was the best choice for his company. Intensive distribution is distribution utilizing many intermediaries and channels.

____

g) Trent was in charge of materials handling for the company. Materials handling is the logistics of handling inventory within a warehouse.

____

h) The company decided to go with exclusive distribution. Exclusive distribution is distribution involving only one intermediary.

____

Check your answers in the Answer Key.

In the News 15.2

Step by Step

Andrew Wahl

Deliver us from chaos: Here's how the Descartes DeliveryNet saved one company tens of millions of dollars

Here's how it used to be in the bad old seat-of-the-pants way that Sweden's Ericsson AB, the global communications giant, sought to serve its customers and make money. Say something went wrong with a remote relay tower belonging to a telecom client of Ericsson's radio tower division, which sells and installs the infrastructure that carries cell-phone signals. A replacement part was needed. The telecom got in touch with a service rep in the field, who then ordered the part from one of Ericsson's big warehouses. The part was out of stock. It had to be ordered from the supplier and be delivered to an Ericsson distribution centre. Then it got loaded onto a truck or an airplane. At that point, both the customer and the service rep lost track of it. They couldn't be sure exactly when the part would arrive at the tower site. That made it impossible to pre-book installation. And of course, Ericsson didn't see a dime until the part was installed.

The bad old days aren't all that old. Ericsson first implemented the Descartes DeliveryNet system in 1998, in its radio tower division. In the months since then, the software has enabled Ericsson to accelerate its order-to-cash cycle from weeks to days.

Ericsson, its customers and its 800 field-service workers can all access the status of any part at any time during its journey. A customer simply sends an electronic order to Ericsson, which then forwards the order to one of its approximately 300 suppliers. When the supplier sends the part off to the customer, information on its whereabouts is automatically posted to Ericsson's DeliveryNet, housed on a Descartes server in the Netherlands. That way, all parties can check on its progress, using either a Web browser or Descartes software, which runs on a Unix-based workstation. Vehicles carrying the part are tracked via global positioning systems (GPS), and every time one passes through a distribution centre, its status gets updated on the system. Because field-service workers know exactly when to expect the part, they can arrange to have it installed as soon as it gets to the customer.

It's all called "logistics visibility." It spells speed. It means customers get service more quickly. And Ericsson gets paid a whole lot faster, too.

Source: Andrew Wahl, "Step by Step," *Canadian Business* Magazine, April 2001. Courtesy of *Canadian Business* Magazine.

For the complete article, visit
www.canadianbusiness.com/shared/print.jsp?content=14523

Exercise 11

Read the article, "Step by Step," above. Pay particular attention to the "way things used to be" and the "way things are now" at Ericsson AB. Sort the following lists into the order in which they occur in the article. Number the correct order in the spaces provided.

The way things used to be

_____order part from supplier

_____can't pre-book installation until arrival time is known

_____everyone loses track of the part

_____Ericsson doesn't get paid until part is installed

_____service rep orders part from warehouse

_____part is loaded on a truck or airplane

_____don't know when the part will arrive

_____contact field-service rep

_____part is out of stock

_____replacement part is needed

_____part delivered to Ericsson distribution centre

_____something is wrong at a remote relay tower

The way things are now

_____pre-book installation

_____supplier sends part off to the customer and posts info on DeliveryNet

_____send electronic order to Ericsson supplier

_____something is wrong at relay tower

_____replacement part is needed

_____Ericsson gets paid

_____everyone knows exactly where the part is and when it will arrive because of GPS tracking

Check your answers in the Answer Key.

Exercise 12

The following terms deal with distribution methods. Use the terms to fill in the spaces in the definitions below.

channel conflict
direct channel
distribution channel
distribution mix
sales agent/broker

a) The ____________________ is the movement of a product from manufacturer, through any number of intermediaries, to the end-user.

b) The perception by one channel member that another channel member is interfering with the first member's ability to achieve its distribution goals is called a ____________ ________________.

c) A ____________________ is a channel of distribution that consists of producer and end-user with no intermediaries.

d) A ____________________ is an intermediary who profits through connecting sellers with buyers and providing both with information in order to facilitate a sale.

e) The ____________________ refers to the channels and intermediaries through which a company distributes its products to consumers.

Check your answers in the Answer Key.

Test Your Knowledge 15

Use your new knowledge and skills to solve the clues and complete the puzzle!

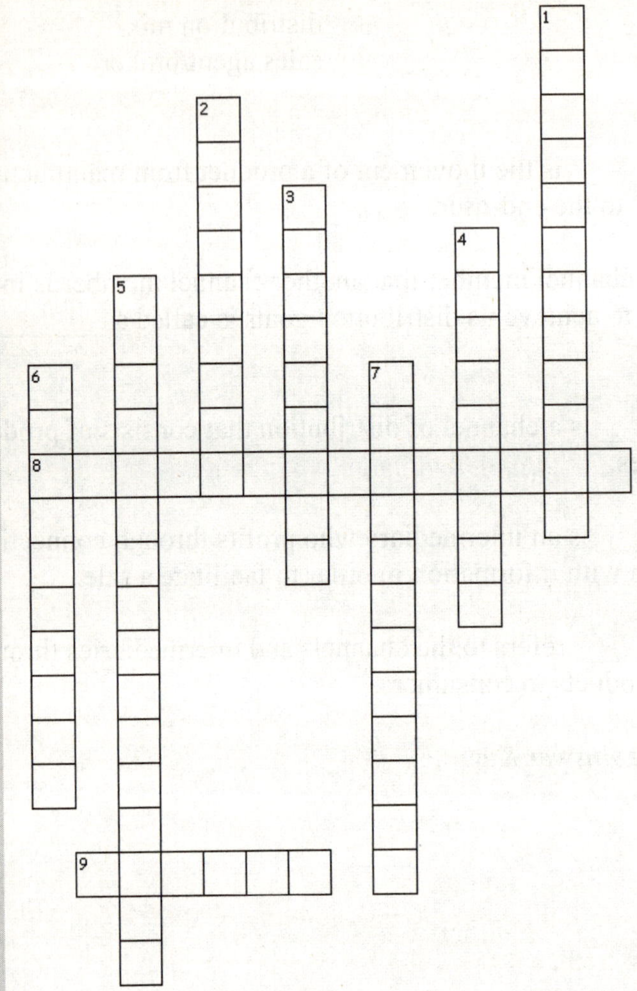

Clues

Across

8. The function of physically moving goods.
9. A ____________ channel is a channel of distribution that consists of producer and end-user with no intermediaries.

Down

1. A ____________ channel is the movement of a product from manufacturer, through any number of intermediaries, to the end-user.
2. That part of the distribution system that sells directly to the end-user.

3. ____________ control is the system of managing the type and quantity of goods to fill the needs of customers accurately, fully, and promptly, without retaining unused surpluses.
4. The activities performed in order to ensure the delivery of the right product, in the right quantity, to the right place, at the right time, and with the least cost possible.
5. A cargo-handling system that transports products from the manufacturer in large metal containers that remain unopened until they reach their final destination.
6. The use of different types of transportation to move a product from one place to another.
7. An individual or firm who comes between the manufacturer and the end-user to facilitate distribution.

Check your answers in the Answer Key.

Answer Key

Chapter 1

Exercise 1

a) recession (or depression)
b) recovery
c) peak
d) trough

Exercise 2

a) Genuine Progress Indicator (GPI)
b) aggregate output
c) standard of living
d) GDP per capita
e) nominal GDP
f) Gross Domestic Product (GDP)
g) real GDP
h) Gross National Product (GNP)

Exercise 3a

a) command economy/market economy
b) deficit/surplus
c) deflation/inflation
d) profit/loss
e) supply/demand

Exercise 3b

a) deflation/inflation
b) command economy/market economy
c) supply/demand
d) deficit/surplus
e) profit/loss

Exercise 4

a) entrepreneur
b) capital
c) information resources
d) competition
e) natural resources
f) labour
g) factors of production
h) profit
i) risk

Exercise 5

a) ii
b) iv
c) iii
d) i

Exercise 6

a) output market
b) competition
c) factors of production
d) demand

Exercise 7

a) so
b) but/yet
c) or
d) and
e) nor
f) for
g) but/yet

Exercise 8

a) and
b) (comma) but
c) (comma) so
d) or
e) for
f) and
g) (comma) but

Exercise 9a

a) economy
b) gross domestic product

Exercise 9a (cont'd)

c) inflation
d) inflation
e) GDP
f) economy/GDP
g) inflation
h) GDP/economy/economy

Exercise 9b

a) Statistics Canada
b) increased interest rates
c) U.S. dollar
d) monthly
e) no

Test Your Knowledge 1

a) unemployment
b) productivity
c) deflation
d) stabilization
e) inflation
f) monetary
g) stability
h) balance
i) fiscal
Mystery Word: economics

Chapter 2

Exercise 1

a) EU
b) WTO
c) NAFTA
d) GATT
e) IMF

Exercise 2

a) comparative
b) national competitive
c) absolute

Exercise 3

a) trade deficit
b) balance of payments
c) trade surplus
d) balance of trade

Exercise 4

a) that
b) whose
c) why
d) when
e) which
f) whom
g) where
h) what
i) who

Exercise 5

a) who
b) which
c) that
d) that
e) that
f) that
g) that
h) whom
i) that

Exercise 6

a) x
b) i
c) v
d) vi
e) ii
f) iv
g) viii
h) iii
i) vii
j) ix

Exercise 7

a) Scenario 5
b) Scenario 1
c) Scenario 4
d) Scenario 6
e) Scenario 3
f) Scenario 2

Exercise 8

a) embargo
b) subsidy
c) cartel
d) local content law
e) quota
f) tariff
g) dumping

Exercise 9

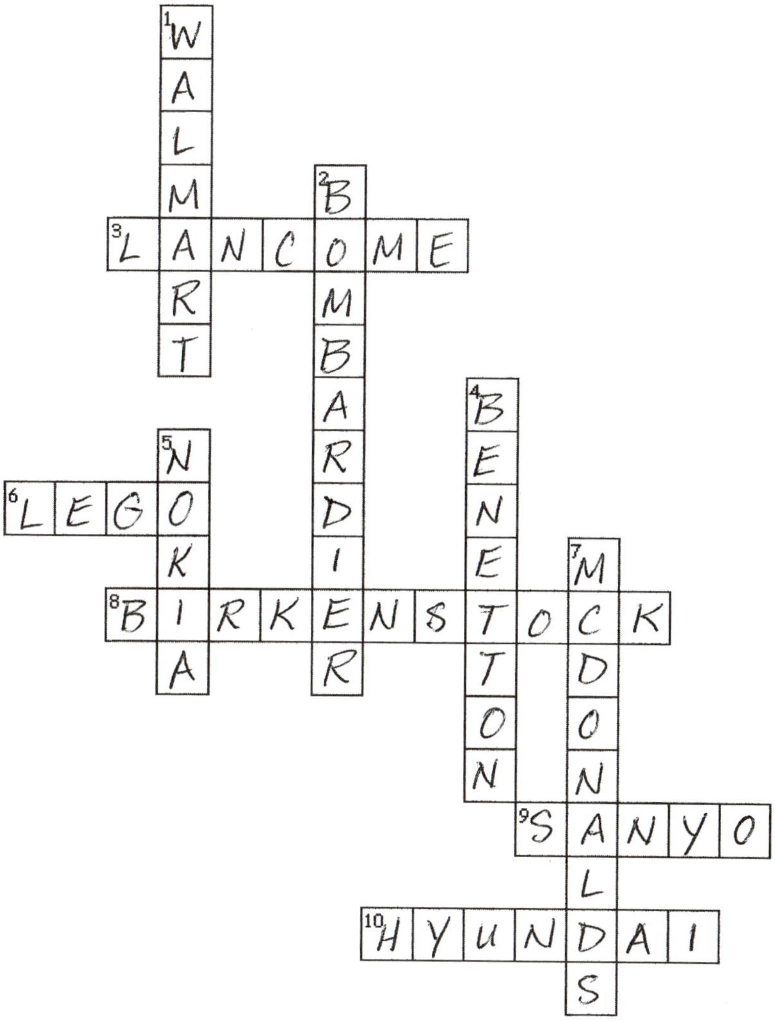

Exercise 10

a) ethanol producers
b) international forum
c) potential
d) global
e) sugar cane
f) corn
g) Brazil
h) produces
i) cheaper
j) international trade
k) technical quality standards

Test Your Knowledge 2

1. b) trade deficit
2. a) which
3. b) subsidy
4. c) an absolute advantage
5. b) the first letters of a title or noun phrase
6. d) joint venture
7. c) Canada, the United States, and Mexico
8. b) World Trade Organization
9. a) licensing
10. b) contract manufacturing

Chapter 3

Exercise 1a

a) double taxation
b) public corporation
c) chief executive officer
d) tender offer
e) inside directors
f) preferred stock
g) initial public offering
h) board of directors
i) corporate governance
j) limited liability

Exercise 1b

a) initial public offering
b) inside directors
c) preferred stock
d) public corporation
e) limited liability
f) corporate governance
g) double taxation
h) board of directors
i) chief executive officer
j) tender offer

Exercise 2

a) with
b) on
c) before
d) to
e) about
f) in
g) for
h) beside
i) under
j) of

Exercise 3a

a) __4_ franchises

b) __2_ sole proprietorship

c) __5_ succession planning

d) __1_ entrepreneur

e) __3_ partnership

Exercise 3b

a) in
b) of
c) with
d) at
e) on

Exercise 4

a) iv
b) iii
c) viii
d) vi
e) i
f) ii
g) vii
h) v

Exercise 5

a) to
b) from
c) of
d) of
e) with; for
f) for; of
g) of
h) of

Exercise 6

Entrepreneur Survey Results

If your score is between -
51–75: You have the characteristics required to become a successful entrepreneur.
26–50: You possess some of the characteristics necessary for successful entrepreneurship, but may have to "grow" the others before venturing into your own business.
0–25: Entrepreneurship is probably not for you. However, there are many jobs that require great team-players who contribute to the overall success of the company.

Exercise 7

a) success
b) dedication
c) market demand
d) competence
e) failure
f) managerial
g) weak control
h) insufficient

Exercise 8

a) iii
b) iv
c) ii
d) i

Exercise 9

a) public corporations
b) institutional investors
c) Shareholders may withhold their vote
d) Under the new system, boards of directors have the discretion to reject the director's offer of resignation.
e) The CCGG is asking companies to voluntarily change their policies because it is easier than lobbying the federal government to change legislation governing all director elections.
f) Companies that adopt the new system will see a substantial increase in investor confidence in the activities of their boards of directors.

Exercise 10

a) microenterprise
b) business plan
c) unlimited liability
d) strategic alliance
e) limited partner
f) subsidiary corporation
g) cooperative
h) outside director
i) employee stock ownership plan
j) inside director

Exercise 11

Business Plan Section	**Items**
Executive Summary	• explanation of the business strategy
Background	• brief history of the company • form of ownership
Marketing	• "industry" overview • promotional strategy • distribution strategy • competitive analysis
Production and Manufacturing	• all production processes • production facilities and equipment needed • inventory requirements
Finance	• capital sources • cash-flow forecast • break-even analysis
Human Resources	• assignment of responsibilities • the training / skills needed
Appendices	• detailed financial statements • detailed management biographies

Test Your Knowledge 3

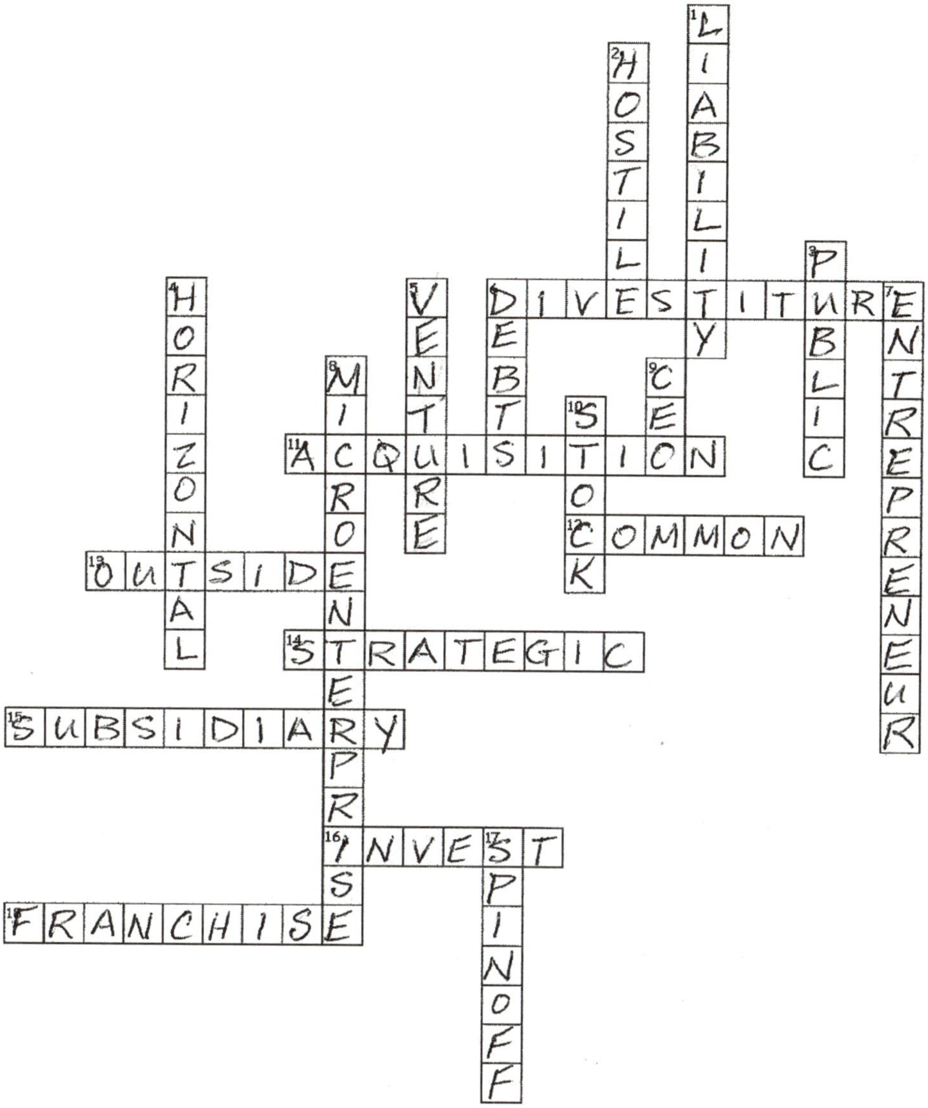

Chapter 4

Exercise 1a

a) obstructionist stance
b) defensive stance
c) accommodative stance
d) proactive stance

Exercise 1b

a) proactive
b) defensive
c) obstructionist
d) accommodative

Exercise 2

a) pollution
b) recycling
c) toxic waste
d) acid rain

Exercise 3

a) v) all of the above
b) the same old, the new trick, the fundraiser, and the concert
c) Africa and America
d) i) rebrand
ii) altruism
iii) corporate sponsors
iv) donate
v) emcee
vi) prohibit
vii) cynicism
viii) imperative
ix) conspicuous compassion
x) genocide
xi) griping and sniping

Exercise 4

a) until
b) although
c) while
d) because
e) if
f) after

Exercise 5

a) before, until
b) while, although
c) if
d) unless
e) while, although
f) since (later time)
g) because, since (reason or cause)
h) because, since (reason or cause)

Exercise 6

a) _3_ accommodative stance
b) _4_ acid rain
c) _9_ consumerism
d) _11_ ethics
e) _7_ organizational stakeholders
f) _5_ pollution
g) _2_ proactive stance
h) _10_ recycling
i) _8_ social audit
j) _1_ social responsibility
k) _6_ toxic waste

Exercise 7

compliance-based ethical codes	integrity-based ethical codes
c	a
e	b
f	d
h	g

Exercise 8

a) organizational stakeholders
b) consumerism
c) social audit
d) collusion
e) whistle blower
f) insider trading

Test Your Knowledge 4

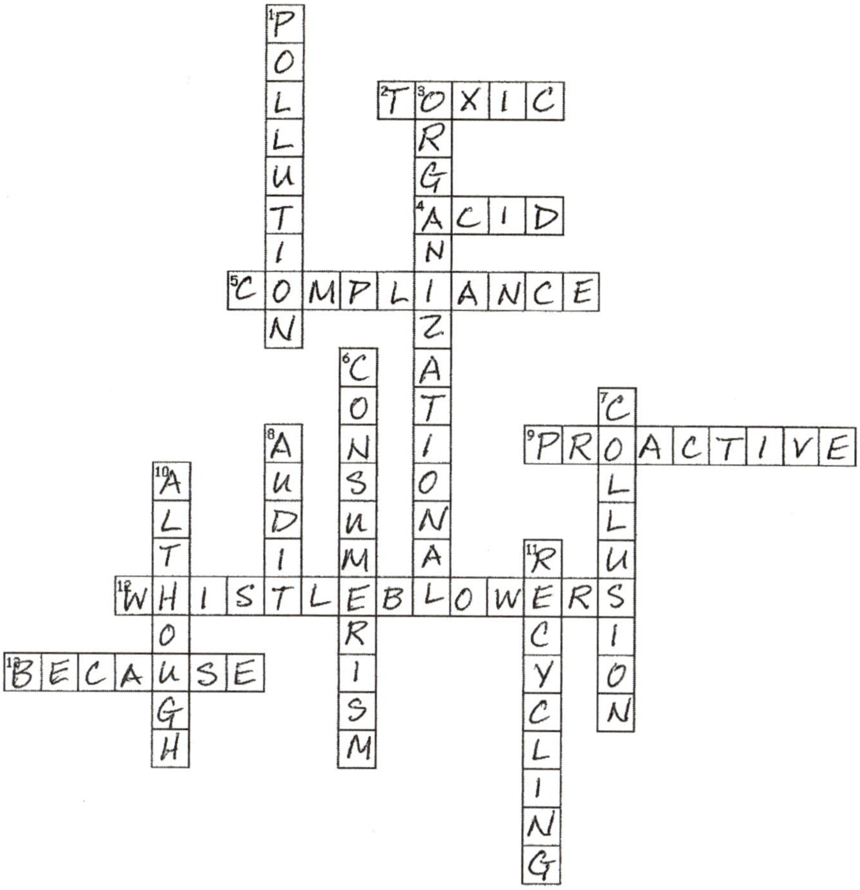

Chapter 5

Exercise 1

a) planning
b) leading
c) organizing
d) controlling

Exercise 2

a) middle management
b) top management
c) supervisory management

Exercise 3

a) supervisory management
b) middle management
c) top management

Exercise 4

a) chain of command
b) departmentalization
c) delegation
d) specialization
e) accountability
f) authority

Exercise 4 (cont'd)

g) responsibility
Mystery Word: organize

Exercise 5

a) must
b) can
c) might, may
d) should
e) should
f) must

Exercise 6

a) iii) crisis planning
b) v) managing outcomes
c) ii) top management
d) iii) controlling
e) ii) contingency planning

Exercise 7

a) might, may
b) could
c) might, may
d) should
e) should
f) can
g) could

Exercise 8

a) __8__ brainstorming
b) __10__ SWOT analysis
c) __3__ technical skills
d) __1__ authority
e) __6__ problem solving
f) __9__ PMI
g) __2__ accountability
h) __7__ decision making
i) __4__ human relations skills
j) __5__ conceptual skills.

Exercise 9

a) S
b) T
c) W
d) O
e) O
f) S
g) T
h) W
i) S
j) O

Exercise 10

a) delegation
b) accountability
c) authority
d) responsibility

Exercise 11

a) staff authority
b) committee and team authority
c) line authority

Exercise 12

a) divisional organization
b) project organization
c) functional organization
d) international organization

Exercise 13

a) food, metal refining, real estate investments, surgical supplies, and industrial plumbing and drainage
b) sale of part or all of the company
c) Lamson & Sessions and Quanex
d) Wendy's; Arrow
e) board of directors
f) board of directors

Test Your Knowledge 5

a) chain of command
b) board of directors
c) authority
d) middle managers
e) SWOT analysis
f) mission statement
g) strategic planning
h) tactical planning (operational planning)
i) operational planning (tactical planning)
j) PMI
k) contingency planning

Chapter 6

Exercise 1

a) human relations
b) turnover
c) morale
d) job satisfaction

Exercise 2

a) If he goes downtown, he will take the subway.
b) She will take the position if they offer it to her.
c) If they sell their house, they will buy a new one.
d) He will complete the project if she takes her vacation next week.
e) If you get the job, you will be happy.

Exercise 3

a) If she wants the job, she will need to get her CFA. (She will need to get her CFA if she wants the job.)
b) If management treats their employees well, the employees will have high morale. (The employees will have high morale if management treats their employees well.)
c) If he motivates his employees, his department will have a low turnover rate. (His department will have a low turnover rate if he motivates his employees.)
d) If their job is challenging, they will like it. (They will like their job if it is challenging.)
e) If morale in our department is high, turnover will be low. (Turnover will be low if morale in our department is high.)

Exercise 4

a) I
b) E
c) I
d) I
e) E
f) E
g) E
h) E

Exercise 5

a) distributed leadership
b) VP of people support
c) animosity
d) 1001 Leaders
e) created partnership councils
f) winner of a "Canada Top 100 Employer Award"

Exercise 7

a) __11_ intrinsic rewards

b) ___6_ job satisfaction

c) ___8_ empowerment

d) ___3_ distributed leadership

e) ___7_ turnover

f) ___9_ motivation

g) __10_ extrinsic rewards

Exercise 7 (cont'd)

h) __5__ goal-setting theory

i) __1__ managerial style

j) __4__ management by objectives

k) __2__ free-reign leadership

Exercise 8

a) theory X
b) equity theory
c) hierarchy of needs theory
d) expectancy theory
e) theory Y
f) two-factor theory
g) theory Z

Exercise 9

a) theory X
b) expectancy theory
c) goal-setting theory
d) equity theory
e) democratic leadership
f) two-factor theory
g) classical theory of motivation
h) theory Z
i) contingency approach

Exercise 10

a) F
b) T
c) F
d) T
e) F
f) F
g) T
h) T
i) T
j) T

Test Your Knowledge 6

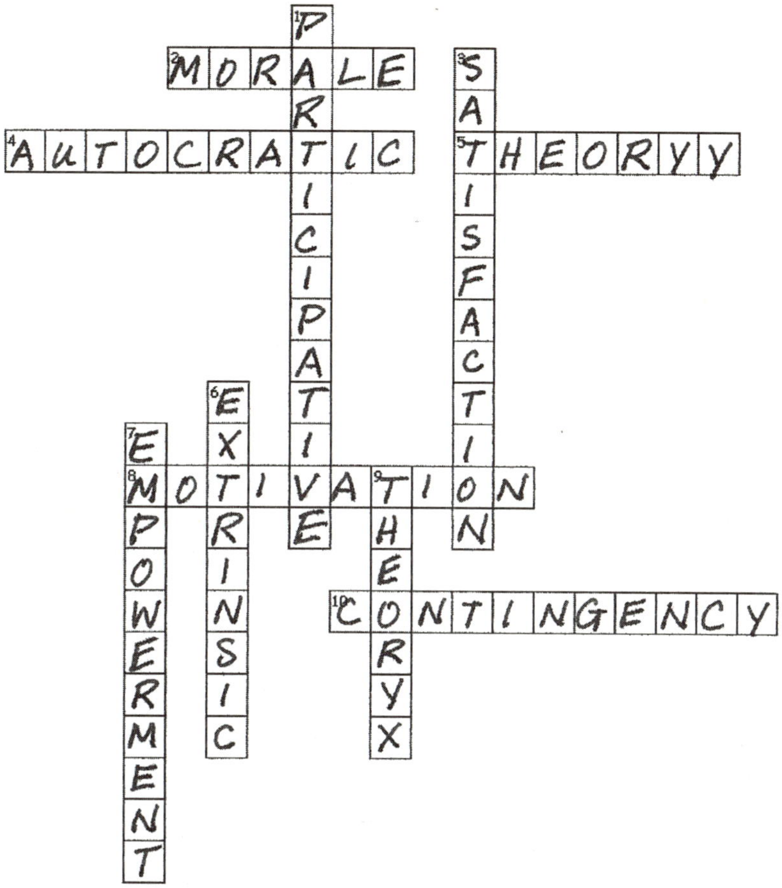

Chapter 7

Exercise 1

a) job analysis
b) replacement charts
c) job description
d) employee information systems
e) job specification

Exercise 2

Step 1 __e)__, Step 2 ___a)__, Step 3, __b)__, Step 4 __c)__, Step 5 __d)__

Exercise 3

a) external recruiting
b) validation
c) assessment centre
d) selection
e) internal recruiting

Exercise 4

a) vestibule training
b) orientation

Exercise 4 (cont'd)

c) systematic job rotations and transfers
d) cross-cultural training
e) on-the-job training
f) apprentice program
g) off-the-job training
h) management development

Exercise 5

a) downsizing
b) expanding
c) employees
d) lay off
e) infrastructure
f) fair
g) job sharing
h) innovation/profitability
i) efficient/focused
j) real changes/locked.

Exercise 6

a) If he liked his job, he would be happier.
b) The managers would hire him if he had more experience.
c) We would accept the merger if the other company gave us more guarantees.
d) If it was Thursday, the human resources manager would be here by now.
e) The team would work better if they knew each other better.

Exercise 7

a) If our company wanted to expand, we would need more resources.
b) The management would change their policies if they wanted to be more inclusive.
c) Tabitha would work harder if she liked her job.
d) Chris would change his habits if management asked him to.
e) If Jorge and Kiko quit, the company would need to hire a few new employees.

Exercise 8

a) iii
b) vii
c) ii
d) iv
e) i
f) v
g) vi

Exercise 9

a) 10 motivation
b) 7 cross-cultural training
c) 2 merit pay
d) 5 fringe benefits
e) 1 flex-plan benefits
f) 9 increase production
g) 11 job satisfaction
h) 8 mentoring system
i) 6 equitable approach
j) 4 human resources management
k) 3 cafeteria-style benefits

Exercise 10

a) profit-sharing plan
b) gain-sharing plan
c) merit pay
d) skill-based pay
e) job evaluation
f) piece-rate incentive plan
g) salary

Exercise 10 (cont'd)

h) knowledge-based pay
i) wages

Exercise 11

a) fringe benefits
b) flextime plan
c) cafeteria-style benefits
d) wellness program

e) worker's compensation
f) compressed workweek
g) job sharing
h) employment insurance

Test Your Knowledge 7

a) job description
b) job specification
c) cafeteria-style benefits
d) flextime plan
e) salary
f) gain-sharing plan
g) orientation
h) systematic job rotations and transfers
i) management development
j) cross-cultural training
k) performance appraisal
l) 360-degree feedback

Chapter 8

Exercise 1

Goods Production	Service Operations	Combination
a)	c)	b)
d)	f)	e)
h)	g)	j)
	i)	

Exercise 2

a) place utility
b) time utility
c) form utility
d) ownership utility

Exercise 3

Analytic Process	Synthetic Process
a)	b)
d)	c)
g)	e)
h)	f)
j)	i)

Exercise 4

High-Contact System	Low-Contact System
b)	a)
d)	c)
e)	f)
i)	g)
j)	h)

Exercise 5

a) If I had wanted that job, I would have applied.
b) If we had been more aggressive, we would have made the sale.

Exercise 5 (cont'd)

c) They would have approved the proposal if he had submitted it.
d) The company would have made more money if the market had improved.
e) If the factory had produced less, there would have been a shortage.

Exercise 6

a) If he had been here, he would have enjoyed the party.
b) They would have bought these desks if they had known about the sale.
c) He would have presented his proposal if he had come to work.
d) If we had given him more training, he would have understood the job better.
e) If she had stayed at the office for lunch, she would have gotten tired faster.

Exercise 7

Would apply	Would not apply
c)	a)
d)	b)
i)	e)
k)	f)
l)	g)
	h)
	j)

Exercise 8

a) iv) research and development
b) iii) statistical quality control
c) ii) ISO 14000
d) i) logistics
e) iii) showcase the technology in order to sell it to other nations
f) iv) Germany and Japan
g) i) China

Exercise 9

a) __10_ supply chain
b) _2, 9_ quality
c) ___7_ ISO 9000
d) ___5_ material requirements planning
e) ___1_ robotics
f) __11_ capacity
g) ___4_ MRP II
h) ___8_ productivity
i) ___6_ total quality management
j) ___3_ inventory control.

Exercise 10

a) transportation
b) holding costs
c) supplier selection
d) logistics
e) purchasing
f) warehousing
g) inventory control
h) lead times

Exercise 11

a) enterprise resource planning (ERP)
b) intermittent process
c) process manufacturing
d) materials requirement planning (MRP)
e) assembly process
f) continuous process
g) just-in-time (JIT) inventory control

Exercise 12

a) mass production
b) competing in time
c) mass customization
d) lean manufacturing
e) flexible manufacturing

Test Your Knowledge 8

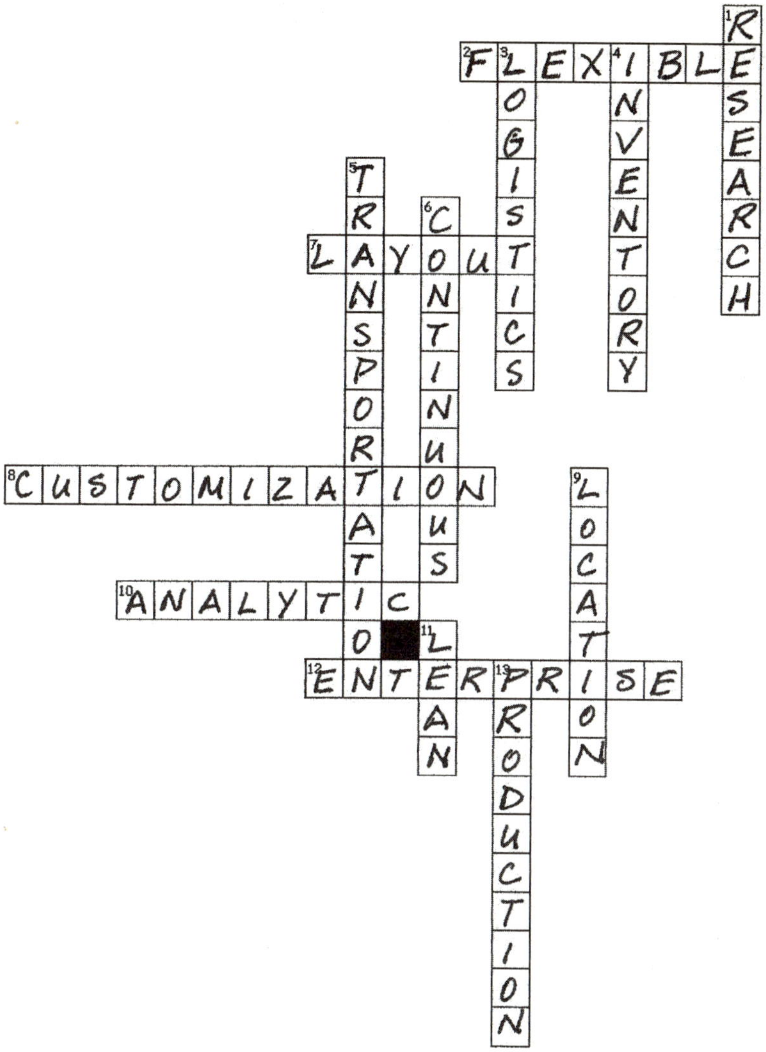

Chapter 9

Exercise 1

data	information
a)	b)
d)	c)
f)	e)
g)	h)

Exercise 2

a) fax machine
b) voice mail
c) electronic mail
d) electronic conferencing
e) groupware

Exercise 3

a) the internet
b) World Wide Web
c) internet service provider (ISP)
d) intranet
e) extranet
f) web server
g) browser
h) search engines
i) directories
j) firewall

Exercise 4

type of software	letters	
word-processing programs	f)	j)
electronic spreadsheets	g)	k)
presentation graphics software	a)	i)
desktop publishing software	c)	l)
Portable Document Format (PDF)	b)	e)
computer graphics programs	d)	h)

Exercise 5

a) in addition
b) next
c) therefore
d) however

Exercise 6

a) first
b) however
c) for instance
d) also
e) on the other hand
f) in conclusion

Exercise 7

a) Blunder #2
b) Blunder #5
c) Blunder #1
d) Blunder #3
e) Blunder #4

Exercise 8

a) however
b) rather than
c) in other words
d) although

Exercise 8 (cont'd)

e) for example
f) in general

Exercise 9

a) provide a better work–life balance.
b) because there won't be any interruptions.
c) makes telework a cultural challenge.
d) is also a challenge.
e) employees have self-discipline.
f) understand objectives.

Exercise 10

a) additionally
b) although
c) that is
d) however
e) overall

Exercise 11

a) __2__ computer graphics software
b) __8__ electronic mail system
c) __6__ extranet
d) __4__ HTML
e) __1__ information
f) __5__ intranet
g) __3__ LAN
h) 7,9,10 PDF

Exercise 12

a) client-server network
b) client
c) local area network (LAN)
d) server
e) wide area network (WAN)
f) multimedia communications systems

Exercise 13

a) information
b) internet
c) intranet
d) database
e) WAN
f) electronic
g) LAN
Mystery Word: firewall

Test Your Knowledge 9

a) ISP
b) browser
c) LAN
d) electronic spreadsheet
e) word-processing programs
f) presentation graphics software
g) electronic conferencing

Chapter 10

Exercise 1

a) chartered accountant (CA)
b) bookkeeping
c) accounting
d) certified general accountant (CGA)
e) audit
f) certified management accountant (CMA)
g) forensic accountant
h) private accountant

Exercise 2

a) liabilities
b) financial statement
c) liquidity
d) assets
e) balance sheet
f) cash-flow statement

Exercise 3

a) operating expenses
b) revenue
c) net income
d) cost of goods sold

Exercise 3 (cont'd)

e) double-entry bookkeeping
f) gross profit (gross margin)

Exercise 4

a) They said they will have the reports done before you leave for the day.
b) The forensic accountants said that they have to check your net income before they could come to any conclusions.
c) She told me that she needs to get her work done before she can see me.
d) I asked the accountants how long it would be before the next financial statement.
e) The top managers said that their revenues for this quarter haven't been as high as they would like.

Exercise 5a

a) bankruptcy
b) cash-flow statement
c) malfeasance
d) forensic accountant
e) private accountant
f) fiduciary duty
g) compliance

Exercise 5b

a) The firm's CEO said that, on behalf of Dare to Dream, he would like to apologize to their shareholders, creditors, and the public.
b) The detective in charge of the investigation said that their investigation is completed and it is likely that those responsible will go to trial.
c) Prime Minister Stutsky said that he feels that corporate heads carry a great deal of responsibility in modern society.

Exercise 6

a) Institute of Chartered Accountants of Ontario. They are the professional body that governs the province's chartered accountants
b) three senior Deloitte & Touche LLP auditors
c) Livent is known for Broadway shows such as *Phantom of the Opera* and *Ragtime* as well as its executives who are charged with criminal fraud
d) its unrealistic because they are being paid by the very people who they would have to accuse of wrongdoing
e) any fraud, theft, or "material breach of any fiduciary duty" must be reported to the authorities within three days
f) the threat of doing hard time in jail

Exercise 7

a) by not prosecuting for securities fraud
b) as the "Wild West"
c) long-dormant, tantamount to no prosecutions at all, and shocking
d) not "to bring lawbreakers to justice" but to "promote the integrity of the capital markets and foster confidence in them"
e) first, eliminate traditional power structures; second, create an independent enforcement agency to initiate proceedings against these scam artists; and third, assess heavy penalties for those who are found guilty

Exercise 8

a) ___3_ private accountant

b) ___5_ liquidity

c) ___7_ audit

d) ___2_ forensic accountants

Exercise 8 (cont'd)

e) ___1_ revenues

f) ___9_ double-entry bookkeeping

g) ___8__financial statements

h) ___6_ malfeasance

i) ___4_ fiduciary duty

Exercise 9

assets	liabilities
a)	b)
c)	e)
d)	g)
f)	i)
h)	k)
j)	l)

Exercise 10

a) asset
b) bankruptcy
c) fiduciary
d) bookkeeping
e) audit
f) financial
g) budget
Mystery Word: account

Test Your Knowledge 10

a) certified general accountant (CGA)
b) financial statement
c) balance sheets
d) bookkeeping
e) double-entry bookkeeping
f) liquidity
g) liabilities
h) budget
i) gross profit (gross margin)
j) fiduciary duties

Chapter 11

Exercise 1

a) venture capital
b) debt financing
c) commercial paper
d) line of credit
e) interest
f) loan
g) promissory note

Exercise 2

a) financial management
b) financial plan
c) financial control
d) acquisition
e) finance

Exercise 3

a) collateral
b) budget
c) owner's equity

Exercise 4

a) insider trading
b) prospectus
c) bear market
d) equity financing
e) capitalization
f) common stock
g) initial public offering (IPO)
h) dividends
i) preferred stock
j) bull market

Exercise 5

a) The acquisition of the smaller company wasn't approved.
b) Insider trading is disapproved of.

Exercise 5 (cont'd)

c) The new budget was drawn up yesterday.
d) The company's capitalization was analyzed.
e) A lot of venture capital was given to @Work.

Exercise 6

a) Hexcorp bought most of the shares.
b) Doll Face Beauty Salon gave a promissory note to the supplier.
c) A scandal in the finance industry caused the bear market.
d) [Sam] developed a cash-flow forecast for the company.
e) [The bank] gave Steve a $5000 line of credit.

Exercise 7

a) Starlims Technologies Ltd.

i) laboratory information management systems

ii) 2.1 million shares

iii) between $13.50 and $15.50 per share

iv) Tel Aviv, Israel

v) $25.5 million

vi) general corporate purposes, including working capital and capital expenditures; also acquisitions and investments

vii) Oppenheimer and JMP Securities LLC are underwriting

viii) "LIMS"

b) Blackstone Group LP

i) private equity firm

ii) no number provided

iii) between $29 and $31 per share

iv) New York.-based

v) between $3.87 billion and $4.13 billion

vi) to help tap new sources of capital for multibillion-dollar acquisitions

vii) Morgan Stanley, Citigroup Inc., Merrill Lynch & Co., Lehman Brothers Holdings Inc., and Deutsche Bank AG

viii) "BX"

c) Starent Networks Corp.

i) hardware and software in support of wireless networks

ii) 10.5 million shares

iii) between $9 and $11 per share

iv) Tewksbury, Mass.-based

v) $81.9 million

vi) working capital and other general purposes including developing new products, sales and marketing activities, and capital expenditures

vii) Goldman Sachs and Lehman Brothers

viii) "STAR"

Exercise 8

a) about $6 billion in cash
b) online advertising
c) premium
d) acquisition
e) $40 billion/20 percent
f) Google Inc./Yahoo/advertising
g) first half
h) market capitalization

Exercise 9

a) __11_ bull market

b) ___9_ equity financing

c) 3,6,8_ acquisition

d) ___2_ IPO

e) __12_ capitalization

f) __10_ risk/return trade-off

g) ___7_ financial control

h) ___5_ commercial paper

i) ___1_ prospectus

j) ___4_ stock

Exercise 10

a) budget
b) venture capital
c) interest
d) collateral
e) loan
f) line of credit
g) prospectus
h) initial public offering (IPO)
i) stock

Test Your Knowledge 11

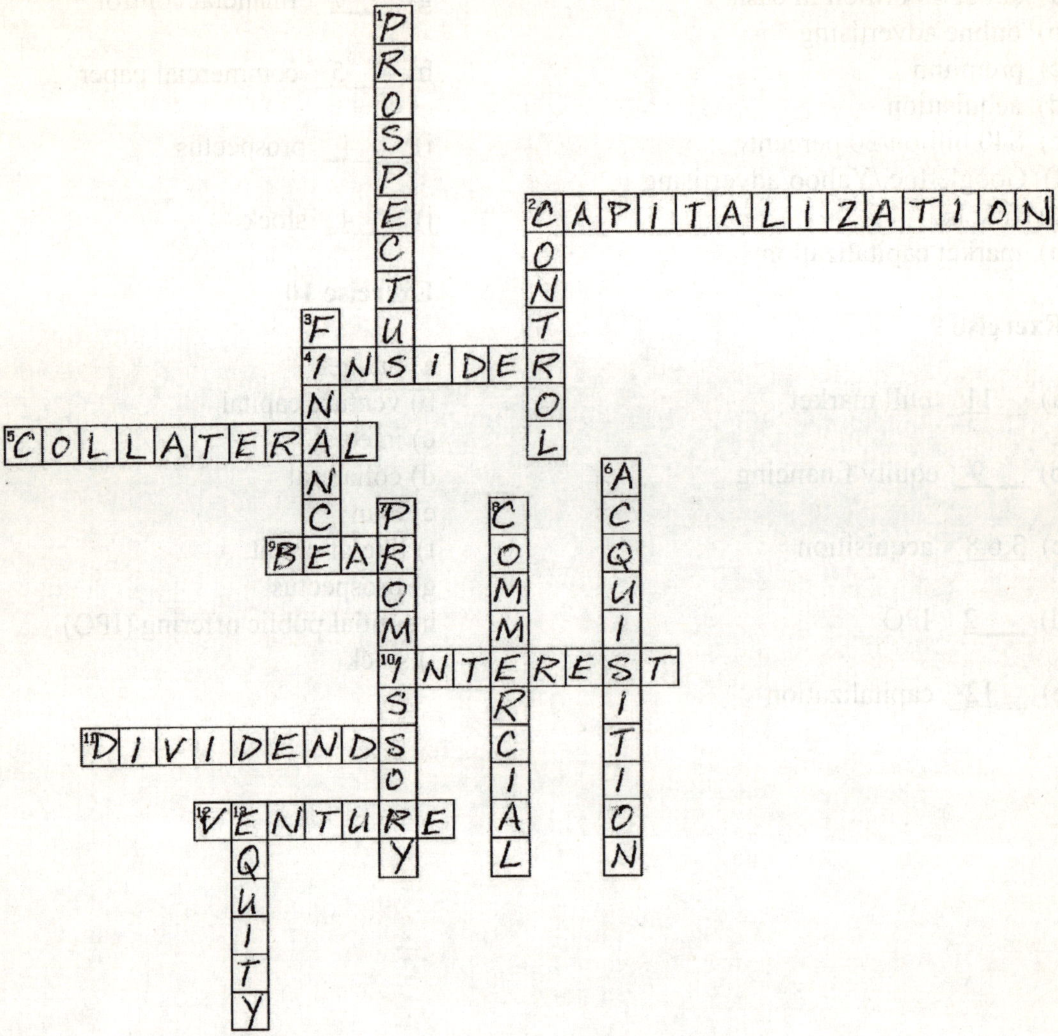

Chapter 12

Exercise 1

a) product
b) promotion
c) price
d) consumer goods
e) marketing concept
f) utility
g) marketing mix
h) value
i) place (distribution)
j) services
k) industrial goods

Exercise 2

a) target market
b) primary data
c) product differentiation
d) market research

Exercise 2 (cont'd)

e) relationship marketing
f) secondary data
g) marketing segmentation
h) marketing plan
i) demographics

Exercise 3

a) rational motives
b) early adopters
c) brand loyalty
d) emotional motives

Exercise 4

a) Mind Marketing uses market research, a study of consumer needs, to develop its strategies.
b) ShowMe Marketing markets products and services, intangibles that can be purchased, for various companies.
c) Consumers often buy products for emotional motives, motives based on feelings or impulses.
d) Marketers often use secondary data, information obtained through previous research, in their development of marketing plans.
e) Some marketing campaigns focus on utility, the ability of a product or service to satisfy a want or need.

Exercise 5

a) a computer-generated world
b) a computer-generated representation of themselves called an "avatar"
c) because avatars are buying stuff in real dollars
d) a young, tech-forward demographic
e) market their brand in a way that works in the virtual world
f) we know that they are a small group, global, tech-savvy; potential early adopters for your brand

Exercise 6

a) **Second Life**, the much-hyped computer-generated world created by San Francisco-based Linden Lab Inc., is popular with users.
b) Second Life "residents" create an **avatar**, a computer-generated representation of themselves, and spend time almost as they would in the real world.
c) Users spend almost one million **Linden dollars**, the in-world currency, every day.
d) **Reuters**, a news agency, assigned a full-time employee to cover Second Life goings-on.
e) Users generate most of the **content**, anything from furniture to high fashion, designing then selling or trading their creations.

Exercise 7

a) have a patriotic fervor.
b) an oft-bellowed phrase.
c) although most of it is fairly routine.
d) are sports fans.
e) type of consumer behaviour.
f) of consumers.

Exercise 8

a) **Rick Singer**, director of worldwide sponsorship marketing at IBM, claims that sports content has a timeliness to it.
b) Canadians like **content snacks**, short hits that are quickly downloaded and absorbed.
c) **KPMG**, an accounting giant, has decided that consumers have already picked the cellphone as their preferred converged media device.

Exercise 8 (cont'd)

d) This year, NCAA and **CBS**, NCAA's broadcast partner, streamed the NCAA's basketball tournament for free on the association's website.

Exercise 9

a) __10_ utility

b) ___4__ primary data

c) ___8_ brand

d) ___7_ early adopters

e) ___9_ value

f) ___1_ consumer goods

g) ___3_ market research

h) ___6_ target market

i) ___5_ secondary data

j) ___2_ industrial goods

Exercise 10

a) market research
b) consumer behaviour
c) primary data
d) emotional motives
e) product differentiation

Exercise 11

a) **"The Ritual Master,"** an exhaustive compilation of all those minuscule, repeated details that add up to a day in our lives, was created last year.
b) Last month, executives unveiled their **findings**, an enormous survey of human behaviour compiled to help their clients sell us stuff.
c) Our **rituals**, the small steps we take from morning till night, were the focus of the study.
d) The Chinese, however, embrace the notion of "**appointment sex**," sex at scheduled times.
e) **Andrew Robertson,** president and CEO of BBDO Worldwide, says that the study will be used to see how client brands can be fit into consumers' lives.

Exercise 12

a) products
b) services
c) market research
d) primary data
e) secondary data
f) emotional motives
g) rational motives
h) marketing plan
i) brand loyalty
j) product differentiation
k) early adopters

Test Your Knowledge 12

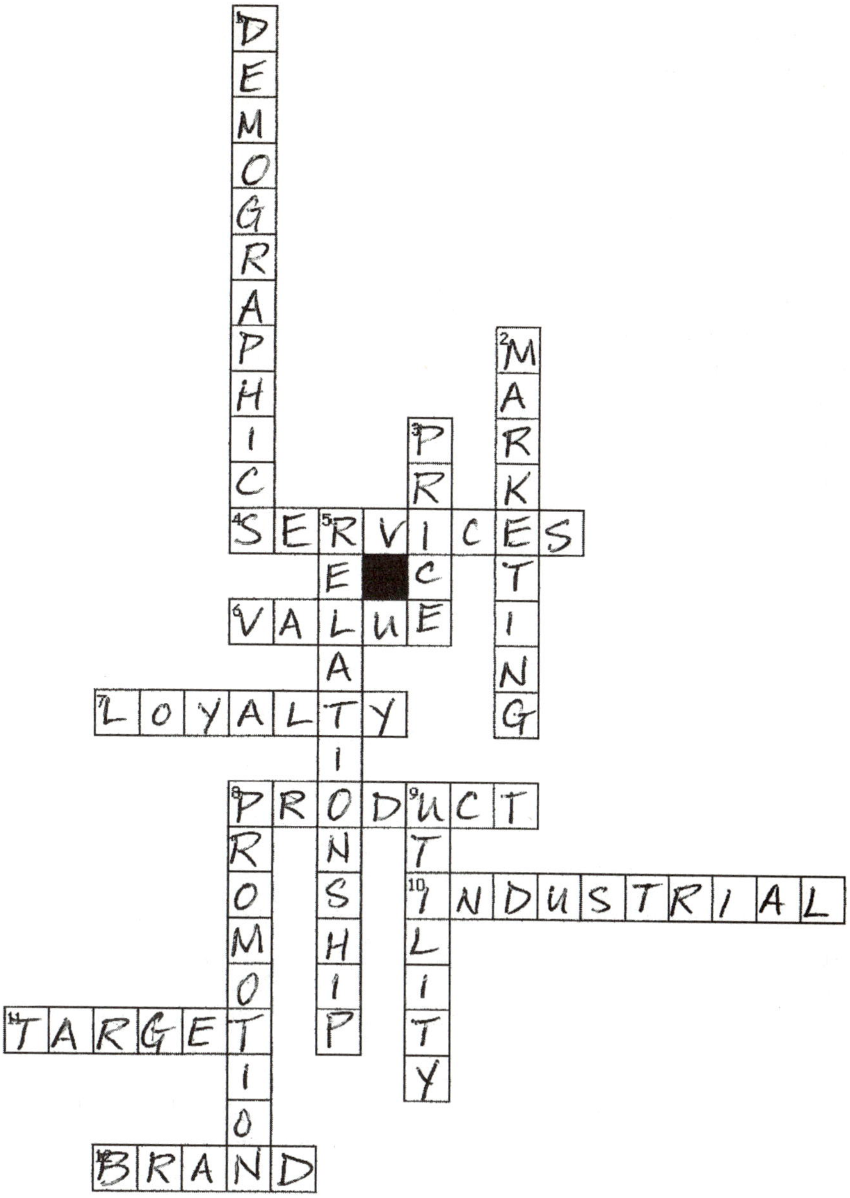

Chapter 13

Exercise 1

a) viral marketing
b) sales promotion
c) publicity
d) word of mouth
e) trade shows
f) public relations

Exercise 2

a) publicity
b) word of mouth
c) product positioning

Exercise 3

a) product positioning
b) point of differentiation
c) brand equity
d) brand loyalty
e) product mix
f) product line
g) market test
h) branding

Exercise 4

a) branding
b) brand loyalty
c) specialty goods

Exercise 5

a) for
b) and
c) , but
d) so
e) nor
f) or

Exercise 6

a) that
b) which
c) why
d) where
e) who
f) what
g) when

Exercise 7

a) before
b) with
c) to
d) after
e) for
f) about

Exercise 8

a) while
b) after
c) because
d) although
e) until
f) if

Exercise 9

a) product line
b) product life cycle
c) advertising

Exercise 10

a) product line
b) market test

Exercise 11

a) product positioning
b) branding
c) product line

Exercise 12

a) brand loyalty
b) product positioning
c) personal selling

Exercise 13

a) word of mouth
b) point of differentiation
c) publicity

Exercise 14

a) point of differentiation

Exercise 14 (cont'd)

b) advertising
c) brand loyalty

Exercise 15

a) introduction stage
b) growth stage
c) maturity stage
d) decline stage

Exercise 16

a) __9__ product positioning

b) __7__ decline stage

c) __10__ sales promotion

d) __1__ advertising

e) __4__ growth stage

f) __6__ promotional mix

g) __8__ branding

h) __3__ introduction stage

i) __2__ product life cycle

j) __5__ maturity stage

Exercise 17

a) Crocs produces colourful clog-like footwear.
b) Snyder is concerned that Crocs may be susceptible to being a one-hit wonder.
c) Benefits to consumer—any three of the following: soft, comfortable, lightweight, grip slippery surfaces, don't stink on sweaty feet.
d) Nurses, teachers, and gardeners wear Crocs. They are also worn by at least one Israeli soldier and an Orthodox Jew. "Everyone from toddlers to grandmas."
e) Profit more than tripled last year, and Crocs are sold in 80 countries throughout the world.
f) Crocs is at the "maturity" stage in the product life-cycle, and Snyder is planning to diversify.
g) Snyder has chosen acquisitions to achieve his goal—Crocs has already made several acquisitions and will continue to look for opportunities.

Test Your Knowledge 13

a) personal
b) branding
c) point
d) word
e) maturity
f) decline
g) trade
Mystery Word: product

Chapter 14

Exercise 1

a) price-skimming strategy
b) odd–even pricing
c) penetration pricing strategy
d) everyday low pricing (EDLP)
e) price leadership
f) price lining
g) non-price strategy

Exercise 2a

a) fixed costs
b) break-even analysis
c) variable costs
d) break-even point

Exercise 2b

a) variable costs
b) break-even analysis
c) fixed costs
d) break-even point

Exercise 3

a) discount
b) seasonal discount
c) cash discount
d) quantity discount
e) trade discount

Exercise 4

a) customer relationship management software via the Web
b) 85 percent of its revenue comes from the U.S.
c) they were expecting the rise in the dollar and engaged a financial consulting firm to review their cost structure
d) they did not raise their price
e) they increased capacity/volume, which protected their margins without having to raise prices

Exercise 5

a) Bravado manufactures maternity and nursing lingerie
b) 85 percent of its products are exported to the U.S.
c) yes, they did anticipate the rise, so they based their profitability on a higher-valued dollar
d) no, they felt there was no room to raise prices
e) they looked at forging better and bigger relationships with their existing customers and increasing their online sales, where margins were significantly higher

Exercise 6

a) biotech
b) U.S. dollars
c) nothing in the article mentions price changes
d) working harder on investor relations, improving efficiencies and margin rates, and enjoying the cheaper prices of chemicals and plastics from the U.S.

Exercise 7

a) Trafford is an on-demand publishing house
b) 85 percent of its work is comprised of exports
c) they are worried about a sudden drop in the dollar
d) no, however they are thinking of increasing prices for their U.S. customers and also adding value
e) opening subsidiaries in England and Ireland, and improving efficiencies and enhancing service have been their solutions

Exercise 8

a) customer-contact centre for the funeral industry and the clinical-research industry
b) 95 percent of sales are in U.S. dollars
c) no, and as a consequence lost $280.00 in profit last year
d) no, but are considering doing so by about 10 percent
e) conducted a client-by-client analysis of profitability, introduce a time-based billing system to replace their current transaction-based system, and pushing for growth

Exercise 9

1. Facebook is selling banner ads and marketing opportunities

Exercise 9 (cont'd)

2. the pricing units are "newsfeeds"
3. variable costs
4. how many consumers see the newsfeed item
5. definitely not—you do not have sufficient information.

Exercise 10

a) ___8_ odd–even pricing

b) ___6_ mark-up

c) ___1_ pricing

d) ___9_ seasonal discounts

e) ___7_ price lining

f) ___2_ break-even point

g) ___3_ fixed costs

h) ___5_ unit price

i) ___4_ variable costs

Exercise 11

a) might
b) should
c) can
d) must

Exercise 12

a) If she is a senior, she will get a discount. (She will get a discount if she is a senior.)
b) If we buy 12 dozen muffins, we will get a quantity discount. (We will get a quantity discount if we buy 12 dozen muffins.)
c) If his variable costs are low, his break-even point will be low. (His break-even point will be low if his variable costs are low.)
d) If she pays cash, she will get a cash discount. (She will get a cash discount if she pays cash.)
e) If they work in the industry, they will get an industry discount. (They will get an industry discount if they work in the industry.)

Exercise 13

a) If she was a senior, she would get a discount. (She would get a discount if she was a senior.)
b) If we bought 12 dozen muffins, we would get a quantity discount. (We would get a quantity discount if we bought 12 dozen muffins.)
c) If his variable costs were low, his break-even point would be low. (His break-even point would be low if his variable costs were low.)
d) If she paid cash, she would get a cash discount. (She would get a cash discount if she paid cash.)
e) If they worked in the industry, they would get an industry discount. (They would get an industry discount if they worked in the industry.)

Exercise 14

a) If we had used a non-pricing strategy, our sales would have increased.
b) Our variable costs would have been lower if we had used a cheaper supplier.
c) We would have launched the new product if we had had a larger market share.
d) If we had priced it better, it would have sold.
e) If we had been a price leader, we would have priced products higher.

Test Your Knowledge 14

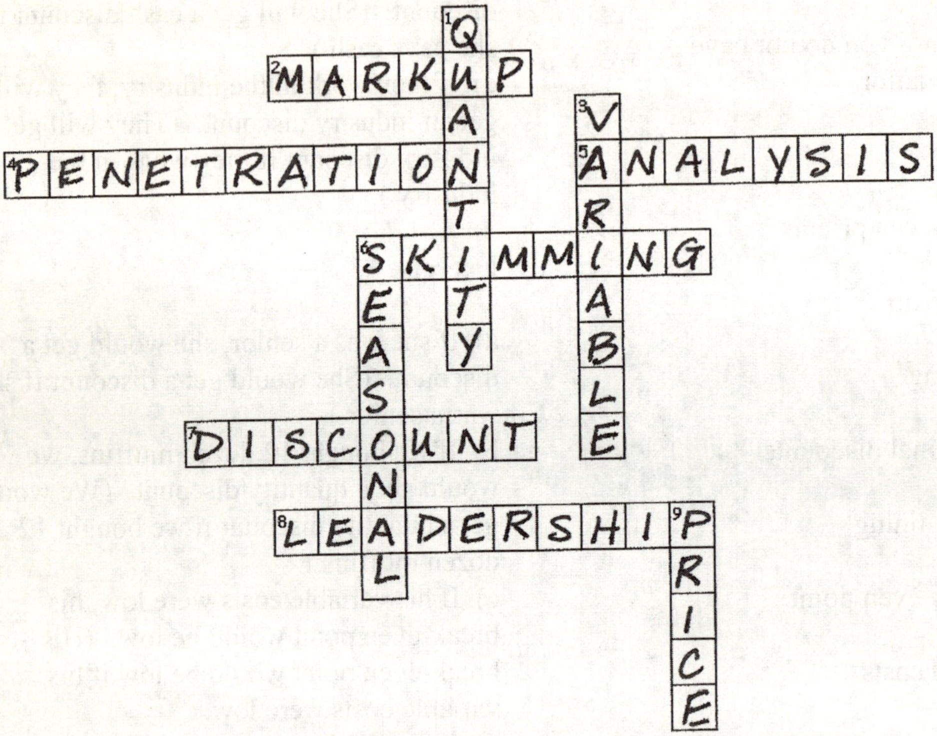

Chapter 15

Exercise 1

a) e-intermediary
b) internet-based retailing
c) e-catalogue
d) electronic order
e) electronic storefront

Exercise 2

a) transportation
b) containerization
c) logistics visibility
d) global positioning system (GPS)
e) intermodal

Exercise 3

a) intensive distribution
b) selective distribution
c) hub
d) exclusive distribution

Exercise 4

a) when your company sells its products or services through multiple channels
b) everyone may become alienated
c) i) vague and outdated sales agreements; ii) the internet has left your reps and agents selling in the same market; iii) the toll-free number makes it difficult to sort out who gets credit for the order

Exercise 4 (cont'd)

d) i) complaints from customers about different prices for same product; ii) distributors complaining about predatory pricing; iii) sales from distributors dropping quickly
e) make it very clear who gets paid for what, when, where, and for how much, based on dollar volume, head-office location, or product mix
f) seek input from both your agents and sales team and then communicate the rules clearly to each

Exercise 5

a) ___8_ electronic order

b) ___6_ e-intermediaries

c) ___1_ retailers

d) ___3_ electronic storefront

e) ___2_ internet-based retailing

f) __10_ inventory control

g) ___9_ distribution channel

h) ___7_ vertical marketing system

i) ___5_ e-catalogue

j) ___4_ materials handling

Exercise 6

a) wholesaler
b) retailers
c) intermediary
d) materials handling
e) inventory control

Exercise 7

a) furthermore
b) however
c) instead of
d) consequently
e) generally
f) for example

Exercise 8

a) The exporter said that he was going to have to use an intermodal transportation system.
b) The sales agent said I should start using a global positioning system (GPS) with my transportation system.
c) Our transportation manager protested that he didn't forget to send the shipment.
d) The message with the electronic order said that our products are really great.
e) Her broker told her that she needed to rethink her distribution mix.
f) The man whispered that he didn't know how to do this.
g) I asked her did she think he would help with her distribution problem.

Exercise 9

a) Management established the distribution mix.
b) The customer submitted the electronic order.
c) The manufacturer contacted the intermediary.
d) Overproduction created the channel conflict at Hexcorp.
e) The marketing team formatted the e-catalogucs.
f) The retailers contacted the wholesalers.
g) My business partner chose my e-intermediaries.

Exercise 10

a) The exporter has an intermodal transportation system, a system involving multiple modes of travel.
b) The trucking industry was experiencing a channel conflict, an overload of distribution channels.
c) The Big Drip, a popular chain of coffee shops, engages in direct selling.
d) Legally Binding, a producer of handmade books, uses an electronic storefront to sell its goods.
e) www.shopalot.com works as an e-intermediary, an electronic distributor, for multiple manufacturers.
f) Salih decided that intensive distribution, distribution utilizing many intermediaries and channels, was the best choice for his company.
g) Trent was in charge of materials handling, the logistics of handling inventory within a warehouse, for the company.
h) The company decided to go with exclusive distribution, distribution involving only one intermediary.

Exercise 11

The way things used to be

6 = order part from supplier

11 = can't pre-book installation until arrival time is known

9 = everyone loses track of the part

12 = Ericsson doesn't get paid until part is installed

4 = service rep orders part from warehouse

8 = part is loaded on a truck or airplane

10 = don't know when the part will arrive

3 = contact field-service rep

5 = part is out of stock

2 = replacement part is needed

7 = part delivered to Ericsson distribution centre

1 = something is wrong at a remote relay tower

The way things are now

6 = pre-book installation

4 = supplier sends part off to the customer and posts info on DeliveryNet

3 = send electronic order to Ericsson supplier

1 = something is wrong at a relay tower

2 = replacement part is needed

7 = Ericsson gets paid

5 = everyone knows exactly where the part is and when it will arrive because of GPS tracking

Exercise 12

a) distribution channel
b) channel conflict
c) direct channel
d) sales agent/broker
e) distribution mix

Test Your Knowledge 15

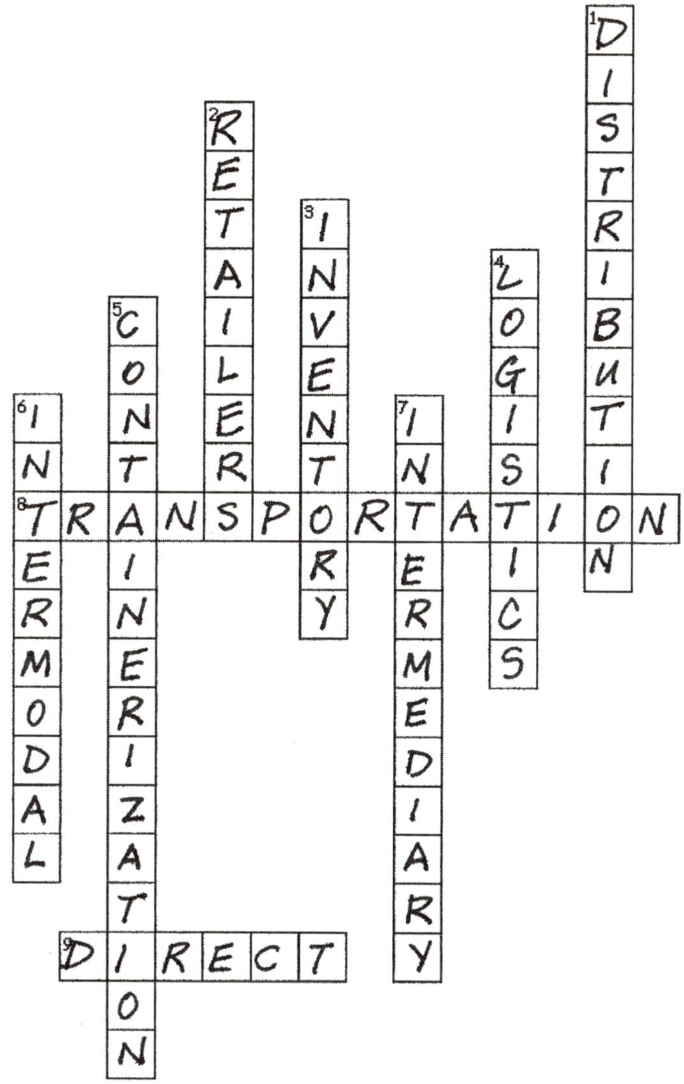

Glossary

absolute advantage a situation in which a country is able to produce a product at a lower cost than any other country or when only one country is able to produce the product.

accommodative stance a company that complies with legal and ethical mores and may even go beyond the expected.

accountability the responsibility of an individual or team to complete the task assigned.

acid rain the expulsion of sulphur into the environment by businesses and government-run power plants.

acquisition the purchase and assimilation of a smaller firm.

advertising any non-personal, sponsor-identified activity communicating information about a product, service, idea, or firm.

aggregate output the quantity of goods and services produced by an economy during a specific period of time.

analytic process a process in which a substance is broken down into its component parts.

apprentice program a type of on-the-job training that includes on-site job instruction, classroom instruction, and often leads to a trade certification.

assembly process a production process or part of a process that involves putting parts together to create a finished product.

assessment centre a set of practical management tasks performed by job applicants and evaluated by management experts.

authority responsibility for the final outcome of tasks completed by others and the right to change those outcomes.

autocratic leadership a style of leadership in which managers dictate outcomes and expect employees to comply without question.

balance of payments an accounting of the difference between funds flowing into and out of the country as a result of transactions with other countries or nationals.

balance of trade an accounting of the difference between the value of a country's exports and imports.

bear market a period of time during which investors believe that stock prices will fall and act on that belief.

board of directors a group of people elected by shareholders to assume legal responsibility and oversee the management of the corporation, including directing the vision and overall objectives of the corporation, the selection and hiring of corporate officers, and monitoring the finances and operations.

brainstorming a free-association exercise in which there is no censoring of ideas, but a free flow of possible solutions to a specific problem.

branch office is part of a company that operates in foreign markets but under the same management structure as its domestic operations.

brand the reputation or image of a product or service that consumers have come to identify with a name or symbol representing the reputation or image; often tied to performance.

brand equity the value-added that a brand gives a product.

brand loyalty a customer's insistence upon purchasing a brand regardless of quality or performance issues; consumer satisfaction demonstrated through repeated purchases.

branding a device, such as a symbol, phrase, name, or design, used to distinguish a firm's products from those of the competition.

break-even analysis an evaluation of the relationship between total revenues and total costs to determine the profitability at various output levels.

break-even point the precise number of units that must be sold at a given price before the firm covers both its fixed and variable costs.

browser a kind of computer software that enables users to access documents on the World Wide Web.

bull market a period of time during which investors believe that stock prices are on the rise and act upon that belief.

business the activity of earning a profit through the provision of goods or services.

business cycle the pattern of peaks and troughs that occur in all economies over time.

business ethics behavioural standards established within businesses and acted upon by managers and employees.

business plan usually undertaken by new ventures, it represents the overall business strategies and how those strategies will be implemented.

business practice law laws and regulations that restrict the way in which we conduct business in a country.

business-to-business websites (B2B) the selling of products or services to business users rather than to consumers or end-users.

cafeteria-style benefits consists of a "menu" of valuated benefits from which employees may choose a fixed amount.

capacity the number of goods or service that can be produced under existing conditions.

capital the funds necessary for the running of a business.

capital structure the balance between a firm's debt and equity financing.

capitalism an economic system in which all or most of the factors of production are controlled privately and operated for profit.

capitalization a firm's dollar or market price per share on a specific day multiplied by the number of common shares outstanding.

cartel a group of producers whose goal is to control the supply and pricing of the product they are producing.

cash discount an incentive for customers to pay cash rather than use a credit card.

chain of command the decision-making authority that emanates from the top of a company to the bottom.

channel conflict the perception by one channel member that another channel member is interfering with the first member's ability to achieve its distribution goals.

chief executive officer selected and hired by the board of directors, the CEO is responsible to the shareholders, the board of directors, the employees, and other stakeholders for the company's performance.

classical theory of motivation the assumption that employees are only motivated by money.

client an access point in a client-server network; usually through a computer.

collateral committing an asset that can be seized by the lender for non-payment of the loan.

collusion the collaboration of two or more companies in illegally manipulating the price or supply of goods.

command economy an economic system in which all or most of the factors of production are government-controlled.

commercial paper a method of acquiring short-term funds by selling unsecured notes for less than face value to be repurchased within 270 days of issue.

common stock shares in a company whose owners have last claim on the corporation's assets and profits, but who are entitled to vote.

communism an economic and political system in which all of the factors of production are government-controlled.

comparative advantage a situation in which a country is able to produce some products at lower cost or better than some other products.

competition businesses competing with each other in the marketplace to win consumers and to satisfy their needs.

compressed workweek a workweek in which employees work longer hours for fewer days of the week.

computer graphics programs software that enables the creation of graphic art.

computer-aided design (CAD) utilization of software in the design of new products or in the improvement of existing products.

computer-aided manufacturing (CAM) utilization of software to design and control the machinery used in producing goods.

computer-integrated manufacturing (CIM) the combination of robotics and flexible manufacturing with other computer-driven systems for design, inventory control, transportation, etc.

conceptual skills the ability to think in abstractions and to picture the entire organization with all of its component parts and derive constructive relationships among those parts.

conglomerate merger the joining of two firms who have been operating entirely different businesses.

consumer behaviour observation and recognition of why consumers of products or services purchase what they do.

consumer goods products purchased for personal use.

consumer price index (CPI) the measure of the value of a typical "basket" of goods and services purchased by a consumer in a given month.

consumerism activist movements that demand safe products, the right to complete product information, the right to be heard by producers, and the right to free and fair competition among producers.

containerization a cargo-handling system that transports products from the manufacturer in large metal containers that remain unopened until they reach their final destination.

contingency approach a management approach that expects each situation to require its own unique approach.

contingency planning developing a back-up strategy in case changes of plans are required.

continuous process a production process that involves longer runs and usually a single product.

contract manufacturing a situation in which a foreign manufacturer produces products under a domestic company's brand; provides an opportunity to test the market.

controlling that part of a manager's responsibilities that focuses on evaluating performance and making adjustments where necessary in order to accomplish organizational goals.

convenience goods products or services that are purchased often and are used quickly; little time is spent either in looking for them or in comparing prices.

co-operative initiated by a group of people for the purpose of benefiting from group buying power in the form of lower prices, and also includes the equal distribution of any profits that remain at the end of the year.

corporate governance the responsibilities of and the relationships among the shareholders, board of directors, and senior managers within the corporation.

corporate philanthropy a company's financial support of causes that come within its sphere of interest.

corporate social responsibility(CSR) a company's interest in improving society by engaging in supportive activities in its community.

crisis planning the mechanisms in place to deal with emergencies as they may arise.

cross-cultural training usually initiated when employees are preparing to move to a foreign subsidiary and will be experiencing significant cultural change in doing so. Preparing employees for this inevitability eases the transition, enhances performance, and supports retention.

data detailed information obtained through research methods to assist in some kind of useful analysis.

database a storage system for related data that is organized for ease of access.

database management programs software programs that process requests from users for specific data, avoiding redundancy.

debt a financial obligation to a person or institution, usually with a set rate of interest and a set time for repayment.

debt financing covering long-term expenditures by borrowing outside of the company.

decision making the process of recognizing problems and finding the most appropriate solution to the problem.

decline stage final stage of the product life cycle where sales continue to fall and where a decisions must be made about whether to remove the product from the market or at least to reduce or discontinue promotional support.

defensive stance a company that operates within the legal parameters regarding social responsibility and environmental responsibility but does nothing more.

deficit a situation in which a government spends more than they gather in taxes during a given year.

deflation a period during which prices for goods and services are falling.

delegation placing the responsibility of completing a task or a function in the hands of a subordinate.

demand the quantity of goods and services that consumers are willing and able to buy during a specific period of time.

democratic leadership this form of leadership seeks out input from employees, but retains the authority to make the final decision.

demographics the identification of groups through observation and analysis of characteristics such as age, income, ethnic background, race, gender, marital status, and religion, for the purposes of segmentation.

departmentalization the separating of functions within an organization into separate units.

depression when a severe decline in the GDP persists for six or more months.

desktop publishing computer software that enables the creation of online magazines, annual reports, and other large undertakings completed in-house under a protected protocol.

direct channel a channel of distribution that consists of producer and end-user with no intermediaries.

directories systems that list information on the World Wide Web using categories and subcategories instead of user-inputted key words.

discount a reduction in the price by the seller in order to persuade the customer to purchase.

distribution channel the movement of a product from manufacturer, through any number of intermediaries, to the end-user.

distribution mix the channels and intermediaries through which a company distributes its products to consumers.

divestiture occurs when a firm divests itself of or sells off a portion of its business operations.

dividends a pro-rated distribution of profits to stockholders.

double taxation shareholders experience this because the company in which they have invested pays corporate taxes and they, the shareholders, must then pay taxes upon any dividends received.

dumping the practice of selling a product for less in a foreign market than at home.

early adopters purchase a product early in its life cycle, they are opinion leaders, are respected, and have influence over their peers.

e-catalogues internet-based retailing that allows consumers and business customers to view product and service details.

economics the study of how a nation produces and distributes its resources among its citizens.

e-intermediaries intermediaries who either disseminate internet-based information for consumers and/or facilitate the distribution of internet products to the end-user.

electronic conferencing a system that allows people in multiple locations to communicate simultaneously by voice, video, or text.

electronic mail a system that sends computerized information electronically to other computers.

electronic order purchasing goods or services via the internet for end-users or the extranet for business-to-business transactions.

electronic spreadsheets computer software programs (such as Microsoft Excel) that enable users to create programmable, interactive grids for a number of different applications—accounting, etc.

electronic storefront an interactive website where consumers are able to acquire information about products, place an order to purchase, and pay for that purchase.

embargo the prohibition, by a government, to export or import a certain product. This can also apply to a prohibition against trading with a particular country.

emotional motives buying decisions that are not based on logic, but on impulse.

employee information system lists the qualifications and skills of all of the people currently working for an organization.

employee stock ownership plan an employee benefit in which employees earn shares in the company, with voting rights while stock is held in trust.

employment insurance employees and employers both pay into this plan that provides a minimum income for employees who are between jobs.

empowerment giving employees the authority to make decisions regarding customer service and other problems that may arise within their work environment.

enterprise resource planning (ERP) a computerized operations system that integrates the production of multiple firms.

entrepreneur a person who undertakes to open and operate a new business venture and assumes all of the opportunities and risks involved in doing so.

equity financing issuing stock or retaining earnings in order to cover long-term expenditures.

equity theory suggests that employees weigh what they accomplish in their work against what others accomplish.

ethical behaviour behaviour that mirrors the standards of what is considered right and acceptable in a society.

ethics standards of behaviour that dictate what is right or wrong, acceptable or unacceptable in a society.

Euro a currency used among most of the signatory countries of the European Union.

European Union (EU) the establishment of a trade agreement among 27 European nations.

everyday low pricing (EDLP) a strategy used by large department stores to compete on keeping prices consistently low.

exchange rate the comparison of the value of one currency to the value of another.

exclusive distribution the situation in which the distribution of a product involves only one intermediary.

expectancy theory suggests that employees work toward attaining rewards that they believe are attainable.

exports goods produced in one country and then transported and sold in other countries.

external recruiting the process of soliciting applications for a position from qualified people outside of the organization. The process could include advertising, hiring an executive search firm, or holding a job fair, among other techniques.

extranet an internal network that permits outsiders limited access to specific network areas.

extrinsic reward recognition of a job well done, such as praise, pay increase, or promotion.

facility layout the physical organization of machinery and equipment within an operation.

facility location the geographical position of an operation.

factors of production the resources utilized to create goods or services: capital, labour, natural and information resources, and entrepreneurship.

fax machine a machine that makes a digital copy of visual information and sends it over a telephone line.

finance that area of business practice in which decisions are made regarding long-term investments and the funds to secure them.

financial control comparing a firm's actual financial performance with the financial plan.

financial plan a strategy for reaching financial goals in the future.

firewall a software or hardware barrier in a computer set up to prevent unauthorized access to a system.

fiscal policy The raising or lowering of taxes or government spending in order to maintain a stable economy.

fixed costs the expenses that are unchanged with the quantity of products that are produced and sold.

flexible manufacturing allows the facility to produce several different products using the same production line.

flextime plan allows employees to choose what hours they will work around the organization's core business hours for which all employees must be at work.

foreign direct investment when a person or company directly purchases or creates assets in a foreign market.

foreign subsidiary a company set up in a foreign country, but owned by the domestic parent company.

franchise an arrangement that allows the purchase of rights to operate under the brand and the operations system of an established firm.

free trade usually a negotiated agreement among several countries to allow free trade among the signatories to the agreement but not with other countries.

free-market economy an economic system in which the factors of production, distribution of goods and services, and economic growth are largely controlled by the market.

free-reign leadership a style of leadership in which managers act as advisors to employees who make the final decisions.

friendly takeover an acquisition in which both companies are pleased.

fringe benefits the fixed benefits included in the package offered by the organization to employees.

gain-sharing plan a compensation plan that rewards employees for increasing productivity or reducing costs and thereby increasing the profits of the organization.

General Agreement on Tariffs and Trade (GATT) a forum through which member countries may negotiate reduction or elimination of trade barriers.

general partner a person who is involved in the day-to-day management of the firm and whose liability is unlimited.

genuine progress indicator (GPI) "same accounting framework as GDP ...adds in the economic contributions of household and volunteer work ...subtracts factors such as crime, pollution, and family breakdown." See www.rprogress.org—a more accurate picture of our progress as a nation.

global positioning system (GPS) a worldwide satellite navigation system, a commercial application of which is to precisely locate goods travelling by land, sea, or air at any time during the transit.

globalization the increasing integration of markets and economies throughout the world.

goals outcomes that a company strives to achieve.

goal-setting theory suggests that employees perform more effectively when they are aware of goals that are quantified, attainable, and time sensitive.

goods production the activities of a firm that result in tangible goods.

gross domestic product (GDP) the total value of goods and services produced, using domestic factors of production, in a specific period of time by a country.

groupware a system that allows for immediate electronic communication between people on multiple computers.

growth stage at this stage of the product life cycle, the product is attracting buyer attention, sales are climbing, and the product begins to generate a profit.

hierarchy of needs theory developed by Abraham Maslow, it suggests that people must have their basic needs met before they can begin to fulfill higher-level needs.

high-contact system a situation in which the consumer is physically present within the system at time of delivery of the service.

horizontal merger direct competitors joining to form one company.

hostile takeover an acquisition in which the company being bought out resists the acquisition by the other company.

hub a central place from which all or most of a company's products are distributed.

human relations the relationship between employers and employees that facilitates mutual respect or the lack thereof.

human relations skills the skills necessary to work well and effectively with others.

human resources management the tasks of attracting, hiring, training, motivating, and evaluating employees who will be engaged in achieving organizational goals.

imports products bought from other countries to sell in the domestic market.

independent agent a person or company that conducts business on behalf of an exporter in foreign markets.

industrial goods products purchased to use directly or indirectly to produce other goods.

industrial policy a long-term plan developed by government and business to secure sustainable industrial development.

inflation a widespread increase in the prices of goods and services over time.

information the knowledge that is transmitted through a computer system or systems including the internet.

initial public offering (IPO) the first time that stock in a particular company is available for sale to the general public.

inside directors any member of a corporation's board of directors who is fully employed within the corporation.

insider trading profiting on the stock market by using knowledge that is not available to others.

intensive distribution the situation in which the distribution of a product involves many channels and many intermediaries for maximum exposure.

interest the cost of borrowing money.

intermediary those individuals or firms who come between the manufacturer and the end-user to facilitate distribution.

intermittent process a production process that involves shorter runs and multiple products.

intermodal the use of different types of transportation to move a product from one place to another.

internal recruiting the process of identifying potential job applicants from within the organization. This may include the use of employee information systems.

international firm a company that conducts a large part of its business in foreign markets.

International Monetary Fund (IMF) an organization that promotes trade, lends short-term funding to member nations, and assists troubled nations with longer-term loans.

internet the international public data communication network linked by networks around the world and serving millions of computers.

internet service provider (ISP) a firm that provides consumers with access to the internet via dial-up, DSL, or wireless connections.

internet-based retailing the marketing of products and services to end-users through the internet.

intranet a private network set up to serve a single organization and made secure from outsiders.

intrinsic reward the personal satisfaction of having done a job well.

introduction stage at this stage of the product life cycle, the product is new to the market and the concentration in promotion is on building prospective customer awareness and showcasing the product's benefits; expenses are high and profit will not be seen until the growth stage.

inventory control the system of managing the type and quantity of goods to fill the needs of customers accurately, fully, and promptly, without retaining unused surpluses.

invest to purchase stock in a publicly traded company, to lend venture capital as a silent partner.

ISO 9000 a certification by the International Organization for Standardization that a company has met quality-management requirements.

job analysis a systematic review of all the jobs within a given organization.

job description lists all of the duties and responsibilities associated with a position.

job evaluation is an assessment by an organization of the value of a certain position within the organization. This can help management to determine compensation for that position.

job satisfaction the enjoyment and satisfaction derived from performing one's job.

job sharing is a relatively new concept that involves two employees working together to fulfill the role of one employee, sharing hours, compensation, and limited benefits.

job specification lists all of the skills and qualifications needed to perform effectively in a given position.

joint venture/strategic alliance a company that creates a partnership with a company in a foreign market in order to produce and sell goods there.

just-in-time (JIT) inventory control a control system designed to economize on storage space by arranging for parts and supplies to arrive just in time to go to the assembly line.

knowledge-based pay rewards employees for the acquisition of new knowledge that will enhance their contribution to the organization.

labour human resources and the skills and talents that they bring to a workplace.

leading that part of a manager's responsibilities that focuses on motivating and mentoring employees to reach their highest potential.

lean manufacturing manufacturing that uses minimal levels of materials and labour.

liability money owed to others.

licensing when a company gives foreign companies exclusive permission to produce and sell its product.

limited liability an investor's liability is limited to the investments they have made in the corporation; their personal investments cannot be touched.

limited partner a person who shares in the ownership of the company, does not participate in the day-to-day operations, and who is only liable for the amount they have invested in the company.

line of credit the bank makes a specified amount of unsecured loan available to a firm to draw funds on as needed.

loan (secured, unsecured) secured through committed collateral; unsecured does not require collateral.

local area network (LAN) a network that covers a single building, an organization, or a small area.

local content law a law that requires that locally sold products must also be partially made in the country where they are sold.

logistics the activities performed in order to ensure the delivery of the right product, in the right quantity, to the right place, at the right time, and at the lowest possible cost.

logistics visibility through an extranet application, allowing all of the players in the channel to view the logistics process at any time during the transit of the goods.

low-contact system a situation in which the consumer does not have to be physically within the system in order for the service to be delivered.

management the responsibility of planning, organizing, leading, and evaluating a part or all of a company's resources in order to achieve the company's goals.

management by objectives (MBO) an approach to management that involves every level within the organization in the goal-setting process.

management development providing training and mentoring to exceptional employees to groom them for promotion and added responsibilities within the organization.

market price the price determined when supply and demand are balanced.

market research a comprehensive study of consumer needs and how the firm can best fill those needs.

market segmentation focusing on specific customer traits and dividing the market according to those categories.

market share the percentage of sales revenue of the firm compared to the total sales revenue for the entire industry.

market test/test market this is a marketing research technique in which a specific geographic area is chosen, based on its demographics and their relation to the projected target market, and the product is sold in that area for a specific time. The resultant sales are then used to project how the product may sell over a larger area.

marketing the function in business of planning, pricing, promoting, and distributing products or services to satisfy consumer wants and needs.

marketing boards organizations that artificially control or manipulate the supply or pricing of agricultural goods.

marketing concept the adoption, by an entire firm, of the goal to satisfy both present and future customers' needs at a profit.

marketing mix the strategic use of product, price, promotion, and distribution in the marketing of a product or service.

marketing plan a strategic map that includes a situation analysis, marketing objectives, identification of target markets, positioning, and action steps.

markup the amount, usually a percentage, added to the cost of goods sold to determine selling price.

materials handling the logistics of handling inventory within a warehouse.

materials required planning (MRP) a computerized production management system that predicts necessary production materials based on sales forecasts.

maturity stage at this stage in the product life cycle, sales begin to slow while profits are at their highest levels. By this point competition begins to eat away at sales and eventually causes sales, and therefore profit, to begin to fall.

merger two companies coming together to form a new company.

merit pay compensates employees for higher job performance and contributions to the success of the organization, generally involving an increase in salary.

microenterprise a small business usually run on a part-time basis.

middle management managers who put strategies into action, supporting and implementing major decisions.

mission statement a company's reason for being (*raison d'être*) or the guiding principles under which it operates.

mixed economies an economic system in which some of the factors of production, distribution of goods and services, and economic growth are controlled by the market and some are controlled by the government.

monetary policy the management, by a central bank, of the nation's money supply and interest rates.

monopoly a market or industry in which there is only one producer of a particular product or service.

morale the way in which employees experience their work environment as either negative or positive.

motivation the subtle influences that prompt people to behave the way they do.

multimedia communications systems systems that enable the use of audio, video, and interactivity to create a more compelling message.

multinational firm a company that structures its operations for the international market and is not firmly connected to any particular domestic market.

national competitive advantage a situation in which a country takes advantage of favourable demand and factor conditions, related and supporting industries in place, and strategies, structures, and rivalries that promote efficiencies at home to support involvement in international trade.

national debt the amount of money that a government owes its creditors.

non-price strategy emphasizing the quality or uniqueness of a product in order to encourage purchases.

North American Free Trade Agreement (NAFTA) a trade agreement among the U.S., Canada, and Mexico made in 1993.

objectives the breaking down of organizational goals into achievable activities.

obstructionist stance a company that has no interest in social or environmental problems.

odd–even pricing an over-used form of psychological pricing that prices products at just less than a dollar amount such as $2.99 instead of $3.00.

off-the-job training usually takes place in a classroom with lectures, videos, case studies, role plays, and demonstrations to assist employees in understanding job requirements.

oligopoly a market or industry in which there are a few very large sellers who have the ability to influence price in order to maximize profits.

on-the-job training an informal process through which employees are shown how to perform a task by another employee or by a supervisor at the work site.

operational planning strategies and tactics for fulfilling the day-to-day goals of the organization.

operations management managing the transformation of resources or raw materials into finished products.

organizational stakeholder any individual, company, or community that is directly affected by the operations of the organization.

organizational structure the lines along which an organization constructs its span of control. These can be horizontal, vertical, or a matrix.

organizing that part of a manager's responsibilities that focuses on the utilization of resources in order to achieve organizational goals.

orientation an introduction to all of the aspects of a new job, including departmental policies, benefits, parking, performance expectations, and the use of any equipment.

outside dircctors members of a board of directors who are not fully employed by the corporation.

owner's equity the net proceeds if a firm were to sell all of its assets and pay all of its debt.

parent corporation a company that owns a subsidiary.

participative leadership a method of empowering employees in order to give them a say not only in how they do their job, but also in how the company is run.

partnership two or more people who hold ownership in a company and share in the operational and financial responsibilities.

penetration pricing strategy the decision to set the initial price very low in order to sell as many units as possible.

per capita income a country's average income per person.

personal selling one-on-one communication between a salesperson and a potential customer.

piece-rate incentive plan rewards employees for each completed unit of production.

place (distribution) the part of the marketing mix that involves movement of the product from where it is produced to where the consumer can purchase it.

planning that part of a manager's responsibilities that focuses on methods to achieve organizational goals.

PMI (Pluses, Minuses, Implications) creating a three-column grid in which all of the pluses, minuses, and implications are listed for evaluation.

point of differentiation how a firm's product or service differs significantly and beneficially from that of the competition.

pollution the releasing, by businesses, of harmful substances into the environment.

portable document format (PDF) a type of electronic document created by software, often used for desktop publishing, that renders documents in a fixed, protected format that is translatable across many different display programs.

preferred stock shares in a company whose owners have first claim on the corporation's assets and profits but have no voting rights.

presentation graphics software software that enables the creation of animated, interactive slides (Powerpoint, etc.) to be used in business presentations.

price the amount of money or other consideration exchanged for use or ownership of a good or service; the part of the marketing mix that involves determining a value for a product that serves the client's profit needs and the customer's purchasing needs.

price leadership the firm that establishes industry prices that other companies follow.

price lining the decision to price similar products at different price points in order to differentiate them from each other.

price-skimming strategy the decision to set the initial price at the highest point that people would be willing to pay in order to maximize profit.

primary data information obtained through initiating new research.

private corporation a business whose stock is owned by a small group of individuals, often family, and is not traded on a stock exchange.

proactive stance a company that operates in such a way that every decision is considered in light of the implications for the social responsibilities toward employees, the community, and the environment.

problem solving finding solutions to the day-to-day issues that arise in the workplace.

process manufacturing a production process or part of a process that changes or refines a substance.

product a good, service, or idea consisting of tangible and intangible attributes that satisfy consumer needs; that part of the marketing mix that involves creating a good, service, or idea that leads to the needs satisfaction of customers.

product differentiation the features of a product or service that make it distinctively more appealing to consumers than other existing products.

product life cycle the profit-producing stages a product goes through in the marketplace, including introduction, growth, maturity, and decline.

product line products that are similar in terms of needs satisfaction, are used together, appeal to the same customer group, and are distributed in the same manner.

product mix the product lines that a company offers for sale.

product positioning the image a firm wants its product or service to hold in the consumer's mind.

productivity the measure of how efficiently resources are converted into finished product.

profit-sharing plan a compensation plan that divides a fixed percentage of the organization's annual profits among all employees.

promissory note a form of trade credit in which buyers sign an agreement of repayment before receiving the merchandise.

promotion that part of the marketing mix that designs ways in which to gain consumers' attention and prompts them to buy.

promotional mix how a firm combines advertising, personal selling, sales promotion, and publicity to sell its products or services.

prospectus required for registration with a securities exchange, this is a detailed statement including information about a firm, its management, its operations, and the purpose of the initial public offering.

protectionism the practice of establishing quotas or tariffs in order to protect domestic industries.

public corporation a business whose stock is traded on a stock exchange.

public relations news releases created by a firm to enhance their own image with the public.

publicity information about a product, service, cause, or firm that is made available to the public through a communication medium.

quantity discount buying in large quantities means a lower price for the purchaser.

quota a limit placed on the quantity of a certain good or type of good that can be brought into a country.

rational motives buying decisions based on logical evaluation of product features and benefits.

recession an economic situation in which there has been a decline in the GDP for two or more consecutive quarters.

recruiting attracting people who are both interested in and qualified for a specific position within the organization.

recycling the utilization of waste materials to create new and useful products.

reinforcement theory the theory that the behaviour of an employee is affected by positive or negative reinforcers.

relationship marketing a marketing strategy that focuses on long-term relationships with both customers and suppliers.

replacement chart lists all of the important management positions within an organization, who fills them, the time they will likely leave the position, and possible replacements from within the organization.

responsibility the obligation to perform the task assigned.

retailers that part of the distribution system that sells directly to the end-user.

risk/return trade-off the degree of risk and the expected rate of return on financial instruments.

salary a fixed amount of compensation rewarded at regular periods of time, often bi-weekly or monthly, for doing a job.

sales agent/broker an intermediary who profits through connecting sellers with buyers and providing both with information in order to facilitate a sale.

sales promotion a short-term incentive offered in order to promote sales.

search engine web-based software that allows users to access documents on the World Wide Web using key words.

seasonal discount lower prices offered for off-season merchandise.

secondary data information obtained through previous research done either by the firm or by others.

selection the process of evaluating the information collected about applicants and making equitable decisions based on the best interests of the organization.

selective distribution the situation in which the distribution of a product involves a limited number of intermediaries and channels.

server a computer that manages a client-server network.

service operations a process that creates a combination of the tangible and the intangible components of a unified service such as a movie theatre or a bus ride.

services intangibles that can be purchased.

shopping goods goods or services that are not purchased often, are somewhat expensive, and prompt consumers to spend some time comparing prices.

skill-based pay rewards employees for the acquisition of new skills that will enhance their contribution to the organization.

small business usually owned and managed by one person and with fewer than 50 employees.

social audit an analysis of how a company is meeting its social responsibilities and how any funds allocated to social causes are being utilized.

socialism an economic and political system in which the main factors of production are government-controlled, but less important industries can be operated by privately owned firms.

sole proprietorship a business in which one person is entirely responsible for the liabilities incurred.

specialization dividing production into parts and assigning those parts to individuals.

specialty goods goods or services that are quite expensive and are purchased rarely, prompting consumers to search for the exact item to fill their needs.

spinoff setting up one or more strategic business units as new corporations.

stability a state of economic equilibrium in which the amount of available money in the system grows at approximately the same rate as the number of goods and services produced.

standard of living the total amount of goods and services that can be bought by people with the money they earn.

stock a portion or share of ownership in a company.

stock (common, preferred) common—have voting rights, but in terms of claim on assets are last in line; preferred—have no voting rights, but have first claim on a firm's assets and profits.

stockholders (or shareholders) members of the general public who have purchased stock in the company.

strategic alliance a situation in which two or more companies join, temporarily, to complete a specific undertaking. (See **joint venture**.)

strategic planning generation of high-level strategies for the optimization of resources in fulfillment of organizational goals.

subsidiary corporation a company owned by another company.

subsidy government aid to domestic producers in order to help them compete in foreign markets.

supervisory management managing the day-to-day operations of a business.

supply the quantity of goods and services that producers are willing and able to offer for sale during a specific period of time.

supply chain the movement of resources into the system, the movement of information, resources, and processes in the system, and the movement of finished products to the consumer.

SWOT analysis analysis of a company's internal strengths and weaknesses and its external opportunities and threats in order to aid in strategic planning.

synthetic process a process in which a number of substances are combined in order to produce the final product.

systematic job rotations and transfers a management training strategy that involves moving new managers through all of an organization's operations in order to ensure a comprehensive understanding of all aspects of the business.

tactical planning taking strategic plans and breaking them down into manageable pieces that are then implemented in the short-term.

target market a group of people with similar wants and needs that can be expected to react to marketing efforts in a similar way.

tariff a government-imposed tax on some imported goods.

technical skills those skills needed to perform specific specialized tasks within an organization.

teleworking/telecommuting giving employees the option of doing all or some of their work away from the organization's traditional workplace.

tender offer often a bid to take over the company, this is an offer made directly to shareholders and would be above the current dollar value of the stock.

theory X this theory assumes that people dislike work, will avoid it whenever possible, and are motivated by fear or money.

theory Y this theory assumes that people like work, seek responsibility, and are motivated by both extrinsic and intrinsic rewards.

theory Z this theory sees the organization as a family in which co-operation and shared values are highly prized and are the factors that motivate employees.

top management corporate managers involved in long-term planning and goal setting, administering all major decisions, and representing the company in the business world.

total quality management (TQM) an organization-wide commitment to the complete elimination of defects in the manufacturing process.

toxic waste traces of radioactive or chemical particles released into the environment.

trade credit the selling firm granting credit to the buying firm.

trade deficit a situation in which a country is importing more than it is exporting; this is considered an unfavourable balance of trade.

trade discount a discount on the list price granted by a manufacturer or wholesaler to buyers in the same trade.

trade shows a promotional tool, used widely in B2B, to display and demonstrate new technologies and products for sale.

trade surplus a situation in which a country is exporting more than it is importing; this is considered a favourable balance of trade.

training and development opportunities provided by employers for employees to learn new skills and to improve current skills in order to enhance performance.

transportation the means through which resources and finished products are moved from one place to another.

turnover the number of employees who leave an organization and have to be replaced over a given period of time.

two-factor theory developed by Frederick Herzberg; suggests that certain conditions must be present in order for employees to work harder at their jobs.

unemployment the percentage of people within an economic system who are actively looking for work and who are unemployed.

unethical behaviour behaviour that mirrors the standards of what is considered wrong and unacceptable in a society.

unit cost the cost to produce one unit of a product or service.

unlimited liability an investor's liability includes not only the debts incurred by the business, but also the personal property of the investor.

utility the way in which a product or service fills a need. Four aspects of utility are time, place, possession, and form.

validation the process of evaluating the types of information collected about job applicants according to its potential ability to forecast job performance.

value a comparison of a product's or service's benefits versus its costs.

variable costs the expenses that change with the quantity of products that are produced and sold.

venture (as in business venture) to undertake the financial risks involved in owning or investing in a new or shaky business with the view of profit.

venture capital a loan granted on the potential of a new or expanding firm.

vertical marketing system (VMS) usually uses an extranet linking all of the members in a distribution channel to enhance communication, coordination, and efficiency.

vertical merger a joining of two companies that have had a seller–buyer relationship.

vestibule training employees receive training in a simulated work situation away from the job site.

viral marketing a promotional strategy that uses the internet to create product awareness.

wages compensation based on a fixed hourly rate for doing a job.

warehousing the storage of resources and finished products.

wellness program a program that gives employees strategies and tools for maintaining and improving their overall health.

whistle blower an individual within a company who draws attention to unethical or illegal practices within the company.

wholesalers intermediaries who sell to retailers or other intermediaries, but not to the end-user.

wide area network (WAN) a network that connects computers over a large geographic area via telephone or satellite.

word of mouth recommendations and opinions about product value through casual conversation.

word-processing programs computer software that enables the construction of simple documents and files.

worker's compensation a plan paid for by employers that covers the health-care expenses of employees who suffer a work-related injury or illness.

World Bank an international financial organization giving low-interest loans to developing nations.

World Trade Organization (WTO) an international forum for negotiating trade agreements and settling trade disputes.

World Wide Web the system of interlinked documents using a standardized method of storage and accessed throughout the internet.

"AS IS" LICENSE AGREEMENT AND LIMITED WARRANTY

READ THIS LICENSE CAREFULLY BEFORE OPENING THIS PACKAGE. BY OPENING THIS PACKAGE, YOU ARE AGREEING TO THE TERMS AND CONDITIONS OF THIS LICENSE. IF YOU DO NOT AGREE, DO NOT OPEN THE PACKAGE. PROMPTLY RETURN THE UNOPENED PACKAGE AND ALL ACCOMPANYING ITEMS TO THE PLACE YOU OBTAINED THEM. THESE TERMS APPLY TO ALL LICENSED SOFTWARE ON THE DISK EXCEPT THAT THE TERMS FOR USE OF ANY SHAREWARE OR FREEWARE ON THE DISKETTES ARE AS SET FORTH IN THE ELECTRONIC LICENSE LOCATED ON THE DISK:

1. GRANT OF LICENSE and OWNERSHIP: The enclosed computer programs and any data ("Software") are licensed, not sold, to you by Pearson Canada Inc. ("We" or the "Company") in consideration of your adoption of the accompanying Company textbooks and/or other materials, and your agreement to these terms. You own only the disk(s) but we and/or our licensors own the Software itself. This license allows instructors and students enrolled in the course using the Company textbook that accompanies this Software (the "Course") to use and display the enclosed copy of the Software for academic use only, so long as you comply with the terms of this Agreement. You may make one copy for back up only. We reserve any rights not granted to you.

2. USE RESTRICTIONS: You may not sell or license copies of the Software or the Documentation to others. You may not transfer, distribute or make available the Software or the Documentation, except to instructors and students in your school who are users of the adopted Company textbook that accompanies this Software in connection with the course for which the textbook was adopted. You may not reverse engineer, disassemble, decompile, modify, adapt, translate or create derivative works based on the Software or the Documentation. You may be held legally responsible for any copying or copyright infringement that is caused by your failure to abide by the terms of these restrictions.

3. TERMINATION: This license is effective until terminated. This license will terminate automatically without notice from the Company if you fail to comply with any provisions or limitations of this license. Upon termination, you shall destroy the Documentation and all copies of the Software. All provisions of this Agreement as to limitation and disclaimer of warranties, limitation of liability, remedies or damages, and our ownership rights shall survive termination.

4. DISCLAIMER OF WARRANTY: THE COMPANY AND ITS LICENSORS MAKE NO WARRANTIES ABOUT THE SOFTWARE, WHICH IS PROVIDED "AS-IS." IF THE DISK IS DEFECTIVE IN MATERIALS OR WORKMANSHIP, YOUR ONLY REMEDY IS TO RETURN IT TO THE COMPANY WITHIN 30 DAYS FOR REPLACEMENT UNLESS THE COMPANY DETERMINES IN GOOD FAITH THAT THE DISK HAS BEEN MISUSED OR IMPROPERLY INSTALLED, REPAIRED, ALTERED OR DAMAGED. THE COMPANY DISCLAIMS ALL WARRANTIES, EXPRESS OR IMPLIED, INCLUDING WITHOUT LIMITATION, THE IMPLIED WARRANTIES OF MERCHANTABILITY AND FITNESS FOR A PARTICULAR PURPOSE. THE COMPANY DOES NOT WARRANT, GUARANTEE OR MAKE ANY REPRESENTATION REGARDING THE ACCURACY, RELIABILITY, CURRENTNESS, USE, OR RESULTS OF USE, OF THE SOFTWARE.

5. LIMITATION OF REMEDIES AND DAMAGES:IN NO EVENT, SHALL THE COMPANY OR ITS EMPLOYEES, AGENTS, LICENSORS OR CONTRACTORS BE LIABLE FOR ANY INCIDENTAL, INDIRECT, SPECIAL OR CONSEQUENTIAL DAMAGES ARISING OUT OF OR IN CONNECTION WITH THIS LICENSE OR THE SOFTWARE, INCLUDING, WITHOUT LIMITATION, LOSS OF USE, LOSS OF DATA, LOSS OF INCOME OR PROFIT, OR OTHER LOSSES SUSTAINED AS A RESULT OF INJURY TO ANY PERSON, OR LOSS OF OR DAMAGE TO PROPERTY, OR CLAIMS OF THIRD PARTIES, EVEN IF THE COMPANY OR AN AUTHORIZED REPRESENTATIVE OF THE COMPANY HAS BEEN ADVISED OF THE POSSIBILITY OF SUCH DAMAGES. SOME JURISDICTIONS DO NOT ALLOW THE LIMITATION OF DAMAGES IN CERTAIN CIRCUMSTANCES, SO THE ABOVE LIMITATIONS MAY NOT ALWAYS APPLY.

6. GENERAL: THIS AGREEMENT SHALL BE CONSTRUED AND INTERPRETED ACCORDING TO THE LAWS OF THE PROVINCE OF ONTARIO. This Agreement is the complete and exclusive statement of the agreement between you and the Company and supersedes all proposals, prior agreements, oral or written, and any other communications between you and the company or any of its representatives relating to the subject matter.

Should you have any questions concerning this agreement or if you wish to contact the Company for any reason, please contact in writing: Permissions, Pearson Education Canada, a division of Pearson Canada Inc., 26 Prince Andrew Place, Toronto, Ontario M3C 2T8.